# Hope and

A Life of Dame Clara Butt

## by Maurice Leonard

"There is Nature...there is Art...and there is Clara Butt." *Sir Herbert Tree*

"A woman archangel might sing like that – at some enchanted princess out of a fairy-tale." *George du Maurier*

Published by

Victorian Secrets Limited
32 Hanover Terrace
Brighton BN2 9SN

www.victoriansecrets.co.uk

*Hope and Glory: A Life of Dame Clara Butt* by Maurice Leonard

Copyright © 2012 by Maurice Leonard

Maurice Leonard has asserted his right under the Copyright, Designs and Patents Act 1988 to be identified as the author of this work.

Cover design by Mathew Keller (www.mathewkeller.com)
Composition by Catherine Pope

All internal images from the author's own collection unless otherwise stated.

All rights reserved. The use of any part of this publication reproduced, transmitted in any form or by any means, electronic, mechanical, photocopying, recording, or otherwise, or stored in a retrieval system, without prior consent of the publisher, constitutes an infringement of the copyright law.

A catalogue record for this book is available from the British Library.

ISBN 978-1-906469-38-2

## Contents

| | |
|---|---|
| Prologue | 5 |
| 1 - Birth at Sea | 11 |
| 2 - Unlike Any Other Voice | 17 |
| 3 - Gold in Her Throat | 22 |
| 4 - Audition Time | 27 |
| 5 - A Unique Instrument | 31 |
| 6 - Albert Hall and West End Debuts | 37 |
| 7 - Royal Patronage | 46 |
| 8 - Queen Victoria | 49 |
| 9 - Paris | 60 |
| 10 - Samson et Delila | 63 |
| 11 - Dicing with Death | 71 |
| 12 - America and Romance | 85 |
| 13 - Marriage | 96 |
| 14 - Australia | 102 |
| 15 - The Recording Star | 130 |
| 16 - South Africa | 136 |
| 17 - Australia Again | 139 |
| 18 - War | 150 |
| 19 - Opera at Last | 162 |
| 20 - Family Tragedy | 167 |
| 21 - Enter Mrs Ponder | 175 |
| 22 - The Mystic East and Empire Day | 179 |
| 23 - Scandal | 186 |
| 24 - Refusing to Give In | 196 |
| Epilogue | 204 |

| | |
|---|---|
| Sources | 209 |
| Appendix A - Dame Clara and George Bernard Shaw | 212 |
| Appendix B - The Lost Chord | 214 |
| Appendix C - Discography | 216 |
| Acknowledgements | 238 |
| About Maurice Leonard | 239 |
| Index | 241 |

# PROLOGUE

I was sitting at my piano one rainy morning, playing *The Harbor Bar* (bar as in a bank of sand not a drinking place), a now seldom performed piece, which ended with the words by Edward Oxenford, "For parting is pitiful pain, only to weep, only to weep, for those who will ne'er come again." The music, suitably melancholic, was written by Madame Sainton-Dolby, of whom I had never heard. The song matched the mood of the weather. It was included in a battered, if once handsome, volume entitled *Galaxy of Song,* published well over one hundred years earlier, and which I'd owned for years although I don't know how I got it.

It also contained pictures and mini-biographies of the singers who had popularised the songs all those years ago. Mme Sainton-Dolby, a singer as well as a composer, was depicted looking well-nourished, as was the fashion then, with full lips and bright eyes. She was draped in lace, as though some net curtains had fallen on her head and then been secured by a rose. I Googled her, feeling this an unchivalrously anachronistic thing to do. Charlotte Sainton-Dolby (1821-86) must have been quite something, an English contralto for whom Mendelssohn had written a cycle of *Six Songs* (Opus 57) and the contralto role in *Elijah*. He had also invited her to sing with the Swedish Nightingale Jenny Lind at a concert he had conducted in Leipzig. It was said Sainton-Dolby did not have the strongest voice in the world but sang with great artistry. She was for many years Britain's leading oratorio and concert contralto until her retirement in 1870.

It was through Mendelssohn that she had met her husband, the French violinist Prosper Philippe Sainton, who became a professor at the Royal Academy of Music and did much to popularize the classics as, indeed, did Madame Sainton-Dolby herself. She had written much besides *The Harbor Bar*, including several cantatas, two of which are *The Legend of Dorothea* (patron saint of gardeners who is murdered by Theophilus in the hope she might send him roses from Paradise) and *The Story of the Faithful Soul* for female voices.

Many of the singers in the *Galaxy of Song*, in fact the majority, were contraltos. There was Marietta Alboni, later the Countess Pepoli (who sometimes sang baritone parts and was adored by Rossini, who personally coached her, and she sang with Jenny Lind at his funeral; Rossini considered the contralto voice to be the "foundation stone of all music"); Ernestine Schumann-Heink (Czech-born but a national treasure in America), Annie Louis Cary, Augusta Mary Wakefield, Gloria Trebelli and so on. They were all stars, but standing head and shoulders above her competitors – literally, she stood 6' 2", and people were smaller in Victorian times – was Dame Clara Butt, the apotheosis of the contralto and as uncompromising as her name suggests.

The contralto is the lowest of female voices, usually ranging a couple of octaves, or less, above F below middle C. In the past, a contralto, by selectively choosing her programme, could scrape by with a range of a little over an octave (the late singer-pianist Nina Simone, who would have been classified as a contralto had she chosen to sing "classical" music had a mere eleven tones), the two octaves cited above was more than serviceable for most singers. Dame Clara had three. It was not just the range, it was the quality of the voice, rich and full, strong throughout its compass, and it had enormous volume, vying even with the organ at the Albert Hall. Sir Thomas Beecham swore that on a clear day she could be heard in France. Certainly she could be heard miles away when she sang in Hyde Park on Empire Day and other occasions, and no patriotic function was complete without a Butt appearance. Dame Clara was sometimes accompanied by the band of the Coldstream Guards and easily soared above them. "Play up boys, I can't hear you!" one frustrated band leader was heard to shout at his musicians. Elgar was so impressed he wrote *Land of Hope and Glory* for her. For all its might, her instrument was versatile. When not booming across the stratosphere it was capable of delicacy, shading every nuance of what she sang, and she could sing with great sentimentality.

Today, contraltos are thin on the ground. From the darlings of the concert hall they have plummeted virtually away. Janet Baker, now retired, is one of our best loved opera and concert singers. Although billed as a mezzo, she sang much of the contralto repertoire, preferring to stay with Elgar and Mahler, rather than the Sullivan and Molloy so appreciated by Clara Butt. Her career took off in 1956 when she came second in the Kathleen Ferrier Memorial Competition – by an awful coincidence it was the same year she was struck by a bus, giving her concussion and persistent back problems. Nevertheless, her career lasted through to the 1980s. Nowadays, there is the feted Polish Ewa Podles, hurtling through Rossini with coloratura[*] panache enough to bring the great man back from his grave in ecstasy. But she is a rarity. Music is no longer written for such voices. The contralto register is no longer trained as a matter of course. Why?

Kathleen Ferrier was an international contralto soloist and I wrote her biography over twenty years ago,[†] when people who had heard her sing in their youth were elderly but still treasuring their memories, and had their records to prompt them. I interviewed her singing teacher, Roy Henderson, who gave me home-made apple pies with a cup of tea – at getting on for ninety he'd been up the tree in his garden to pick the apples the day before. He told me: "If you only knew Kathleen through her records you only knew half of what she did, you had to see her to understand what she was all about."

---

[*]  Coloratura is an elaborate and agile ornamentation of a melody, and therefore the province of flexible singers.

[†]  *Kathleen*, Hutchinson 1988

He could have been speaking of Butt, who painted and acted out every song she sang. Today she would be considered mawkish, twee even (although her voice was anything but twee), but in those days of home entertainment and song cycles with titles such as *Cautionary Tales* it was exactly what was wanted. She could switch from the secular to the sacred in an instant, from *A Fairy Went A-Marketing* to *Abide with Me* and take her listeners with her. And this in the vast auditorium of the Albert Hall.

I wrote about Ferrier not because she was a contralto but simply because she was a magnificent singer whose records have always lifted me to a higher plane. There's something spiritual about the way she sings. Ferrier was a lovely woman, beautiful to look at, possessed a sumptuous voice and was a unique interpreter. She was also brave. She introduced Mahler's *Das Lied von der Erde* to English-speaking audiences, shortly after the Second World War when German was an unpopular, even hated, language. *Das Lied* was well after Butt's time but she would never have sung it anyway. Although starting out in oratorio, once in her stride, she preferred shorter, more immediate items, such as *The Holy City* or *The Lost Chord*. Their voices, too, were as different from each other's as their repertoires and the times in which they lived.

But they had much in common. Both had large, adoring audiences and resolutely stuck to the concert platform in preference to the opera house. Both appeared in only one opera, *Orfeo ed Euridice*, which they sang in limited Covent Garden seasons. Both had principally male teachers, although in Kathleen's case Roy Henderson was more coach than teacher; she was virtually self-taught. Both had that essential ingredient for all stars, the common touch, and liberally sprinkled their recitals with popular items which some musical snobs felt unworthy of them. Both died prematurely, slowly and painfully of cancer, Kathleen at forty-one and Butt hanging on, often in agony, till she was sixty-three. Both refused to give up, performing right to the end.

I became fascinated by Butt, spending days at the British Library, reading all I could about her, and listening to her records. She became, if not an obsession, then something close to it. I loved the way she sang, her famous "gear change", which would have purists wringing their hands in horror, and the way she would hurtle from head voice to chest in a brutal manner (she knew exactly what she was doing and her audiences clamoured for it). Yet she could sing the Brindisi from *Lucrezia Borgia* with the utmost delicacy. Butt frequently reduced audiences to tears, particularly during the First World War when emotions were running high. It was all very heady.

Madame Sainton-Dolby had piqued my initial interest, but, with no disrespect to her, I switched my allegiance to Dame Clara. What a strange, sad and brave life I discovered.

# CHAPTER ONE

## Birth at Sea

She was almost born on the English Channel on a stormy winter's day. Had her seafaring father, skippering the boat on which his pregnant wife was a passenger, not put into emergency dock at the Sussex village of Southwick, she might have arrived, sans midwife, on the ocean. Then a fishing village, Southwick is now a suburb of Brighton and Hove.

Her parents, who had eloped a few years earlier, came from nautical families. Shipbuilder's daughter Clara Hook had run off with twenty-one-year old trawlerman and sometime oyster dredger, Henry Albert Butt, when she was sixteen. His family had earned their living from the sea for generations and he was to keep up the tradition. They met when he was employed at her father's yard in Shoreham, near where she had been born. Neither family forgave their children for eloping, each blaming the other for it. They disapproved of the marriage and were never reconciled.

Henry Butt was headstrong, both emotionally and in business, but, whereas his wife could be impulsive (otherwise she would not have eloped with Henry or travelled with him at sea while heavily pregnant) she was the steadier of the two. Henry was quick to make decisions which were not always the wisest, as his future business ventures would testify. Their marriage, however, was solid, based on love, and produced eleven children. No theatrical blood could be detected in Henry's lineage, yet his daughter Clara was to become one of the most flamboyant stars of her era. The element of show business which flooded through Clara's veins came, genetically, from her mother, who was the granddaughter of humourist Theodore Hook, son of James Hook, composer and performer of popular songs. His *'Twas Within a Mile of Edinboro' Town* endured through many generations and was included in the repertoire of the celebrated Adelina Patti, notably when she was performing in that city.

Theodore wrote music himself including, at sixteen, the opera *The Soldier's Return*. His fondness for cruel and elaborate practical jokes, however, caused a hiatus in what could otherwise have been a glittering career. The Berners Street Hoax of 1809 was the most infamous of his pranks. Taking a bet that he could make any house the most talked-about in London, he chose that of a hapless Mrs. Tottenham (some say he had a grudge against her) at no. 54 Berners Street. Unbeknownst to her, he sent out 4,000 invitations and orders for deliveries to her address for the same time on the same day. Among the notables invited were the Archbishop of Canterbury, the Governor of the Bank of England and the Lord Mayor, all of whom turned up with hundreds of others and a flotilla of delivery men. Fights broke out and police had to quell the riot.

Fortunately for Theodore, the Prince Regent had taken a liking to him and, to get him out of the way, made him Accountant General of Mauritius. It is said he knew nothing of accounts, but he certainly knew enough to help himself to £12,000 of public funds, and was promptly arrested. He went on, however, to found the magazine *John Bull* and to publish several successful books. Maybe it was fear of this scandal resurfacing that later made Mrs. Butt wary of drawing attention to her family.

The future Dame Clara Butt was born in hastily arranged lodgings at 4 Adur Terrace, Southwick on 1 February 1872. Just over two months later, on 3 April, she was christened Clara Ellen at the nearby

Wesleyan church, famous for its font shaped like a giant clamshell. She was the Butts' second child, a sister for two-year-old Henry Albert, known as Bertie. The Butts had run away to Jersey after their marriage, as Henry was of Jersey stock, and moved back there in 1874 when Clara was two, staying until 1878. Then they moved to Totterdown in Bristol, where Henry got a job as a shipbuilder. By this time they had another four children, Frederick, Herbert, Albert and Frances.

After another son, Wilfred, was born they moved to Sydney Terrace and then to 94 Coronation Road, Southville, where they lived from 1886 till 1893. The house, still standing, now bears a plaque commemorating Dame Clara's residence there. It is not a blue plaque put up by the council but a white one paid for by devotees. This came as a surprise to the current resident, Barbara Thorne, who had no idea of the illustrious former inhabitant until admirers knocked at the door a few years ago and explained what they wanted to do. She readily cooperated but admits, "I couldn't muster a lot of interest ... now, had it been Elvis!" There used to be a blue plaque, put up by the Southwick Urban Council, commemorating Clara's birth, on the Adur Terrace house but the homes have since been demolished to make way for a lorry park.

Clara considered Bristol her home town and the Bristolians still claim her as their own. Even today there is an immense measure of pride in her association with that city and, as recently as 2008, a programme entitled *An Audience with Dame Clara Butt* was given there. Staged at a pub and performed by locals, it was fully covered by the *Bristol Evening Post* under the headline 'Dame Clara Butt Remembered'. Not many artistes can claim that level of appreciation nearly eighty years after their death. Mrs. Sheila Keevill, who lives in Bristol, regularly lectures on her and has a collection of memorabilia. The Bristol Museum houses the brooch presented to Dame Clara by the people of Bristol on her wedding day.

Both Clara's parents were keen amateur singers. Some said Clara Senior was almost as good as her daughter, and three of her siblings turned professional, although whether they would have done this without their sister's success is anyone's guess. Having said that, her sister Ethel, was exceptionally talented. Using her mother's maiden name of Hook, she made some of the earliest sound recordings.

The sea was in Clara's blood and she was to spend much of her life crossing it. She regularly embarked on lengthy world tours, her family ensconced with her in her staterooms and a retinue of staff – chefs, dressers, hairdressers, valets, company managers and the like – accommodated elsewhere, as were her forty or so trunks of clothes. Her love of the ocean is unexpected, given she nearly drowned as a child. Mrs. Butt had engaged a nanny, who must have been inexperienced and not too bright, as she encouraged baby Clara to swim by throwing her into the sea. A breaker carried her out and the terrified nanny had to quickly grab her, otherwise she might have drowned. A quivering, soggy mess, the tiny Clara was dried in a panic and clutched to her nanny's bosom. Clara never did learn to swim, and nearly met with a watery end on several other occasions. Mrs. Butt kept the nanny on – with six children her hands were full, and she needed all the help she could get. Moreover, there was not much money in the house, and the girl was cheap.

Clara's first Bristol school, which she started when she was eight, was Bath Road Academy, a handsome old building shaded by a purple lilac tree. Clara liked school, was a good pupil, and got on well with her class mates. For all her latter-day hauteur she was, in fact, a good mixer, well imbued with *esprit de corps* at that age. Although she was to grow into a *grande dame*, an important part of her public persona, there was no hint of this manner during her early years. Clara took her first music lessons about this time. A Miss Adelaide Fincken, a friend of her father's, gave her piano lessons. This was not a sign of budding musicianship, simply what refined young ladies did, as they were expected to entertain their families. Miss Fincken taught Clara at home under the strange admonition from Mrs. Butt to "Be firm with the child," the mother perhaps aware that her daughter would prove a handful. Clara was loath to practice; she enjoyed playing songs but could not be bothered with exercises. Endless repetition of tuneless notes bored her. She loved melody, particularly melodic hymns and would churn those out on the piano at length. It was a love that was never to leave her. Had she not been musical she could have been a missionary, such was the depth of her religious belief, and this materialised in her love of sombre spiritual items. When she became a star she was to capitalise on this spirituality, transporting her audience to the same rapture. As queen of the concert platform, no one could sing about death and meeting their maker quite like Clara.

Like the sea, Christianity was also in her genes. Her father Henry was religious, too. He belonged to the Bible Christian Society and took Clara with him to the meetings. Clara loved to go and would sometimes play hymns on the piano there. It was at a Bible Christian service that she first heard *Abide with Me,* a piece that she was later to make virtually her own personal anthem, albeit to a different tune. Even as a child the words inspired her. They were written by curate Henry F. Lyle in 1847, in death agony, watching a sunset over Torbay, just three weeks before he died of tuberculosis. She was an enigmatic child. According to Clara, as she told her biographer Winifred Ponder, she was dreamy but not shy. She wore her thick dark hair in plaits and had big dark eyes. There was Spanish blood way back and she seems to have inherited her sultry looks from this ancestor.

Bertie, her elder brother, contracted diphtheria when he was ten. As he and Clara shared a bed, sleeping nose to feet, he passed it onto her. It was a highly infectious and potentially lethal disease affecting the throat, making swallowing and breathing difficult. Both children hovered near death, and the Butts were terrified their other children may catch it. Bertie, tragically, died and it looked for a while as though Clara might follow him into an early grave. Although more fortunate than her brother, Clara was cursed with the legacy of heart problems. For all her robust, even ebullient, adult appearance she was dogged by a weak heart which could manifest itself when she was stressed, forcing her to withdraw from concerts and rest. Convalescing from diphtheria, Clara suffered a painful accident. Her brother, Freddie, was with her in the kitchen where a pot of stew was bubbling on the stove. He pushed past her, knocking it off, and the scalding contents fell on Clara's legs. The pain must have been excruciating. Fortunately her father was to hand, but, as he tore the stockings off his screaming daughter, the scalded flesh came off with them. Infection set in and, at its height, there was talk of amputation – an exceptionally risky procedure in the late nineteenth century that meant an almost certain death. It was nearly a year before Clara could return to school and Mrs. Butt had to employ a governess for her, an expense she could ill afford.

The family's bad luck continued when Henry's business partner was killed at sea. Henry had recklessly invested his entire capital with this man and lost most of it as a result. He was a superstitious man, as were many sea-farers, and blamed this bad luck on a mirror he had broken a few days earlier. He believed that he would have to suffer seven years of bad luck. While he was not completely ruined, his fortunes never fully recovered. The family lived in straitened circumstances until Clara made the big time and could help support them, which she did all her life.

## CHAPTER TWO

## Unlike Any Other Voice

"That strange sweet voice. Not in the least ... like a child's voice, and unlike any voice, child's or woman's ... ever heard." This is the first known reaction to Clara's childish singing, related by Miss Fincken to Winifred Ponder as she was researching her biography *Clara Butt: Her Life Story*. Mrs. Ponder was told to consult Miss Fincken by Clara herself, so some partiality may be expected. According to Miss Fincken, Clara's mother had asked her to hear her daughter sing, and to give her singing lessons if she felt it worthwhile, in addition to her piano lessons. Clara sang Handel's *Angels Ever Bright,* which her mother had chosen, and Miss Fincken did think it worthwhile. Singing was included in Clara's musical curriculum, as it was for hundreds of youngsters throughout the country.

The lessons seem to have inspired her mother, too, and she began singing again as an amateur, something that had lapsed during her multiple pregnancies. Both she and Henry enjoyed singing, when they had time, sometimes in choirs and sometimes as soloists. In 1884 Mrs. Butt fell in love with the newly published *Love's Old Sweet Song* by the Irish composer J. L. Molloy, who wrote *The Kerry Dance* and *Little Tin Soldier.* It was hummed, sung and played at all hours in the Butt household. The sentimental lyric of G. Clifton Bingham, which yearned for the "dear, dead days beyond recall" touched a nerve with the nation and its popularity swept the Western world. It has more or less, accepting the vagaries of fashion, stayed there ever since. Few people have never heard it. It may have been those warm, childhood memories that made Clara keep the song in her repertoire. She originally learnt it at her mother's knee but regularly included it in her concerts.

Clara had probably also heard it sung by the popular contralto Antoinette Sterling, who introduced it to the public and, according to biographical notes by Lady Mary Sinner-Hendrickson, "lived her life doing good deeds". She was a favourite of the composer Gounod, who would sometimes accompany her on the piano in recital, as would his pupil, the temperamental Saint-Saëns, with whom Clara was later to share an intense professional ambition to sing his opera *Samson et Delila*. Antoinette Sterling sang for the ailing Liszt, just before he died, but by then he was so battered by life and the failure of his last London recital, that he refused to accompany her or to play anything. The mere sight of a piano made him ill. The American-born Madame Sterling signed the temperance pledge and considered opera morally suspect. Clara had no moral objection to it, but she was simply too tall. At her full height of 6' 2", without shoes or headdress, she would tower above any male partner, making them, and the opera, look ridiculous. Although initially despondent, Clara eventually abandoned her operatic ambitions, instead making the wise decision to concentrate on concerts. She was a good actress and put this to use in her recitals. For some critics she did this too vividly at times, but her public loved it.

Another link between Clara and Sterling was that, although sincere Christians, they had a streak of mysticism in their character. Both turned towards Theosophy at the end of their lives, influenced by the socialist reformer turned mystic Annie Besant, then President of the Theosophical Society. The Society was the inspiration of its co-founder, the Russian-born Madame Blavatsky, who claimed to have received her occult lore from sometimes discarnate Eastern mahatmas. It is doubtful the coarsely-spoken, but witty, chain-smoking Madame Blavatsky, tipping the scales at eighteen stones, would have attracted either lady herself; quite the reverse – she would have alarmed them, but the articulate and immaculately-tailored Mrs. Besant won them over.

Another star contralto who would have influenced Clara was Janet Patey, of whom critic Herman Klein ungallantly wrote "[her] absence of facial charm was more than atoned for by the ravishing quality of her voice". Samuel Butler added that she was "strikingly like Handel in the face". Not the most flattering of compliments, but she was dearly loved by the public.

A contributory reason for the popularity of contraltos was the accessibility of what they sang. Although not many could sing like Madame Patey, the range presented fewer hurdles for the amateur. After a concert, sheet music could be bought and the songs sung at home. Anyone, no matter how rough their voice, could have a go. The same could not be said for coloratura soprano pieces. Most households owned a piano and, usually, someone could thump out a tune. Clara's parents also attended concerts whenever they could and took their musical daughter with them, so she saw many popular singers of the day, albeit from cheap seats.

Miss Fincken taught Clara what she could but realised she needed more specialised tuition. Another neighbour, a Miss Brooks, was an amateur soprano and Clara was handed over to her. Miss Brooks, without thinking too much about it, cultivated Clara's upper register and trained her as a soprano. Some believe the reason Clara had such an extensive range was due to this early cultivation of her upper register, but that is unlikely. It was something with which she was born. Ranges can be extended, and notes added to the voice, but these seldom last and Clara's range never deserted her, even at the painful end. No teacher, however, could manufacture that extraordinary timbre she was to develop in her lower register. Miss Brooks probably did not know the lower notes were there, so did not exploit them. The same is true today when the contralto register is largely ignored. Who knows what marvellous voices lie undiscovered?

Every Sunday afternoon Clara went to Wedmore Vale Methodist Church Sunday School. Word had spread of the talented child and it was here she sang her first song in public – *Two Children Out in the Cold*. As she later told the *Bristol Times*, she was "a very little girl" and was wearing new shoes that squeaked when she walked on stage, embarrassing her, and increasing her nerves. Her "poor little voice was very weak" but after the applause she felt better, forgot her squeaky shoes and sang out. Returning to the church in 1928, as a celebrity, she reminded the congregation of that debut. It was the one and only time her vocal apparatus was described as "little" or "weak" and only then by its owner. It was at Wedmore Vale Church that she first heard the revivalist evangelist Rodney "Gipsy" Smith who made her burst into tears. "I found myself crying bitterly", she said. "I was told I had been saved. I didn't know from what I'd been saved, or why I should cry, but crying I was."

In 1884, when Clara was twelve, she moved to South Bristol High School. The headmistress, Miss Cook, called to see Mrs. Butt one day, about school matters, when Clara was singing in the next room. She assumed it was one of the Butt sons and casually remarked what a nice voice he had. Amid much merriment the situation was explained. Clearly the lower tones were already there in embryonic form, even if Miss Brooks had not heeded them. But Miss Cook did heed them and could not credit it when Mrs. Butt told her Clara was being trained as a soprano. She henceforth kept a proprietary ear on Clara's singing.

Clara became South Bristol High's star singing pupil and sang at school events and Christian Bible evenings, usually performing hymns, school songs or the less romantic ballads of the day. These were in whatever key suited her, neither specifically soprano nor contralto, whatever was comfortable. She became something of an infant phenomenon. Although dedicated to her music, there was another side to her nature, a boisterous side at times. Clara was athletic and particularly enjoyed tennis, making her a popular girl, her size also a useful asset for the hockey team. As she grew older Clara's voice grew stronger and Miss Cook believed something should be done about it. She also was sure her pupil was no soprano.

An evening came when Clara reached the same conclusion. She was taken to a recital by the contralto Belle Cole. Miss Cole, born in New York, was about to settle in England, where she lived for many years between her world tours. As had many before her, Clara fell under her spell and knew the sounds Cole made were the sounds she wanted to make. Sounds she could make and work on. Clara would be a contralto.

## CHAPTER THREE

# Gold in Her Throat

Dan Rootham was a respected choirmaster in the Bristol area. Son of Cyril Rootham, Cambridge musician and composer, he was organist of St. Peter's Church and conductor of the Bristol Festival Choir. A fine bass, he continued singing into his eighties. Miss Cook, racking her brains as to how she could best help Clara, contacted Rootham who agreed to audition her, subsequently taking her on as a pupil. On first hearing he knew Clara was a contralto and trained her as such. She was not his only pupil, but one in whom he took a distinct interest. He soon placed her as a chorister in the Festival Choir. This was a fine training in itself and stood her in good stead when she turned professional and performed as a soloist in the great oratorios.

Rootham was the right teacher at the right time and an expert at developing young voices. Due to his success with Clara, he was later to coach the young Eva Turner before she launched herself as one of the world's greatest dramatic sopranos, described as the "ideal" Turandot and possessing a voice of "enormous proportions". He clearly liked big voices and is recorded as having told Clara she had "gold in her throat". This proved true, both artistically and financially.

Someone who was described as having silver in her throat, due to the clear, bell-like quality of her voice, was the future Queen of Covent Garden, Dame Nellie Melba. However, on 1 May 1886, about the time

Clara was entertaining the Bible Christians and school friends, the twenty-five-year-old Mrs Charles Armstrong, as she then was, arrived at Tilbury docks from her native Australia, on her first visit to England. Although desperate to forge a career in opera, she was unimpressed with the English weather, thinking she would never be able to sing in such a dismal climate. Towards the end of their lives, she and Clara were to become embroiled in a scandal that set the world's newspapers on fire.

By 1887, aged fifteen, Clara was regularly singing with the Festival Choir, under Rootham, in *Messiah*, *Elijah* and the still-living Brahms' *German Requiem*, which he had written nineteen years earlier. She took part in productions which involved soloists such as soprano Lillian Nordica and baritone Sir George Henschel, wonderful artists with whom to be associated and from whom to learn. She studied with Rootham for three years and he established a solid technique upon which to base her mighty voice while giving her plenty of practical experience. She still sang at school, particularly *O Rest in the Lord* from *Elijah,* proudly introduced by Miss Cook. It presents a poignant image, the tall girl with the low voice, singing this sombre piece in front of her fellow pupils, her serious young face registering her dedication.

Clara sang, sometimes with her father, at the Bible Christian meetings, where the majority of the audience had left their schooldays far behind – most were ladies of a certain age wearing the large, ornate hats of the period, unpretentious crucifixes dangling among the ruffs and flounces of their modest décolletages. She also sang at the home gatherings which Mrs. Butt would give, when finances allowed, to show off her eldest daughter. And there were concerts, too. Clara was confident enough to give an evening's entertainment, usually at the invitation of local Christian or affiliated societies, and she could earn as much as a couple of guineas apiece at these, most of which went to the impecunious family.

Although Clara was later to enjoy a glass of wine or two (unlike Miss Sterling she was no advocate of the Pledge), she sang at several temperance meetings. It was at one of these, at the Redcliffe Crescent Chapel, that she met Alice Jenkins, a girl her own age who was to become her friend and regular accompanist. Her concert was divided by an interval, and, in the first half she had not been impressed with the designated accompanist. During the interval she asked Alice, whom she had been told was a pianist, to play for her. She was streets ahead of her accompanist, and, there and then, Clara persuaded her to take over for the second half. There were ruffled feelings as the scheduled pianist was, naturally, humiliated and Alice was diffident about upstaging him. But Clara was insistent. She never grew into a monster, although there were those who said she did when she became famous, but she would never tolerate musical inadequacy – anything that threatened her artistic status was, if possible, eradicated.

Their first song after the interval was Frederic H. Cowen's *Light in Darkness*. She knew, at once, she had made the right decision about Alice. It is a difficult piece and she sight-read it perfectly, despite having had no rehearsal. Little is heard of the Jamaican-born Cowen today, but he was popular in his time. He was known as the "English Schubert" on account of the over 300 songs he had written, in addition to his orchestral works and cantatas. He and Clara came to enjoy a warm professional association and she often sang his songs. Music assumed a value above all else to her, and she believed it had healing power. Alice became ill and Clara held her hand and sang quietly to her in hospital. Both she and Clara attributed her subsequent recovery to the therapeutic properties of singing. In the last, terrible days of Clara's life she would croon softly to herself to alleviate the pain.

As long as she had Rootham's blessing Clara would sing at any venue that requested her services. Usually her mother went with her and they would drive together in "the pillbox", a tiny horse and trap, ideal for two respectable middle-class ladies, sometimes with Clara at the reins. By this time, Mrs Butt had given birth to ten of her eleven children and, even with Bertie's tragic death, this still left nine at home with the nursemaid. Her final child, Hazel, would be born in 1889.

Clara began to be recognised by strangers. Bristol was getting to know its talented songbird. She loved to look the part for her concerts, and spent time on her appearance, eventually becoming one of the most spectacularly dressed of artistes. As her career swelled, so did her dressmaker's bills. Her taste grew flamboyant, exemplified at the pinnacle of her fame by her famous Grape Dress, festooned with bunches of artificial grapes, which her public specifically requested her to wear; it became as much a part of her performance as *Abide with Me*. But in those early days there was not much cash for clothes.

As she was sometimes paid for her concerts, however, Clara could occasionally splash out a pound or so on a new frock. She saw a scarlet satin creation one day, and fell in love with it. Attired in the dress and about to leave for an appearance, she spotted some tomatoes at home. Hearing they were good for the voice, she put a couple in her pocket to eat before the concert. Forgetting they were there, and in the excitement of things, she sat on them in the dog cart. Fortunately, the dress was red, so the unbecoming stain could have looked worse than it did. She hated singing in a dirty dress and, sadly, it was ruined. It was its first and last appearance.

The voice was still developing and could be unwieldy, surprising even Clara at times with its unpredictability. It took time to settle down and she was still unsure of what she could, or could not, do. The same applied to her stage demeanour which, under Rootham's eye, was also developing. Those girlish concerts, often to halls with empty seats, were perfect training. Sometimes she was overcome when singing hymns or sacred songs and had to master her emotions, trying to follow Rootham's advice that a singer needed a warm heart but a cool head. Once, the heel of her shoe snapped off as she was leaving the stage. Not sure what to do, she made a little joke of it which produced a mild laughter of sympathy. Elsewhere, when asked for an encore she called out to her mother, sitting in the front, "What shall I sing?" Mrs Butt reddened with embarrassment, as she always did if her name was mentioned in public. She never did get used to it and, while proud of her daughter, made mild attempts to dissuade Clara from pursuing a public career. With her husband, the entire school, Rootham and much of Bristol against her, she was wasting her time. Clara was by now determined to pursue a singing career.

When Clara was sixteen, Rootham had done as much as he could for her. He entered her to audition for the Royal College of Music in London.

# CHAPTER FOUR

## Audition Time

Although the Royal College of Music was in London's Kensington, Clara took her preliminary examination in Bristol. Hundreds of hopefuls each year vied to get into the prestigious college, so local heats were held to weed out the inadequate. The first lesson applicants had to learn was that music is a tough business. Rootham entered Clara as a scholarship girl, there being no way her parents could have afforded the fees and supported her through her training. News of the examiners was not encouraging, as it included George Riseley, chorister, scion of the Bristol Orpheus Glee Society and assistant organist at Bristol Cathedral. He was no friend of Rootham's – as organists the two men were rivals. Rootham feared that he might, on principle, look unfavourably on any of his pupils.

His fears were realised. Riseley gave Clara not so much a rough ride as an indifferent one. He subjected her to all sorts of, to her, irrelevant prose reading tests before hearing her sing. When she did sing it did not seem to produce much effect apart from puzzlement. Then he languorously asked, "What do you call your voice...?" On hearing the answer he responded, "Yes, I suppose you *could* call it a contralto." He was not the first, nor the last, to be puzzled by it. Clara left convinced she had not done well, only too aware that Riseley's judgement could affect her entire future. But, for all his seeming lack of enthusiasm, he passed her for the main examination which would be held at the Royal College of Music in London in January the following year. This was wonderful news for Clara, her siblings and her father, but it did not fill Mrs Butt with undiluted joy. She was worried about her daughter going off to the wicked city and pursuing a life on the even more wicked stage, expressing reservations as to whether this was a suitable career for a young lady. It was an uneasy Christmas for mother and daughter. Henry, however, was full of confidence, convinced Clara would succeed.

And it was Henry who took Clara to London for the audition. Her appointment at the College was for ten o'clock the next morning and, to ensure they were not late, they stayed the night before in the suburb of Lewisham with his sister. They could not afford a hotel, and it was a good opportunity for the family to get together, those occasions being few and far between. This meant an early start next day. The elements often conspire to dampen spirits when something important is afoot. Nellie Melba had arrived at Tilbury on a leaden day; years later when the ballerina Markova was to dance *Giselle* at the Old Vic, the biggest production the company had undertaken, the fog penetrated the theatre, almost obliterating the stage and preventing many of the audience from getting there. And Clara's big moment took place on a wintry January morning. It was so foggy and icy they feared the train bringing them into town might be cancelled. As it was, when they arrived in London, the horse-driven taxi they caught from the station was involved in an accident. It was with a feeling of relief that Clara saw the huge shape of the Albert Hall looming through the gloom, the College just behind it. They had made it, and were not even late.

Since the contestants were heard in alphabetical order, Clara did not have long to wait. She faced an august panel including Sir George Grove, director of the Royal College of Music and compiler of the encyclopædic *Grove's Dictionary of Music and Musicians,* and Sir Walter Parratt, one of the country's foremost organ teachers and about whom, someone once spitefully wrote, "He knew so much about music that he never wanted to hear any." She would recount the story of her audition, with amusement, all her life. Her opening song was *The Enchantress* by John Hatton, composer of opera, oratorio and songs and an accomplished pianist and singer himself. He had delighted the Americans when on tour by performing a Bach fugue followed by the song, *The Sleigh Ride,* during which he jingled bells attached to his trouser bottoms. *The Enchantress* was, in fact, an excellent, if ambitious, choice for an audition piece. She could thank Rootham for that. Highly dramatic, not to say boisterous, it exposes the range of the voice and the dramatic potential of the singer. Clara went for it with gusto. She clearly shocked the examiners, and this registered on their faces.

Recalling Riseley's affront, Clara thought they were not taking her seriously. *The Enchantress* contains a line "Kings Have Trembled when I came, reading doom upon my face," well within her lower register, and she thundered this out, hitting its low E flat with such force it seemed as though the facing wall trembled. She later recorded the song, capturing its essence of bloodthirstiness. If her audition performance matched the recording then it is indeed understandable that the examiners were stunned. Parratt was the first to speak and, pulling himself together asked, almost timidly, if for her second item she could sing something a little quieter, perhaps something from Elijah? She said she could sing *O Rest in the Lord* but not expecting to sing it had not brought the music with her. The official accompanist did not seem to know it. Clara, still bristling at what she construed as cavalier treatment, asked bombastically, "Surely one of you gentlemen can play?" Eventually, Parratt said he could play *Woe unto Them* (not the most soothing of arias) and she sang that for them instead.

Clara was thanked, asked to wait and then informed she would be told that afternoon whether she had passed, a better system than having to wait anxious weeks for results as can happen today. She was sure she had failed, but there was nothing she could do but wait. She and her father wandered disconsolately out of the college and round the Albert Hall, barely glancing at the imposing building, little dreaming that in the future she would sing there, not just once but often. On that miserable morning it seemed merely another hostile building. They walked round it a few times to pass the time. When it came to lunch they found a little restaurant nearby. Clara didn't feel particularly hungry but, now the audition was out of the way, she consoled herself as best she could with mutton and apple dumplings. They took their time then strolled back to the College and sat down to await the results. A framed certificate facing them on the wall informed them the College had been founded by royal charter with the Prince of Wales as its President – perhaps an omen of the royal patronage Clara was later to enjoy. At the time, however, it offered no comfort. To her surprise, the board wanted Clara to sing again. This was an unexpected result. She regretted her hefty lunch which now sat leadenly in her stomach. With renewed hope she sang and, again, was asked to wait. This time the deliberations were concluded much sooner: Clara had passed and was to become a full-time scholarship pupil. However, the scholarship could not be taken up till she was seventeen and that was not until the following year.

## CHAPTER FIVE

## A Unique Instrument

Clara spent the time singing in Bristol, trying to earn money for her college days. Word got round that she had passed her scholarship and she was enthusiastically congratulated. Although she kept busy, the time dragged. Clara was impatient to start her new life. One of her bookings was from Jimmy and Abigail Chute, who ran Bristol's Prince's Theatre, celebrated for its annual pantomime. Abigail was a socialite and persuaded many of her famous friends, including Ellen Terry, to perform at the theatre to raise funds. Clara, although crippled with nerves, set foot on her first professional stage there, believing it an honour to take part. Within a few years the position was to be reversed – the theatre felt honoured when she sang there.

Clara gave a well-attended farewell concert at the Tyndale Lecture Hall. So keen were the Bristolians for her to succeed at college that they had organised a whip-round, presenting her with some poetry books and a cheque for £60, a substantial amount then. She never forgot their kindness. All through her career Clara responded to charity calls from Bristol.

Clara was to live at Alexandra House, Kensington Gore, a hostel used by the Royal College of Music to house female students. Described as "a stepping stone between school and complete independence" it was to be her first taste of self-sufficiency. Situated right in the middle of the metropolis, it was ideal for youngsters to acquaint themselves with London. Clara shared a room with three piano students. Every morning she would warm up her voice, which must have acted as an alarm call for the others, not to mention much of Kensington. Sometimes it frightened the pigeons off the window sills. In a student house one wouldn't expect much attention would be paid to religious observations, but Clara was requested to sing grace before meals. This was not such an honour as it sounds. It came about because of the good nature of the popular superintendent, a Miss Palmer, for some reason known to the girls as Mixed Pickles. Clara was habitually late for meals but, rather than reprimand her, Mixed Pickles would admonish her hungry other charges, "Now, young ladies, we will wait to commence until Miss Butt comes to sing grace for us." Clara was then obliged to do so, intoning the sombre line, "For these and all thy mercies given," thereby informing the rest of the room that she was late. But there was nothing nasty about it, it was all good-natured fun.

As with school, Clara enjoyed college life, fitting in easily with the other girls and taking part in many productions, often cast as a man. She didn't object to such roles and sometimes, in cahoots with the others and in a borrowed dinner suit, would pretend to flirt with an unsuspecting girl, giving a chaste kiss on the cheek, before telling her she was a woman. Her low speaking voice helped. At a fancy dress party, she appeared as a baby in a nappy carrying a feeding bottle. Clara was undisciplined and irreverent in everything but her music, which seems strange considering the later majestic photographs representing her as the epitome of organised composure. But she admits she was untidy, careless with school books and lost any notes she took. Among her professors was Albert Visetti, novelist Radclyffe Hall's step-father, whom Miss Hall hated with a vengeance. It was entirely reciprocal. In 1928, the year of Visetti's death, Hall published her infamous novel, *The Well of Loneliness,* a sensitive study of lesbianism, which became the subject of a notorious obscenity trial.

Painter Romaine Brooks, one of Hall's friends, later developed a crush on Clara, after seeing her in concert. The ladies subsequently met, as Miss Brooks was wealthy and could afford to hire Clara to sing at her soirees. If she was aware of the extent of Brooks' affection, Clara didn't mention it. She probably never even noticed. Una Troubridge, Hall's partner and chronicler of her troubled life, describes Visetti as "that dreadful, cretinous, lecherous old man," and says he made sexual advances to the young Hall. Hall, herself, called him "my disgusting old stepfather". Notwithstanding his moral dubiousness, Visetti was an expert on singing, having studied with Boito, acted as Adelina Patti's advisor, and had written books on Palestrina and Verdi. He was also the first professor to be appointed to the Royal College of Music's staff. Visetti hit the headlines when he claimed to have witnessed in a Dalmatian graveyard a case of mass tarantism, an hysterical illness then believed to be caused by the bite of the tarantula spider. According to his published report, he saw "girls, women, sick people of all ages, men falling to the floor as though they were real epileptics", performing the "unbridled dance". The dancers were urged on by an abbot on a tombstone, performing somersaults. His creativity could not be faulted.

Clara's second subject was piano which she studied under Marmaduke Barton and with a degree of indifference. Henry Blower was Clara's main vocal teacher and, to this day, a musical prize is awarded in his name. Together they explored her voice. In the long hours at his Kensington studio at the College, he and Clara gradually unravelled its enormous potential. They were helped by its hardiness, immense size and the bounty of nature in providing her with a wide throat. But care was needed in its polish, so as not to stunt its range nor tamper with its natural timbre. As their studies progressed, it dawned on them that she was the possessor of a unique instrument. Every voice is, of course, unique, but voices unique in the qualities essential for fine singing turn up perhaps once in a generation. The *Oxford Companion to Music* tells us, "During the late 19th and early 20th centuries there was a marked tendency to the gradual disappearance of the true deep contralto."

There was no truer, deeper, contralto than Clara. She was the last of her breed, and it is to Blower's credit that he did not follow the trend and try to eradicate her uniqueness in favour of a lighter quality. He nurtured Clara's natural sound, and she was already in love with the inimitability of her own voice. As time went on and contraltos became less extreme in their registers, she made a point of emphasising her lower range.

The collective range of the human voice, male and female, from bass to soprano, is just over five octaves. Peruvian Yma Sumac claimed this entire range, although publicly she sang a span of just over four octaves. The German bass Ivan Rebroff had the same range and could sing through the octaves to soprano. German soprano Erna Sack sang as high as A in altissimo, five tones higher than the top C in *Vissi d'Arte*. Mozart wrote of Lucrezia Aguiari, who sang the C above top C and stunned him by doing so. French soprano Mado Robin has sung as high, sometimes even higher. Other extreme voices include Eugenia Mela, a female tenor, and in the 1930s, a three-year-old Czechoslovakian boy who sang bass. In the 1950s singing teacher Alfred Wolfson taught students to sing every note on the piano, one of them recording all the leading roles in Mozart's *The Magic Flute* from the Queen of the Night with its stratospheric Fs above the stave to Sarastro's aria with F below the bass stave. Wolfson believed voices were restricted by being categorised as soprano, baritone, etc. The trouble with multi-octave voices is there is little written music for them to sing. There are voices today, both male and female, that can emit the highest notes on a piano, but these "whistle" tones, as they are called, are purely sinusoidal and have no musical value. In fact they are quite hideous and musically pointless.

Much has been written, in an admiring fashion, of certain voices having the power to shatter glass. Legendary singing teacher Manuel Garcia's pupil, the bass Luigi Lablache, was one such and, according to the late Dowager Lady Swaythling, Clara was another. This was reported in *The Times* on 5 February 1947 by a Mr J. Mewburn, who said that the Dowager recalled being "at a party once at which Clara Butt sang, and at a certain note 'ping' went a very beautiful glass vase".

Although Clara's reverberating baritone could have placed her with the performers cited above, she had no desire to be a freak singer, and neither did Blower or the College wish to produce one. It is only necessary to listen to her Brindisi from Donizetti's *Lucrezia Borgia* to hear how she had mastered classical technique. Her approach in all she did was schooled and musical. Soon after she was admitted to the College Clara began to suffer from an inflamed throat. She wondered if this could be the result of incorrect teaching, although did not truly believe this. In any case, she was in no position to query it – she knew, as a scholarship girl, how lucky she was to be at the college. In fact, she was diagnosed with tonsillitis and booked into hospital for an operation. Clara was uneasy, and this uneasiness increased to dread as the operation date approached. She went through with it until she was actually lying on the operating table. Then, with the surgeon approaching, she panicked and leapt up, refusing undergo the operation. Clara's fears were entirely rational – a tonsillectomy was a risky procedure until the early twentieth century, when improved surgical techniques meant that bleeding could be better controlled. Fortunately, her throat cleared itself and she was convinced she had made the right decision. Had she not refused the operation the world may never have heard of Clara Butt. So she believed, anyway. Clara occasionally lost her voice in her career, but that is not unusual – professional singers frequently have vocal crises. Throughout her life she suffered other bouts of tonsillitis, laryngitis and adenoid problems, even though she possessed unusually robust vocal equipment among singers. Such interruptions were an occupational hazard.

The College did not approve of students singing professionally but, after the first year, aware of Clara's financial straits, permission was granted for her to give certain paid concerts. She gave several in Bristol, and was also awarded the Morley Scholarship fund, supplying her with extra much-needed money. As a student Clara was allowed concessionary rates at theatres and, being billeted near the Albert Hall, she was a regular there. At a concert in 1892, as she chatted with her friends before the performance started, she was approached by the recently knighted Sir Joseph Barnby, former director of music at Eton College and Principal of the Guildhall School of Music, which had opened twelve years earlier. He was actually looking for Clara. His work is seldom performed now, but that was not the case then. He was a collaborator of Gounod's and a champion of his sacred works. Barnby had written nearly 250 hymn tunes himself, and his oratorio, *Rebekah*, had been successfully performed. He was also conductor of the Royal Choral Society. They had not met, and he had not heard her sing, but he had heard of her – already her fame had spread to the Guildhall, and she had been pointed out to him. He introduced himself, although she knew who he was, and jokingly enquired, "Are you the girl with the big voice?" He asked her to audition the following week as he had her in mind for something special. She, all of a fluster, snatched at the offer with alacrity. Clara could think of nothing else all evening, and the music wafted through her head unheard. She knew she was abusing protocol by auditioning for Sir Joseph, and so did he. The Guildhall (now Guildhall School of Music and Drama) was competition to the Royal College of Music and the schools did not poach each other's pupils. Barnby had sixty-two students under his wing at the Guildhall who would be bitterly disappointed if he chose a pupil from a rival establishment to sing under his baton.

Clara was pretty sure news of the audition would not go down well with the administrators at the College. She was indebted to the college, and to Blower in particular. The concerts she was allowed to give were a concession and not a right, but to audition for Barnby was another matter altogether. Sir Joseph, however, was a man of power. There was no way she was going to turn him down.

## CHAPTER SIX

# Albert Hall and West End Debuts

Sir Joseph was preparing the Royal Choral Society for an Albert Hall production of Sir Arthur Sullivan's cantata *The Golden Legend* on the 7 December 1892, and he was interested in Clara for the role of Ursula, mother of a teenage daughter. Another reason she was to sing so little opera was that, so often, the parts on offer to contraltos were confined to "witches, britches and bitches," hags, male parts or the wicked. Ursula was none of these, but was, nevertheless, considerably older than Clara. Her audition lived up to Sir Joseph's expectations and Clara was offered the role of Ursula and solo appearances in two of his other productions, *Elijah* and *Israel in Egypt*, at a fee of five guineas each. This was fifteen guineas in all, serious money, but dwarfed by the thrill of the engagements. Clara accepted all three, painfully aware that she was not playing fairly with the Royal College of Music and that there would be repercussions.

Clara absorbed this momentous information and then had to confess to the College what she had done. She presented a reasonable, cool exterior but was anything but cool inside. A weak attempt was made to persuade her to renounce the offers but she bluntly refused. Clara left the room while the matter was discussed. Little could be done, actually, as she had made it plain she was going to sing and nothing would be gained by the College expelling her. It was acknowledged that kudos would come to the college with one of its pupils debuting at the Albert Hall, and under Sir Joseph. She was called back and the confrontation was not as dire as it could have been. Permission was granted. Clara had an ally in Blower after she had confided in him that she was to audition for Sir Joseph. He was thrilled and agreed to play the piano for her.

The size of the Albert Hall has reduced many artistes to a state of terror, even Wagner is reported to have been shaken when he first saw it. Clara was spared such a fear, her voice fitted it like a hand in a glove. As an anonymous person remarked, "The Albert Hall was built in intelligent anticipation of Butt's advent." Sullivan, for all his operetta success with his lyricist partner W. S. Gilbert, yearned to handle weightier themes, and *The Golden Legend,* a parable of virtue overcoming evil, based on a Longfellow poem, was one of these. The religiosity of the piece also appealed to Clara, with its dramatic opening stanza of Lucifer trying to tear down the cross from Strasbourg Cathedral. It was popular with the Victorians and there had been seventeen productions alone in 1886, the year of its premiere. Queen Victoria had commanded a performance at the Royal Albert Hall in 1888, after which she invited Sir Arthur to her box and told him she thought he would do well to write a grand opera. He wrote several, but they did not do particularly well.

Patey had created Ursula, and she was a hard act to follow, but the cast with whom Clara would now be singing was hardly less formidable. Soprano Emma Albani, some twenty-five years Clara's senior and at the peak of her powers, was a favourite at Covent Garden and had the good sense to marry its manager. George Henschel was the bass, whom she had supported when a chorister, and the popular Ben Davies was the tenor. Clara's parents came to London for the performance and sat in awe of what had happened to their eldest daughter. Henry was plainly thrilled, her mother was nervous.

The excitement at the College had been so great when it was known she would be appearing at the Albert Hall that it had been decided that, rather than gloss over the fact her debut was under the aegis of the Guildhall, the College would capitalise on her success and showcase her itself. By so doing, the College would, clearly, showcase itself too. After much consideration, and while she had been learning the part of Ursula, the College decided that she should be launched in opera, her eagerness to do this influencing the decision. The Guildhall had already done oratorio and she was engaged to sing two more with Sir Joseph. Opera would be a new venture and it was her first love. The chosen vehicle would be a grand college production of Gluck's *Orfeo ed Euridice*, in which she would, naturally, sing Orpheus. This opera is loosely based on the Greek myth of Orpheus, who, famed for the beauty of his voice, is mourning the death of his wife Euridice. Amore (Cupid) tells him he can go to the underworld and get her back, although with the proviso that he does not look at her until they have returned to earth – if he does, Euridice will be unable to leave. At first, the Furies refuse him entry, but relent when he charms them with his singing. Euridice is delighted when they are reunited, but upset when Orpheus will not look at her, taking this as a sign that he no longer loves her. He breaks down, turning to look at her, and she dies again. Orpheus then sings the show-stopping aria *Che Faro* (What is Life Without Thee?) and Amore reappears to reunite them.

The performance of *Orfeo ed Euridice* was to be staged at the West End's Lyceum Theatre on 10th December 1892, just three days after her *Golden Legend* appearance. This meant she would be debuting at two top London venues within days of each other. Although great things had been expected of her, Clara's success as Ursula was even greater than anyone had anticipated. The Royal College of Music was absolutely delighted. It had all worked out well for the College, and the Guildhall had done them a favour in publicising their new star. Their decision to allow her to sing had been vindicated.

Orpheus was a "natural" for Clara. She was playing a man, so her height was a bonus and she would look superb in the costume. The low tessitura would show off her extraordinary voice to perfection.

The opera was first performed in 1762, the role of Orpheus written for contralto castrato Gaetano Guadagni, favoured by Handel in several of his works. Most castrati glorified in virtuosity, but Guadagni achieved his effects by dramatic rather than coloratura display. He was unusual in that in middle age, when most singers think of transposing down their repertoire, he discovered his upper register and became a soprano. As there are now so few contraltos about, Orpheus is usually sung by a mezzo but it has been done by both tenor and baritone. When the prospect of Ursula had been looming, not to mention its follow-up Orpheus, Clara had been uncharacteristically nervous during rehearsals. Orpheus is an emotionally draining role and she was now required to act with her body as well as her voice. She had not yet control of her emotions on stage and this was clear during rehearsals when she was rehearsing the aria *Che Faro*. She burst into tears and had to stop. Looking up from his score and mistaking this for laughter the conductor, Charles Stanford (Sir Charles from 1902), who taught composition at the College, rapped his baton on the lectern and barked, "Come, Miss Butt, no nonsense please. Stop that laughing." She explained, embarrassedly, that she was not laughing, quite the reverse, but his rebuke stung. He was the last conductor to publicly admonish her and get away with it.

Stanford's criticisms were drowned by a chorus of praise from the press:

> The Orpheus of Miss Clara Butt was more than merely satisfactory – she has a fine contralto voice, full and sweet and of considerable power. It is remarkably even in tone and her transition to the lower notes almost unnoticeable. In fact she has the rare taste not to try and draw attention to the lower notes at the expense of the rest. No doubt she has something to learn, but as she is only twenty, she should become a singer of the highest rank. As actress, though her work was somewhat crude, she showed much natural power and intelligence. Unfortunately her stature - she is over 6 feet and well proportioned – must limit her range of parts in opera. *Pall Mall Gazette*

"We must first speak of Miss Clara Butt, who carried off the chief honours...simply outstanding as the work of a youthful student." *The Era*

"Miss Clara Butt...succeeded...in riveting the attention from the beginning and her fine voice was used to the greatest advantage." *The Times*

"...it is necessary to place her among the very first of vocalists." *Musical News*

"I fancy there will soon be a contest among managers for Miss Butt's services..." *Evening News*

"That she is by far the best singer that has ever come from The Royal College of Music is beyond dispute..." *The Times*

"[She] far surpassed the utmost expectations that could reasonably be entertained" George Bernard Shaw, *The World*

Clara was so successful that, so she told Mrs. Ponder for her biography, she was immediately offered a three-year contract by Sir Augustus Harris, director of Covent Garden. She tells us that, beguiling as this was, she had the sense to know she was not yet ready for such a prestigious appointment. This opinion was endorsed by the Royal College of Music, and this time she listened. But it is unlikely that Harris, a man of experience, made such an offer to an inexperienced singer, however promising. Maybe it was the vanity of a star misremembering the past.

As *Grove's Dictionary of Music and Musicians* puts it: "From that date her success was assured." This, on top of her Albert Hall triumph, brought a flood of offers from agents and impresarios. Being a novice in the field of personal representation she thought a long time about these, listening to what people more experienced than she had to say, before coming to a decision. Eventually, with her prescient business acumen starting to bud – it was never to desert her – she settled for representation by Narciso Vert, described as the "Napoleon" of agents. Vert had been an employee of the George Dolby agency which had had an office above Chappell's, the music publishers, and had taken over when Dolby retired in 1880. Dolby was brother of contralto Charlotte Sainton Dolby. It was the right decision, and she stayed with him until his sudden death in 1905. Even after that she was represented by him to a degree in that he had employed two young men, Robert Leigh Ibbs and John Tillett, who created Ibbs and Tillett, the most successful concert agency in Europe for most of the twentieth century. For years she was their prime client. Ibbs and Tillett went on to represent the likes of Fritz Kreisler, Rachmaninov, Segovia, Myra Hess and Kathleen Ferrier. After John Tillett's death the agency was fronted by his redoubtable widow Emmie Tillett, aka the Duchess of Wigmore Street, where the agency was based. People still quail at the mention of her name.

One of the offers Vert negotiated for Clara was an appearance at the Handel Festival, to be held at the Crystal Palace the following year. She tells us that Sir Augustus Harris repeated his offer of a three-year contract at Covent Garden, which she again refused. She returned to the family for Christmas at Bristol, which had an air of unreality about it after the fast life she had been leading in London. She was still a student, yet represented by a top agent. It was remarkable, and no one could quite believe what had happened. Lanky Clara, just turned twenty, was a star, and she was the coolest of anyone about success. Stardom was different then, altogether more refined, but it never held any disadvantages that Clara could see. Like Maria Callas, she was to the manner born.

The New Year term at the Royal College of Music was equally unreal. Most of her studies were taken up with coaching for professional engagements. She sang in *Israel in Egypt* and *Elijah* at the Albert Hall, with the Royal Choral Society under Barnby, as agreed, and appeared on the bill in several Albert Hall concerts. Unsurprisingly, Clara could get above herself at times. This was unleashed on Sir Walter Parratt, who had a tendency to be sarcastic. He used this tactic on his students for years, but it rankled with Clara. He called her, proprietarily, "my bass," which she did not mind, but she did mind when he publicly criticised her. The showdown came when he remarked, "Do you think you are here for ornament, Miss Butt?" She was singing so much professionally, she tried to rest her voice in class on performance days, and this was such a day. She replied, haughtily, that she was certainly not there for ornament, adding she would never come to his class again, and slammed out of the room. This was unacceptable behaviour from a student, but Parratt had to accept it, and she never did return to his class. This was the man who had auditioned her, and he might have wondered what on earth had happened. Clara was now singing all over the country and made sure Parratt saw a review in the *Newcastle Daily Journal* of a performance she had recently given there: "Without doubt her gifts cannot be surpassed by any vocalist at present before the public." Parratt's student was now a nationally-renowned singer. No wonder her head was turned.

Someone else who felt the sharpness of Clara's tongue was Mr. Hedley, manager of the Royal Choral Society. During a rehearsal he suggested that, during *O Rest in the Lord,* she might like to take a breath at a certain place. When she asked why, he replied it was because Madame Patey did so. He reached for her score to pencil it in. He never got the score, she would not let go of it. She had no need of a breath in the suggested place. A tug of war ensued and Hedley was met with cold disdain from her brown eyes. "I shan't take a breath," she informed him, "not unless I want to, that is. Certainly not because someone else does". These eminent people, who had spent their lives in music, bristled at this lack of respect, but there was little they could do. Her glory reflected on them and they were pleased enough to bathe in it.

More glory fell on the Royal College of Music when it received the following telegram:

I AM COMMANDED BY HIS ROYAL HIGHNESS THE PRINCE OF WALES TO DESIRE A REPETITION OF THE PERFORMANCE OF ORPHEUS AS GIVEN BY THE STUDENTS OF THE ROYAL COLLEGE OF MUSIC AT THE LYCEUM THEATRE IN DECEMBER LAST.

His Royal Highness (later to become Edward VII), Patron of the Royal College of Music, had missed *Orpheus*, but had heard much about Clara. Would the College be kind enough to stage another performance for him? The college and everyone concerned with the opera were delighted. In those days royalty was all, its slightest whim indulged. The royal performance was trumpeted for 11 March 1893.

As the Prince had commanded a repeat performance, the same cast was booked with, for some reason, the exception of Euridice, who had been sung by Maggie Purvis, another College pupil. The conductor, Stanford again, had decided she would be replaced by another student, Mary Turner. Maggie was not the only one to be upset – Clara was furious. She and Maggie were both scholarship girls and had become friends. Clara was having none of it. This decision to replace Maggie was made less than a week before the performance and Clara's outrage was fuelled by the fact that Mary Turner was not a fast learner. Clara knew her and had no quibble about her singing, but was nervous she might not learn the part properly in time and jeopardise the performance. She did not want a change of cast to throw things. She and Maggie were comfortable with each other.

Taking the matter into her own hands she insisted Maggie be reinstated. Told the change was absolute she refused to leave the green room to rehearse, demanding to see the royal telegram. She observed that without Maggie it would not be a repeat performance such as HRH had requested. This was true, although it is doubtful the Prince of Wales would have noticed the difference. Stanford sent for her, "Tell him I am waiting for Miss Purvis, we'll come together" was his answer. She was told Maggie was no longer a cast member. Clara replied tartly that if Stanford wanted a new Euridice then he must find a new Orpheus: "He can't have one without the other." The rehearsal was cancelled. Time was running short and Clara was again summoned before the board of the College. Somewhat more conciliatorily this time, she explained how difficult it would be for her to work with a new singer with such limited rehearsals. Referring to Mary Turner's well known slowness she added, pointedly, that it had taken her a year to learn one act of *Fidelio*.

Stanford's decision was overridden. The board felt it couldn't do much else if it wanted a command performance. For all her arrogance, Clara was relieved. She wanted the performance as much as anyone. But she wanted to be seen at her best, not let down by a weak cast member. She also genuinely thought that Maggie had been unfairly treated. With the exception of Stanford, the cast was entirely on her side, and when Clara arrived for rehearsals next morning she was greeted with a round of applause. She burst into tears, thanking everybody. The cast was as relieved as she that they were not to be denied a command performance. Had the College insisted on Mary Turner, Clara would have been forced to sing. To refuse would have been an unforgiveable insult to the Prince of Wales and she would never have risked such a move. Singers depended on royal patronage, and she could have compromised her prospects. It was thanks to the Prince that she came under the patronage of the most powerful woman of the British Empire, Queen Victoria herself.

# CHAPTER SEVEN

# Royal Patronage

It was a star-studded audience. In addition to the Prince of Wales, royalty was represented in the form of the Duchess of Teck and Princess May. Operatic celebrities included the Italian sisters Sofia and Giulia Ravogli. Giulia, an unusually tall contralto, not unlike Clara, had herself enjoyed a success at Covent Garden with *Orfeo*. It was Ravogli's triumph that had brought the role to the Royal College of Music's attention and the reason why Clara was now singing it in front of the Prince of Wales. Giulia and soprano Sofia were a sort of operatic double act, appearing in *Norma*, *Aida* and many other works together. They were so wrapped up in each other that when Sofia retired, so did Giulia, despite being at the peak of her career. She settled into non-musical life as the wife of society surgeon Harrison Cripps. Giulia had possessed a fearsome lower range (she was dubbed 'Il Tenore' and critic Herman Klein described her voice as possessing an "abnormally full, masculine timbre") with an extraordinary upward extension which lifted her into the soprano territory; she did, in fact, sing several mezzo roles. From her box, Ravogli assessed the strength of the opposition. To know that Ravogli was in the house must have intimidated Clara.

Henry Irving, actor and manager of the Lyceum was also there, and he had lent his theatre to the College for the evening. His performance in *The Bells* had electrified London, running for 151 performances.

Irving's business manager, Abraham Stoker, was also there. A few years later in 1897, under the more familiar name of Bram Stoker, he would terrify the world with his novel *Dracula*, introducing his infamous vampire. Irving escorted leading lady and star of the Lyceum, Ellen Terry, who had lent Clara her dressing room. London was at Terry's feet and this included George Bernard Shaw, who eulogised: "Ellen Terry is the most beautiful name in the world; it rings like a chime through the last quarter of the 19$^{th}$ century."

  Clara, nervous in front of these stars, mistimed one of her moves and accidentally dropped her sword. It was a harmless enough fluff, although she could have died of shame. She managed to pick up the weapon nonchalantly, so that the audience barely noticed it. The one exception was Ellen Terry, who afterwards congratulated Clara on her presence of mind. For a novice to have such command had impressed her. Despite her nerves, *Orfeo* was even more successful the second time round. Clara's dressing room, Ellen Terry's in reality, was cluttered with celebrities afterwards but she could not spend much time with them. She was summoned to the royal box to be congratulated by the Prince of Wales. Still in costume she hurried there, in such a fluster that she was unsure whether to curtsey or to bow. The critics were again full of praise for the young singer:

> Miss Clara Butt, who repeated her striking impersonation of Orpheus, seemed more especially to have derived benefit from her former experience. … Her attitude and gestures were less angular; she bore herself with greater dignity and repose of manner; and an even deeper note of pathos seemed to pervade the utterances of the sorrow-laden hero. Miss Butt thus proved herself a thoughtful and intelligent student as well as a richly endowed singer, and the success of her future career became more than ever assured. Her rendering of Che faro was distinguished by notable beauty of tone and appropriateness of expression[.] *Illustrated London News*

Clara sang at the Hanley and Bristol Festivals in the October of 1893 and more appearances with the Royal Choral Society followed, notably Handel's *Israel in Egypt* conducted by Barnby. This performance was reviewed by George Bernard Shaw, who singled her out as "magnificent" adding "[her] last 14 bars came with the true musical and dramatic passion which reduced all purely technical criticism to a mere matter of detail".

For all her success, Stanford had not forgiven Clara's mutinous opposition to his attempted recasting of Maggie Purvis. They were taking part in a *Messiah* in Leeds and during the performance the baritone whispered something to her. Stanford noticed this and hissed "Do not talk, Miss Butt!" His back was towards the audience but the choir and musicians heard. During the interval she rounded on him: "I will not have you speaking to me as you did just now." He responded, "And I cannot have any chattering on the platform." "You are here to conduct the performance not my behaviour," she retorted, turning on her heel, the manner in which several conversations with Stanford ended. It was his turn to be furious and he swore he would never conduct her again. Unfortunately for them both, he did.

Such was the demand for appearances that, without consulting the College, Clara accepted a tour of America. In the unlikely event that the College would have granted permission, it was a foolhardy venture. Clara was too inexperienced and, as yet, had an insufficient repertoire to undertake such an ordeal. Even seasoned troupers are fazed by such tours and Clara's youthful verve was no substitute for experience. America, however, was a land of glamour and she was agog to see it, and to travel in general. She had heard tales of the success Jenny Lind enjoyed in America during her 1850-52 tour, for which the legendary soprano had been represented by the equally legendary impresario Phineas T. Barnum. Clara, however, was not put to the test. Shortly after *Orfeo*, the strain took its toll and she was rushed to hospital.

## CHAPTER EIGHT

## Queen Victoria

For all her voluptuous appearance Clara was, in fact, a woman of frail health and her childhood diphtheria had left her with a weak heart. She rarely mentions illnesses and in her "official" biography only permits this mention of hospitalisation because is links to an anecdote concerning Queen Victoria. She briefly admits to a surgical operation, but omits to disclose that it was the first of several. By the time Clara came to allow her memoirs to be written she was a follower of Christian Science, a religious movement founded in America in 1879 by Mary Baker Eddy. Part of its doctrine is to deny the reality of sickness and its adherents traditionally refuse treatment. Consequently, any details of Clara's illnesses are hard to find. She would have hated for her medical problems to be discussed publicly, and did her best to ensure no one else knew about them.

Her parents wanted her to convalesce at home but, pleading the beneficial effects of sea air, Clara recovered at St Leonard's, near Hastings. She was taken by ambulance to Henry Blower's home, her teacher at the Royal College of Music. Mrs. Blower revelled in Clara's success, which reflected well on her husband who was still teaching her, and fussed over her like a mother hen. She arranged for Clara to stay in a nearby boarding house with a Royal College of Music friend called Bee Gilligan. This was actually easier for Clara, as she could take things at her own leisurely pace, without the strictures of having to be a polite guest.

Although Clara was devoted to her family, she was more comfortable now in the company of those who understood the pressures of a professional life. Such was her fame that she was introduced to the Blowers' friends under the alias of Miss Linnington. Today, with her striking appearance, and connection with the Blowers, she would have been detected at once. In those less media-frenzied times she got away with it. The Blowers did not suspend their musical activities while she was with them and held their regular soirees where guests sang. They probably hoped she would drop her cloak of anonymity and reveal, to the amazement of their friends, her true identity. This did not happen. Being a bit under the weather Clara was relieved to be out of the public eye for a short while.

Although no one knew she was a professional Clara was invited to join in the singing, out of courtesy. It would have been churlish to refuse and she sang *Barbara Allen*, a popular song of the day. During the evening there had been talk of Blower's pupil, the famous Clara Butt, and how she had conquered the country. She had actually been asked if she knew her, so, to put them off the scent she deliberately sang a bit off pitch. She was not asked to sing again, although several of the others gave encores. In reality it was more difficult for Clara, who had perfect pitch, to sing out of tune than it was to sing in tune. Singing off pitch was also a trick of Kathleen Ferrier's, who was once filmed at a party, slightly squiffy, doing precisely that and accompanying herself at the piano at the same time. Clara's pride, however, would not let her spend the evening as a musical Philistine and, when the guests had thinned out, she sang *Kathleen Mavourneen* in perfect pitch for a sweet old lady who said she loved the song.

The song has an interesting history. The tune was written by Frederick Crouch – the only one of his many compositions now remembered – who sang it all over Britain and America before selling it to a publisher for £10. The publisher is said to have made £15,000 from it. Crouch's daughter, Cora Pearl, became more famous than him by becoming a notorious courtesan. Not particularly beautiful of face, her bosom was greatly admired and has been described as "a marvel of nature".* Clara was to include *Kathleen Mavourneen* in numerous recitals and later recorded it several times. It became one of her best-selling titles and she fully imbues it with the pathos for which its beautiful, sweeping lines call. It was a real Butt favourite.

After a few weeks with the Blowers, and on sick leave from the Royal College of Music, Clara moved on to nearby Brighton, noted for its recuperative air. Her convalescence was interrupted by an exciting telegram from Sir Arthur Sullivan, then conductor of the State Orchestra. He was authorised, by Her Majesty Queen Victoria, to command Clara to sing at a state concert at Buckingham Palace. Sir Arthur's telegram worked wonders, and was a more effective restorative than the Brighton breezes. Feeling much better, Clara hastened back to Bristol and her family, full of the exciting news. She contacted Sullivan, who had been delighted with *The Golden Legend*, and he explained that it was the Prince of Wales, impressed by her Orpheus, who had recommended her to the Queen, who had then contacted Sullivan to arrange for her to hear this new discovery. His own recommendation had done no harm. Her Majesty sang herself and loved to be surrounded by musical people.

Clara took her mother to the palace as chaperone, as no well-bred young lady travelled alone. Mrs. Butt was even more flustered at the prospect than her daughter. Her father was desperate to go himself but appreciated it was more seemly for his rather nervous wife to accompany Clara. Clara's choice of music was, some might consider, not entirely proper for a virginal young lady to sing in front of her monarch, particularly if that monarch happened to be Queen Victoria. Clara loved the music of Saint-Saëns' opera *Samson et Delila*,

---

\* Understandably, she has been much written about and for those who want to know more there is, among others, *The Memoirs of Cora Pearl: The Erotic Reminiscences of a Flamboyant 19th Century Courtesan.*

and nurtured dreams of singing Delila herself one day. She particularly loved the aria *Mon Coeur s'ouvre à ta Voix*, which showed off her vocal range. It is Delila's seduction scene and the music is voluptuous, even erotic. Nobody, however, seems to have suggested its unsuitability to Clara, not even Sullivan, who was making the arrangements. In any case it was Biblical. Clara recorded the aria around 1915 and again when she was on tour in Tokyo in 1931. By that point, she was nearly sixty and ill from the cancer that was to kill her five years later. Her voice does, indeed, show signs of strain (and wear, she had been singing for over forty years by then), but she sails intrepidly through the piece, using her dramatic powers to the full.

Mrs. Butt was not allowed to join the main audience at the palace, but had to stand hidden in a gallery from where she could peep down unobserved, rather like the ladies of a harem. Queen Victoria, swathed in mourning for Albert (although he had died in 1861, thirty years previously) arrived on the arm of her Indian servant Abdul Karim, unloved by the royal household but adored by her. Handsome Karim had started work at the palace as a waiter but within two years had become the Queen's confidant, promoted from servant's quarters to the royal household where Her Majesty sought his advice on state and personal matters. Such was his closeness to Victoria that, on occasion, members of the royal household threatened to resign in protest. None of this swayed the Queen, used to a court atmosphere of jealousy and intrigue, and also to getting her own way. Her devotion to Karim never wavered, nor his to her. After his death, Edward VII demanded that Karim's family return all the royal correspondence and then promptly burned it. Fortunately, his personal diaries were smuggled to relatives and have recently been published, bringing to light this extraordinary cross-cultural friendship.

Queen Victoria entered to a fanfare of trumpets and the orchestra stood to play the national anthem. All bowed as she passed. Mrs Butt nearly swooned with the sumptuousness of it all. Not so Clara who, in the full confidence of her voice, sang Delila's love song in French (which, of course, Her Majesty understood perfectly). Clara finished to silence. This was not a mark of displeasure, it was a state concert and applause was not permitted. At the end of the concert Victoria left, with Karim, to continued respectful silence. A day or so later Clara received a letter bearing the royal crest and enclosing a cheque for twenty-five guineas. The letter was signed by the Queen, who expressed pleasure at what she had heard. Perhaps the erotic music brought back happy memories of Albert? Clara bought a diamond brooch with the money, the first of many items of fine jewellery she was to buy.

Queen Victoria was not the only one impressed by Clara; so too was Sullivan and it reminded him how good she had been in his oratorio. Sullivan and Clara revelled in quasi-religious music and she was often to sing *The Lost Chord*, one of his most popular songs. He wrote the music for it in 1877 at the bedside of his dying brother Fred, an actor who had appeared in several of the Gilbert and Sullivan operas. It was set to a poem by Adelaide Anne Procter which had been published in *The English Woman's Journal* nearly twenty years earlier in 1858 (see p.214). Miss Procter was as popular in her day as Tennyson, and a favourite of the Queen. The song was made popular by Sullivan's mistress, the socialite singer, Fanny Ronalds, known in Paris where she had lived as the "Patti des Salons". Both Sullivan and Mrs. Ronalds had spouses elsewhere, although Mrs. Ronalds was officially separated, but this did not affect the piety of their performances, where he would often accompany her at the piano. They regularly performed the piece in front of royalty. Sullivan himself thought highly of it, and made a specific request that it never be parodied, adding "I have composed much music since then, but I have never written a second Lost Chord." Enrico Caruso notably sang it in 1912 at New York's Metropolitan Opera House at a charity event to raise funds for families of *Titanic* victims. Clara loved *The Lost Chord* and so did her audiences. After singing it for a lifetime she would complain of contemporary music, "What we need now are more songs like *The Lost Chord*, there is something of the grandeur of Beethoven about it."

A further royal command came from the Queen. This time Clara was summoned to the less formal surroundings of Windsor Castle. She sang *Promise of Life,* made famous by Belle Cole, and rather more suitable for the occasion than Delila's aria. Based on a Biblical text, it featured music by Frederic H. Cowen and words by Clifton Bingham, lyricist of *Love's Old Sweet Song.* Clara was accompanied on the piano by composer Francesco Tosti, who was to become a lifetime friend. Sir Francesco, as he later became, was Italian by birth but had settled in London in 1880, where he taught singing to the Queen and other members of the royal family. Previously he had been singing teacher to the Queen of Italy, a highly fashionable figure. Tosti's songs are still sung today, the most famous being *Goodbye!* Her Majesty clearly enjoyed *Promise of Life* and sent for Clara to thank her, telling her, "I have never liked the English language before but in your mouth it is beautiful." This seems a curious thing for a British queen to say, but perhaps she was comparing it to German. The Queen and her late husband had spoken German together, sometimes joined by the German composer Mendelssohn, a royal favourite. Mendelssohn had composed piano pieces especially for the Queen and would play duets with her.

Among the Queen's guests was Empress Frederick of Germany, Queen Victoria's daughter. She took to Clara and, dropping protocol, cordially invited her to call in should she ever be in Germany. Clara was to take her at her word and the two women became friends, until the Empress's untimely death in 1901, less than seven months after that of her mother. Clara remained close to the German royal family until the outbreak of the First World War.

Tosti knew everyone who was anyone in the music industry and introduced them to Clara. With Tosti accompanying, she sang at no fewer than eight royal receptions. She became known as a favourite of the Queen, and hostesses vied with each other to book her to sing in their drawing rooms, hoping for royal tittle-tattle. Clara did not want to become too accessible so kept the duration of these bookings as short as courtesy would allow. Sometimes the brevity was a necessity as she was booked for as many as three engagements a night. She was not exclusive in this regard; the At Home circuit was busy, and all celebrated performers, including Nellie Melba and the violin virtuoso Joseph Joachim, were at it. They virtually tripped over each other crossing Belgrave Square, sometimes performing at the same house, one leaving as the other was entering.

Clara was not always booked as a performer, frequently she was a guest, in which case she took care not to sing, unless by a royal request which she could not refuse. On one such occasion, a royal requested *Mon Coeur s'ouvre à ta Voix* which she had sung for Queen Victoria. There was another, older, contralto present, who had had her own successes but whose palmy days were now behind her. She had intended to sing the piece for royalty and, indeed, had brought the music with her. With the callousness of youth, Clara asked if she might borrow this for Sir Arthur Sullivan, also a guest, to accompany her. This was indignantly refused, the aging diva wanted another, albeit brief, moment of glory for herself. Making light of the refusal, Clara and Sir Arthur performed from memory. This was another triumph for Clara and a night of bitter humiliation for the old timer. The new favourite had taken over. On one occasion the elderly Duke of Teck kept demanding song after song from her and his requests were becoming more and more haphazard. Finally, after some perplexity, it was realised he wanted her to sing the Toreador song from *Carmen*, a lusty baritone aria recounting the thrills of the bull ring. This she could not accommodate.

Clara could sometimes be the target of snobbishness at these functions. At one gathering some drunken blades were daring one of their number (actually Prince George, the future king) to ask her to dance, the point being she was much taller than him. She was aware of what was going on and when eventually she was asked replied coldly, "I'm sorry, sir, either you're too short or I'm too tall." He returned to his group. At another At Home, for which she had been booked with other artistes, she was annoyed when a little old lady kept pestering her as the preceding artistes were performing. As soon as she had finished her own spot she was lionised again. Clara turned away in impatience and was horrified when told she had been talking to the famous novelist Marie Corelli. Clara adored Corelli's fantasy novels; *A Romance of Two Worlds* was among her favourite books, and also Queen Victoria's. The Queen had predicted Corelli's name would live forever. Although no longer a household name, Corelli retains a small but enthusiastic following for her curious blend of fantasy and didacticism. Her real name was Mary Mackay, daughter of a Scottish songwriter, but this was too prosaic for her and she invented many exotic stories about her birth, claiming a spurious Italian heritage. The novelist E. F. Benson later based his character Lucia partly on her. Corelli's home, Mason Croft, was in Stratford-upon-Avon, where she had moved to be near Shakespeare. Such was her fame that she competed with the bard as a tourist attraction, hiring a gondolier to propel her up and down the Avon. Corelli wanted be tall and willowy but was short and dumpy. Consequently, she was only photographed standing on something to elevate her height, her long dresses hiding the prop. Small wonder Clara did not recognise her. When Clara realised she had spurned one of her heroines she rushed back and told her how much she enjoyed her books. The two became friends for life. When Clara became famous she would pop down to Mason Croft to get away from it all. Corelli would write every day from 10-1p.m. while Clara went through her vocal exercises. Over lunch, they liked to gossip about people they knew.

In 1894 writer George du Maurier, grandfather of novelist Daphne du Maurier, published in serial form in *Harper's Monthly*, his melodrama *Trilby*, the story of the evil Svengali who, using his power of hypnotism, turns a French grisette into a brilliant classical singer. Clara was no grisette, but it is largely believed that his inspiration for this tale came after he heard her sing. In book form, *Trilby* sold an impressive 200,000 copies. Since then it has been adapted for stage and screen.* The first London stage production was at the Haymarket Theatre under Herbert Tree with waif-like Dorothea Baird, probably the most popular actress in London, as Trilby. Tree wanted her singing voice to be sung by Clara off stage, but he could not tempt her. In any case, there was no way Clara could commit herself to a long run, she had too many engagements elsewhere. Such was the play's success that it spawned soaps, dances, songs and even toothpaste. Its lasting heritage is the Trilby hat.

About this time Clara met Clara Novello Davies, vocal coach, composer, pianist and founder of the Welsh Ladies Choir which she conducted and took on international tours, winning prizes at the World's Columbian Exhibition in Chicago in 1893 and the Paris Exhibition in 1899. Of humble stock and married to a tax collector, this had not stopped her from climbing the social ladder. She was to become even more famous during the 1930s and 40s as mother of popular show composer and matinee idol Ivor Novello. Madame Davies had acquired her name "Novello" as her father's tribute to soprano Clara Novello, whom he had heard sing in Cardiff and had never forgotten. Madame Davies was a believer in life after death, something which fascinated Clara. In America the Fox sisters, two girls who had heard raps in the night and interpreted these as contact from the spirit world, had given birth to Spiritualism, claiming that the dead still lived in another dimension. Spiritualism was all the rage. Mediums sprang up overnight and society ladies employed them to put them in contact with their dear departed. It was said, but never substantiated, that Queen Victoria herself employed mediums to contact Albert. In this vein, Madame Davies had written the music to a song *A Voice from the Spirit Land*, the words by an unknown Quaker lady, and Clara had included it in a recital she gave in Cardiff with the Cardiff Orchestral Society, to

---

\* In 1931 with John Barrymore and Marian Marsh and 1954 with Sir Donald Wolfit and Hildegard Knef (surely the possessor of the best pair of legs to come from Germany since Marlene Dietrich). This film has the added advantage of the glorious soprano of Elisabeth Schwarzkopf.

whom Madame Davies was honorary accompanist. Madame Davies writes in her memoirs, "Clara Butt and I were destined to a life-long friendship." They had even more in common when they realised that Maggie Purvis, whom Clara had insisted sing Euridice to her Royal Command Orpheus, was now a pupil of Madame Novello Davies. Maggie dubbed them Big Clara and Little Clara.

Davies describes Clara at this time as a "handsome young girl ... who, nevertheless, had an air of shy appeal that went straight to my heart and as an older and experienced musician Clara liked to come to me for advice." Clara was still a student, in her twenties, and working as hard as any full time professional; more so, considering she still had her college studies. Sometimes when she returned to Alexandra House, where she was still staying, she fell into bed exhausted. But she was tingling with excitement. Clara had been applauded in the most eminent drawing rooms in London, surrounded by illustrious figures. Who could ask for more?

For all the glitter of society rooms, there were times when she was aware she was still painfully naive. One of these times happened after a concert, when she was with her mother, and they were about to leave the theatre for a meal. To her surprise a personable young man called at her dressing room and invited them both to dinner. Flattered, she accepted. It would be alright as she was with her mother. He took them to an expensive restaurant and ordered a lavish champagne dinner. When the bill came he informed the waiter, "The young lady will pay." The young lady was too embarrassed and humiliated to refuse. It was a near thing, neither she nor her mother had been anticipating such an extravagant meal and barely had enough between them to scrape together the money.

On another occasion she was called upon to make a little speech after a recital. It was a disaster. Queen of Song she may have been, but at public speaking she was, then, a failure. She knew it and confessed afterwards that she had never felt such a fool in her life. She learnt her lessons in worldliness the hard way and soon needed them. The Royal

College of Music decided to extend her scholarship by another year, making it four years in all. Three months of this would be spent in Paris to study French repertoire. The French extension to her studies was being paid for personally by Queen Victoria. Clearly Clara's Delila had inspired Her Majesty to encourage her to learn more of the French method. Clara was eager to go, but soon came down to earth with a bump. Literally. Before leaving she went on holiday to Staffordshire. She decided to improve her horse riding skills, as all properly brought-up ladies rode. Although she had been on a horse a few times, she was far from expert. She chose an elegant chestnut, a variety notorious for their mettle. She was thrown from the horse mid-gallop, sustaining bruises and a broken ankle. She had to walk around for six weeks with a crutch and her leg in plaster.

This did not stop her fulfilling engagements, although Charles Santley, with whom she was booked to sing *Elijah*, looked aghast as she hobbled onto the platform on her crutch, and protested, with justification, "You can't sing *Oh Rest in the Lord* leaning on a crutch." She took his point and sang unaided. But the audience had noticed the crutch and someone whispered, "Such a wonderful voice, what a pity she's a cripple." Clara was able to sing through her pain. It was still there, and the ankle constantly throbbed, but she was able to detach herself from it and concentrate on her voice. In time she improved and even mastered this technique, which got her through difficult times ahead.

# CHAPTER NINE

# Paris

Clara left for Paris in the autumn of 1893 to study with Henri Louis Duvernoy. Duvernoy, son of minor composer Charles Duvernoy, was an even more minor composer himself and is now chiefly remembered, if remembered at all, for a set of piano exercises. It is a mystery why he was chosen as a coach. But he was a fashionable teacher of the time and knew the French repertoire. Clara did not get on with him and they found they had little in common. By and large, it turned out to be a pretty miserable trip. She could not cheer herself up with any little shopping trips for, although Queen Victoria was paying the bills, this did not mean unlimited expenses; quite the reverse. The monarch was no fool, and did not enjoy a particularly lavish lifestyle herself. There were times when Clara could have wished Her Majesty had not been so desirous to help and had instead left her in England. But there was no way she could renege on royal largesse, however stingy. She was accompanied by Mrs Bindon, the matron from the Royal College of Music, with whom she did not have a particularly harmonious relationship. Episodes that might have struck her as amusing became ordeals. The sight of her prescribed French chaperone-companion did not lift her spirits either – she described her unkindly as a "subnormal hunchback". Her digs were depressing and filthy, but she half expected that from the French. Most English people made similar assumptions in those unenlightened days of travel.

Things bucked up when she became friendly with another student from the Royal College of Music and began spending time with her. They improved even more when she abandoned her digs and her chaperone and fled to Neuilly to live with a friendly French family recommended by her new friend. This could have been a certain Miss Snella, who later moved to England to become companion to Clara. Fond of children, Clara visited an orphanage there, and her heart was touched. A good needlewoman, she made clothes for them and gave them singing lessons, visiting several times, and they called her Auntie Clara. She promised to help them. It was not a rash promise – in her heyday she re-visited and gave several fundraising concerts for the home.

Clara sang while in Paris and her stentorian tones greatly excited the manager of the Folies Bergères, who invited her as his guest to the famous cabaret. She sat at the table of honour with the proprietor. The Folies was then at its height, its glamorous ladies admired throughout the world. Its resident star was Loie Fuller, an American dancer who was to introduce Isadora Duncan to the French. Pioneer of natural movement and improvisation and dressed in the extremity of fashion, Fuller was the embodiment of Art Nouveau in motion. Her admirers included Toulouse-Lautrec, Rodin and, oddly, Marie Curie. The manager saw a future for Clara at the Folies. He loved her height – no show girl could be too tall for the Folies – but she was not to be just a show girl. He saw her as far more than that and excitedly suggested that he would feature her, gorgeously dressed, in a revue of her own. She would enter to a fanfare of trumpets, her own notes competing with theirs. His pleas, like those of Herbert Tree for *Trilby*, were in vain. The world of the *demi-mondaine* was not for Clara. Her voice was a gift from God, and should be used in His service (as well as her own). She was to employ and even pioneer many theatrical techniques and defiantly flirt with the world of Light Entertainment. Feathers, fanfares and fabulous frocks had their place, and were to feature in her performances (to the dismay of some critics) but, above all, she was a "classical" artiste. That would never be forfeited.

Clara was subsequently informed she had been honoured with the Royal Society of Musicians medal as the year's most successful student. A philanthropic body founded in 1738, the Society had included Purcell and Handel among its members. It was expected that Clara should make a visit to London to accept the prestigious medal. Some members of that august body did not take kindly to her response that they would have to wait until she returned to England for her to collect it. She was not being ungrateful, she simply did not have the money for the fare, entertaining little idea of her future life of first-class travel.

# CHAPTER TEN

## Samson et Delila

Clara later returned to England for her first solo recital at London's Queen's Hall. There were also appearances with the Royal Choral Society and various festivals including, in 1894, the Handel Festival. This was followed by another royal recital at Balmoral with soprano Emma Albani. Her fourth scholarship year sped by and Clara barely noticed when she left college as she had been doing so much professional work already. College had, in fact, become rather a rein on her career. She left Alexandra House and took lodgings with Maggie Purvis and her parents in their London home. Clara decided to stop earning in 1896 and invest in the future. She had been working too hard, packing in the At Homes, and was feeling the strain. Friends advised her to take a year off from performing and instead concentrate on studying. Clara admired the Belgium baritone Jacques Bouhy, now a singing teacher based in Paris, and had the opportunity of studying with him for six months. This would mean a return to the city of romance that had afforded anything but romance to Clara, but her studies came first.

Bouhy had created Escamillo in *Carmen* and sung the part of the high priest in *Samson et Delila*, the work in which Clara longed to sing. His knowledge of the opera would be invaluable to her. Among his former pupils were several successful singers, including American contralto Louise Homer. Her triumphs though, according to her autobiography, were in spite of Bouhy who, she claims, tried to "muffle" her voice. The Bouhy method was not for her. Singing is an individual art, and what suits one does not always suit another. There was also the problem of how to finance these studies – she could hardly go back to Queen Victoria, cap in hand. And Clara was still far from wealthy. Although she kept it quiet, the erratic business affairs of her father had taken another tumble and much of what she earned was sent to Bristol to support her family. This was why she had been unable to return to England for the Royal Society of Musicians medal.

The problem was solved by society friends. The hostess Mrs Ronalds got together with Lord Hardwicke and he anonymously deposited £900 in a Paris bank for her: £600 for lodgings and £300 for expenses. She did not find out the identity of her sponsor until years later, when she gratefully repaid the amount. Thanks to their beneficence she was able to make further arrangements. After studying with Bouhy in Paris she would travel to Berlin to study for a further six months with Hungarian soprano Etelka Gerster. She had heard much of the Gerster method and was anxious to benefit from it. In Paris, Clara would also study with French composer Herman Bemberg, a friend of Nellie Melba's who had sung his opera *Elaine* both at Covent Garden and the Metropolitan. Today he is all but forgotten, not even warranting an entry in the *Concise Oxford Dictionary of Opera*. He was rich, handsome and on the guest list of all society ladies. Clara, too was taken with him, and they would jokingly tell friends they were engaged.

Clara lodged at Miss Field's English Hotel. Perhaps it was Bouhy's reminiscences of *Samson et Delila*, but she found she could not keep Saint-Saëns out of her mind and her desire to sing Delila became an obsession. It was more than she could do to be in the same city as the great man and not approach him. Clara knew Saint-Saëns would not welcome being approached, at least not by aspiring female singers. He was past sixty, portly, reclusive and unhappy by the disappointments of what had promised to be a privileged life. His musical successes did not compensate for personal tragedy. When in a depression he would disappear for weeks at a time. He had written his first composition aged three and was giving piano recitals at ten, including concerti by Mozart and Beethoven. His work was admired by Berlioz, Lizst, Rossini and Gounod and his pupils included Fauré and Messager. His father had died when he was a child and he was brought up by a strong-willed mother whom he adored, and with whom he lived until her death in 1888. When younger he had been famous for his parties where he would appear in frocks, singing soprano arias to wild applause. His homosexuality caused much of Saint-Saëns' melancholy and he attempted to "correct" this through marriage. At the age of forty he married a younger woman and they had two children, both of whom died in infancy within six weeks of each other. This unbalanced him for a while and he abandoned his wife but continued to live with his mother. When she died he was suicidal. He spent much time alone with his dogs and would winter in Algeria, then a well-known homosexual haunt. Saint-Saëns was in one of his darkest periods when Clara, bursting with youthful enthusiasm, decided to call unannounced. She was fresh-faced and eager to sing his music.

Clara was curtly, and rightly, informed that the great man was unavailable, but she made so much fuss at the front door that the butler actually went to his employer to explain the upheaval. Naturally enough he declined to see her. She refused to go and eventually, exasperated by the disturbance, Saint-Saëns made his fussy, puffing way to the door. He was even less gracious than the servant and made it clear he certainly did not want to see, let alone hear, an oversized, female student. Clara begged to be allowed to sing *Mon Coeur s'ouvre à ta Voix* to him, promising to leave instantly if he didn't like it. Since it was clearly going to be difficult to get rid of her, and there were tears in her eyes (wasted on Saint-Saëns), he, with ill grace, conceded. It would be quicker than pleading with her. She followed him to the music room, where he sat at the grand piano and thumped out the opening bars. Disregarding this unsympathetic approach, Clara sang with all her heart, her love of the music pouring out. She sang the piece in its entirety and his accompaniment was rapidly modified to suit her voice. He adored it. It was a changed man who rose from the piano stool, inspired with visions of a new Covent Garden production featuring a towering Delila with a strange, dark voice. He saw her height not as a problem but as an asset. She would not look ridiculous, as he knew exactly the tenor with whom to partner her – Albert Alvarez. The imposing Alvarez stood around 6' 8", with a voice and stage presence to match, and he had created several roles for the Paris Opera. Saint-Saëns adored him. Strangely, for such a robust man, he had been trained by male soprano Andrea Martini. Abandoning anything else he was doing, Saint-Saëns began to coach her in the role there and then.

*Samson et Delila* had a chequered history. Originally conceived as an oratorio in 1868, it had taken Saint-Saëns ten years to write. Giving up hope, he had abandoned it for two years until Lizst encouraged him to continue. When finished it was viewed with indifference and no one offered to stage it. The part of Delila was written for, and dedicated to, Pauline Viardot, fourteen years his senior, whom Saint-Saëns admired above all singers. He would often accompany her at recitals. She very much wanted to sing Delila and, in fact, did so in an incomplete form, in 1872 at a private performance before an invited audience with the composer at the piano deputising for an orchestra. Students comprised the chorus and Viardot wore an oriental costume. She was fifty at the time but, as April Fitz-Lyon writes in *The Price of Genius*, "His elderly Delila was in no way incongruous or ridiculous". That said, Viardot's voice was also fifty years old and betrayed signs of the hard use to which it had been put, particularly its middle register. Contemporary reports, however, noted that "its upper and lower notes were wonderfully preserved". Still no one wanted to stage it. Eventually Lizst put it on himself in 1877, and it slowly increased in popularity, with performances in Europe and America. It was not staged in Paris until 1890 and by then Viardot was around seventy and too old to sing Delila. In fact, too old to sing anything much.

Work had started on a production at Covent Garden in 1893

until it was realised the Lord Chamberlain had pronounced a veto on Biblical subjects being represented on stage, although a concert version was permitted. So keen was Saint-Saëns on starring Clara, whom he envisaged as the most exciting Delila since Viardot, that, once her Paris studies were over, he took her to London for discussions with Covent Garden management. To no avail – the Lord Chamberlain had still not changed his mind and no Biblical opera could be staged. It was a bitter disappointment. It was not mounted at Covent Garden until 1909, when Louise Kirkby-Lunn sang Delila. This was as galling for Clara as it had been for Viardot, particularly when she read comments like those made by concert manager Roland Foster: "What a magnificent Delila Kirkby-Lunn made."

From Paris, Clara moved to Berlin, still financed by her unknown sponsor, for six months of study with Etelka Gerster. One thing Clara had drummed into her before meeting Gerster was not to mention her rival Adelina Patti. The divas detested each other. The fact that a vocal crisis forced Gerster to retire prematurely, while Patti was still touring to full houses, did not help. Patti, born in 1843, was probably the most famous singer in the world, but the younger Gerster, born 1855, was not far behind her. They were jealous rivals, which was intensified when J. H. Mapleson had engaged them both for an American tour of *Les Huguenots* during 1883-4, doubtless exploiting their feud to expand the houses. Patti had not been blessed with physical beauty (her face was distressingly plain), but nature had compensated her with an exceptional soprano which she had trained into a superb coloratura. Her parents were singers, too, which had helped open doors. Patti had made her concert debut aged seven and sung her first opera at sixteen, billed as "Little Florinda". She had twenty-five consecutive seasons at Covent Garden, with a clause in her contracts excusing her from rehearsals. She sang what she sang and the cast had to accommodate her. There are several recordings of Patti, made in 1905-6 when she was past her best and her voice, frankly, worn out. But there are some pretty sounds. Patti thought so too when the records were played back to her; she is reported to have kissed the amplification horn and announced: "Maintenant je comprends par ceque je suis Patti!"

Gerster, too, had had a distinguished career. Trained by Matilde Marchesi, who specialised in high, bright voices and whose pupils included Melba, Calve and Mary Garden, she had an early admirer in Verdi who recommended she make her debut in his opera *Rigoletto* at Venice's Teatro La Fenice. She had triumphed then, subsequently appearing many times internationally, making her London debut at Her Majesty's in *La Sonnambula*, before going on to sing *Lucia di Lammermoor*, *I Puritani* and Queen of the Night in *The Magic Flute*. Then tragedy struck. At the age of thirty-five, at the peak of her career and mid-performance of *La Sonnambula*, her voice broke and never mended. There were moments when it flickered back into life, but these were few and unsustainable. Gerster was able to put her expertise to good financial use by opening a school in Berlin, and this was where Clara went to study with her. Like all teachers, Gerster was not infallible – she had dismissed soprano Lotte Lehmann for not responding to her methods and Lehmann, under other teachers, went on to enjoy an international career.

Gerster was by now in her forties. Her daughter assisted her at the school and it was rumoured that it was her birth that had caused Gerster's vocal collapse. If so, it must have been a unique case – plenty of singers give birth and carry on regardless. Certainly she bore her daughter no animosity. In those treasured, tragic, moments when Gerster's voice returned she had the urge to sing. She would accompany herself and, for a few triumphant moments, the voice that had thrilled thousands would ring crystally into the air. Then a croak replaced the trills as her cords collapsed again. She quietly left the piano, her moment of glory finished. She was used to it.

It is unusual, although not unique, for a female singer to be taught by a man, such as Clara had been by Henry Blower and, indeed, Bouhy, – and Kathleen Ferrier by Roy Henderson – and odd that she should have sought further tuition from a coloratura soprano rather than a contralto. Perhaps not so odd given that Clara developed a fine coloratura technique herself, as evinced in the Donizetti *Brindisi*. Her homogenous collection of teachers certainly did no damage to her voice. While in Berlin, Clara decided she would take up Empress Frederick's invitation, issued at one of Queen Victoria's soirées, to call upon her. She did not do exactly that but wrote a letter explaining why she was in the city and recalling her memories of their English meeting. A reply came back post haste inviting her to visit that very evening, after dinner, and to bring some music. The royal carriage would be sent for her. Obviously the Empress was after a free cabaret. There was great excitement at the Gersters' as she chose which songs to take and ran through them with her teacher.

The royal chamber was quite filled with people and musically she was in good company. Among the performers were Mendelssohn's cellist nephew, and the violinist Joachim, who had studied with Mendelssohn and whom Clara knew, having appeared with him at several London functions. All the musicians performed and Clara was complimented, the Empress remarking on a distinct improvement in her technique. She sent her regards to Madame Gerster with whom she was acquainted. The Empress invited Clara to a party where she sang more songs, including *Light in Darkness*, recorded in 1925 but never released, probably because Clara was unhappy about something in the performance. The Empress was deeply touched and entreated Clara to be sure to include sacred songs in her repertoire as "They are sermons in themselves." This was a sentiment with which Clara tended to agree. Clara made other visits to the royal family, where she sang and, if children were present, as they sometimes were, she would sit on the floor with them and make them laugh by making vulgar trumpet noises. The Empress, like Queen Victoria, was creative and had composed songs herself which Clara would sing.

When her Berlin studies ended it was a sad parting. With great temerity she craved a favour from the Empress – would it be possible for her to have a signed photograph? Royal protocol did not permit this but the Empress gave her, instead, a diamond bracelet to add to her jewellery collection – a hint of the great wealth Clara was later to accumulate.

## CHAPTER ELEVEN

# Dicing with Death

Back in England Clara resumed her recitals and life became a round of well-received appearances. As Michael Aspinall observes in the liner notes to the CD set *Clara Butt. A Critical Survey*, "It was becoming increasingly clear that what the public wanted from her, and what she was ever more inclined to give them, was generous quantities of 'ballads' old and new, tuneful songs that lay in a hazily defined and not quite respectable field, somewhere between really *classical* songs and popular music." Just the sort of thing beloved by Queen Victoria.

There were the usual invitations to great houses and the usual horseplay this entailed. On one occasion a group of lounge lizards, in full evening dress, sported with each other as to who could walk the furthest on his hands. They were wildly applauded. In his autobiography, Roland Foster, who was to become Clara's concert manager for her 1912 Australasia tour, explains the relationship between the hirers and the hired: "Professionals were regarded somewhat patronisingly by the upper 10,000, whom only a few top-notchers like Melba, Albani, Clara Butt, the de Reszkes, Paderewski ... who had received the cachet of a royal summons to Windsor Castle could presume to meet on anything like equal terms." Elsewhere he tells us, "One great lady engaging a celebrity for a private function agreed upon a fee of 100 guineas. 'Of course,' she added, 'You will not expect to be introduced to my guests.'" This example shows the importance of Queen Victoria's, and the Prince of Wales' patronage to Clara.

Manners at times could be less that respectful to an artiste. Baritone Peter Dawson tells of an occasion when he was asked by his hostess "Would you like to sing now, Mr. Dawson, or shall we let the guests enjoy themselves a little longer?" Clara once, uncharacterisitically, lost patience and stopped singing, rounding on her stunned audience with, "If you've only come here to talk I'm not going to waste my time singing to you." She stormed off and sent for her cloak, only returning after apologies from her hostess. A favourite of the Queen could behave like that.

On 23 April 1897 Beerbohm Tree opened Her Majesty's Theatre with his production of *Seats of the Mighty*. His actress wife made an introductory speech to the celebrity audience and, after the finale, Clara had the honour of singing the National Anthem. On 26 May she returned to Bristol for a concert at the Colston Hall, topping a bill that included Madame Novello Davies conducting her Royal Ladies Welsh Choir and Herman Bemberg leading the orchestra. As the *Bristol Times and Mirror* for 27 May put it, "A brimming house ... shows the high esteem in which the young Bristolian is held by the residents of her own city. ... Miss Butt, who wore a couple of beautiful decorations given her by the Queen, ascended the platform and was greeted with enthusiastic plaudits." Saving her main repertoire for the second half, she appeared in the first half with Molloy's *Golden Bells*, rather than *Golden Balls* as one misprint had it, after which "the assemblage showered upon the fair vocalist a torrent of applause and recalled her to receive a large basket of beautiful flowers".

*Si Mes Vers avaient des Ailes* was given later, although this delicate song was rather spoiled by trouble in the balcony when an outraged voice could be held yelling "Sit down! Sit down!" She included Schubert's *Der Tod und das Mädchen* and Mme Novello Davies' *A Voice from the Spirit Land*, which Clara loved for its message of eternal life. For this Mme Davies abandoned her baton and accompanied her on the piano.

The *Bristol Times and Mirror* assures us, "Miss Butt grandly unfolded them with a passion and pathos which deeply impressed the audience." Clara ended the show with Donizetti's *Il Segreto* from *Lucrezia Borgia*, and Cowen's *The Voice of the Father*, in which she was, again, joined by the choir. Her encore was Bemberg's *La Ballade du Désespéré*.

Madame Novello Davies was often her accompanist (or accompaniste, as she spelled it on her programmes), receiving a twenty-guinea fee for this service. At one booking they appeared with pianist Harold Bauer. He had studied with Paderewski and went on, in 1908, to give the world premiere of Debussy's *Children's Corner*. They visited dressmakers together and Mme Novello Davies introduced her to her dressmaker, Madame Wyatt of Clifford Street, just off Savile Row, who designed gowns to their specification. Davies claims Clara's "flair for dress [grew] under my guidance".

Clara was booked for an Eisteddfod festival with Davies as her accompanist, and Madame Wyatt made them close-fitting sequined gowns of identical styles – Clara delighted in showing off her splendid figure – but different colours. Mme Novello Davies, or Little Clara as she was now known, wore black, while Clara shimmered in sea green making her look, as Davies says "like a beautiful mermaid". Clara was booked for appearances in Paris with Davies as accompanist, who tells us, "All the guineas Clara and I earned soon went in the wonderful shops we loved to wander through. We enjoyed ourselves immensely therein with no sense of money values." Little Clara may not have had much sense of monetary values, but Big Clara certainly did. Although she was now doing well financially, she was still supporting her family. In time she was to live extravagantly, but that would not be for a while yet. Even so, Clara permitted herself a few indulgencies. After one such expedition the ladies, weighed down by parcels, realised they were lost and had no money for a taxi back to their hotel. Fortune must have been smiling on them, for they were discovered by the imposing form of the bass Signor Foli, who had sung many times at the Paris Opera, and who escorted them home.

The Signor may have been en route to the tables at Monte Carlo where he frequently lost a fortune and had to borrow money himself to get home. An Irishman, his given name was Allen Foley but due to the prevailing fashion for Italian opera he changed it to Signor Foli, never using a first name. He had studied in Italy but performed often in London where he had appeared in more than sixty operas, many times with Patti. One performance had come to an abrupt halt, mid-duet, when a wasp flew into her mouth while she was singing. Foli had burst into laughter. He also owned a parrot which would surprise guests by screaming at them, "Have you any money for me!"

Clara and Davies narrowly escaped death in Paris. One of Clara's sponsors was the Duchesse d'Alencon, sister of the Empress of Austria, who invited them to the opening of a charity bazaar on the rue Goujon at which she and her daughter were officiating. Nearly 2,000 guests, the cream of Parisian society, were expected at the wooden and tarred edifice, newly built for the occasion. One of the main attractions was an immense gas-filled balloon moored in the building and a new invention called cinema. The cinema, which was causing much interest, was due to show a film at 4 p.m. The Two Claras, by then a little spoiled by the many invitations they had received, and having had a lunch appointment elsewhere, decided to give the opening of the bazaar a miss and go the following day, instead taking a carriage ride. They were stopped by the police. The roads were blocked due to a raging fire. It was the bazaar. The cinema projectionist had not been able to see in the darkened room and his assistant struck a match, igniting the gas balloon. In ten minutes the raging inferno had devoured everything. The carnage was truly horrifying, the heat so intense that corpses were unrecognisable. Jewels had melted into scalps and fingers. The Duchesse and her daughter were among the victims. The Duchesse had had her hair positioned by a new lacquer – unfortunately highly inflammable. She was only identified by her teeth, the result of the new technology of forensic dentistry. To this day anniversaries are held in Paris to mark the tragedy. Clara and Mme Novello Davies returned to their hotel to be told the details, such as were known, of the ghastly event. But for their tardiness they would have been among the terrible charred remains. They were not sorry to leave for Fontainebleau, where they were to spend a week with rich businessman Charles Radcliffe and equally rich Herman Bemberg.

Restoring her shattered nerves amidst the sylvan splendour, Clara noticed a group of gypsy caravans. The gypsies soon noticed them and, realising they had wealthy admirers, put on a show of dancing and music. This was just what she needed, and it was a wonderful restorative. "We proved a veritable gold mine to them," Madame Novello Davies tells us. Indeed they did. With Mr Radcliffe footing the bill, the gypsies played for them much of the week, parking outside the hotel so that Clara and party only had to walk outside to be entertained.

Back in London, with the ghastly nightmare of the fire never to leave them, one of the functions for which they were booked was to lunch and then perform at the home of Lady Morgan. Her Ladyship served a magnificent meal for her many guests and Little Clara tells us that she and Clara enjoyed this so much, with a few glasses of wine, that they nodded off on a couch during coffee and had to be woken to perform. Whatever the truth of the snooze, Lady Morgan was so pleased with the performance that she gave both Claras diamond stars as thank you presents. Big Clara often wore hers on the concert platform, set into her hairstyle.

About this time Clara was plagued by sore throats and colds and, at first, put this down to the shock of the Paris tragedy. Her doctor, however, recommended her tonsils be removed. Thinking of her earlier tonsillitis, she refused, but did consent to the removal of her adenoids. The surgeon only agreed to do so on the written undertaking from her that he would not be held responsible if it went wrong.

A European concert tour was planned for 1897 which would cover Berlin, Paris, Budapest and Prague. There was a request to include Russia, and Clara was so excited about this she started to learn the language. Unfortunately she was never able to visit Russia – her bulging engagement book would not permit it. This was a bitter disappointment. The fabulous Imperial Russian court was a lavish patron of the arts. Most of the great singers appeared there, earning more in a week than in a year elsewhere. Gifts were showered on them, jewellery and *objets d'art*. A performance in Russia immediately put an artiste on the map as a world class performer. Both Viardot and Malibran had performed there, Glinka even composing some chamber music based on Malibran's variations to *La Sonnambula* as a memento of her visit. Russia had fine singers of its own, particularly contraltos. Notably famous was the voluptuous Eugenia Zbrujeva. Three years older than Clara, she had made her debut at the Moscow Imperial Opera (the Bolshoi) in 1894, two years after Clara had made her own operatic debut in *Orpheus*. She would have welcomed a chance to compare Zbrujeva's Russian (based on the Italian) method to the British method. She would also have welcomed the chance to hear the Russian repertoire, works seldom performed in England, such as Saint-Saëns *Henry VIII* in which Zbrujeva sang Anne Boleyn, and Mussorgsky's *Khovanshchina*.

It was Queen Victoria's Diamond Jubilee in 1897 and, to mark this glittering occasion, Clara was awarded the Victoria Badge as a token of approval. Many of these badges were issued but Clara's was presented to her directly by Her Majesty. It displayed double images of the royal visage, one of an attractive girl of eighteen and a more severe likeness revealing the strain of her sixty-year reign. Around this time, Clara became friends with The Hon. Mrs George Keppel, better known as courtesan Alice Keppel, great-grandmother of the current Duchess of Cornwall. Alice Keppel became one of the mistresses of the Prince of Wales in 1898 and remained more or less by his side until his death, as Edward VII, in 1910. Extramarital affairs were tolerated among the rich, providing discretion was maintained. Clara, who could be prudish, and whose own demeanour was always within the bounds of rectitude, accepted the morals of her betters without question, like the majority of the population.

## 11: DICING WITH DEATH

Just how prudish she could be on her own territory was demonstrated when she attended a party at the country house of Sir Arthur Sullivan. Several singers were also there, including Nellie Melba and the French bass Pol Plançon, the most admired Mephistopheles of his day. Melba had clearly forgiven, if not forgotten, Sullivan's treatment of her when she had presented her letter of introduction to him upon her arrival in London as an unknown. He had dismissed her with the advice that if she studied for another year he might be able to offer her a small part in *The Mikado*. It had been a lavish party with much champagne. Sullivan had hired a private train to transport his party and, on the way back to London, spirits were high, with games of poker played for high stakes. When the train stopped at London the party disembarked with goodbye kisses all round. Clara was affronted when Plançon grabbed her to plant a friendly smacker on her lips. She responded with a slap round the face that sent him reeling. Melba called Clara a "silly young ass", which she certainly was. This spirited response to a perceived solecism belied Clara's precarious health at the time. Her weak heart was diagnosed as the reason she fainted before a performance in Exeter and, again, at the Queen's Hall, this time mid-concert. She put it down to pressure and ignored it.

Mrs. Butt accompanied Clara on her continental tour. She did not fancy travelling all that distance without some support. Her mother was getting used to the idea of her daughter being a diva and, although bemused by it, came to appreciate the advantages, such as a first-class trip to Europe. Travelling with Clara meant that she was treated like a queen herself. Moving from place to place with her mother, and with no manager in those days, she did not always take enough ready money to cover travel expenses, particularly when she spent so much on clothes. The Butts were about to board a train when, to their horror, they realised they had not brought enough to pay the additional fare for their many trunks. There are two versions of what happened next. Mrs Ponder states that, incredibly, a hotel employee who happened to be on the station recognised Clara and came to her aid, telling her that the

Englishman Sir Arthur Sullivan was at his hotel. Perhaps he could help them? Before he got the chance to do so, an English porter who also recognised Clara, seeing she was in difficulty, offered to lend her some money, which she accepted and for which she wrote a cheque. It seems unlikely, however, that a railway porter would have been carrying that amount of money, and that he could afford to part with it. The other, more plausible, version has Sir Arthur on the platform at the same time as the Butts, where he settled the additional fare. Such hitches did not occur in the future when Clara was to travel with a whole retinue of staff.

In Berlin the German royal family turned up in support. That, and the fact she was a favourite of English royalty, which her promoters took pains to make known, ensured a healthy box office. In Budapest her admirers hired a band to serenade her and unharnessed the horses from her carriage so they might pull her themselves to her hotel. Paris was a sell out, although Clara did not gain a fan in Reynaldo Hahn, composer of some of the finest songs in the French repertoire. His music is designed for light, articulate voices and, whereas Clara could be as articulate and light as any, she could also produce a thunderous, dramatic volume. This was too much for Hahn, who described her instrument as "une voix obscène". This was going a bit far, and rankles with some even today. In his 1977 *The Record of Singing* Michael Scott retorts, "compared with his effete baritone, Dame Clara's mighty alto must have been shocking." This, too, is a little harsh. When war broke out in 1914, Hahn, well past the age of enrolment, voluntarily served in the army as a private. Nothing effete about that. He was a prodigy, and as a child sang and accompanied himself at the scented and scandalous soirées of Napoleon's niece, the Princesse de Metternich. He was to have a love affair with author Marcel Proust and it is said that Proust's masterwork *À la Recherche du Temps Perdu* was inspired by him. Proust himself is recorded as saying, "Everything I have ever done has always been thanks to Reynaldo." His songs are still regularly performed, among the most popular *Si Mes Vers avaient des Ailes* which

## 11: DICING WITH DEATH

he set to a Victor Hugo poem and *L'heure Exquise* to Verlaine's words,* both written in his adolescence. Verlaine is reported to have burst into tears when he first heard the setting. Others have done so since.

Back in England Clara needed a new place to live. Fond of the Purvises as she was, and grateful to them, lodging with them was becoming impractical with her irregular hours and many callers. It was not fair and she was constantly, although unnecessarily, apologising. Their kind attentions were also becoming restrictive. They parted on the best of terms and she took a flat in the more central Hyde Park Mansions, moving in with a friend, a Miss Grant. It would not have been suitable to live unchaperoned. Her finances had so far improved that she could now afford to rent a country cottage, with the hope of her family spending holidays with her. She and Miss Grant spent hours touring the countryside in a dog cart inspecting properties. These happy circumstances were brought to an abrupt end when the horse Clara was driving bolted. The cart overturned and she was thrown and knocked unconscious, damaging her head. The spot was isolated and Miss Grant, who had not been hurt, panicked. She could not revive Clara and blood was pouring from her skull. In desperation she ran for two miles before she found help. Clara was concussed and unconscious for twenty-four hours, then confined to bed for six weeks. She was cheered during her convalescence by a get well telegram from Queen Victoria. Battered and bruised, she still appreciated the attentions of royalty.

As soon as Clara recovered, too soon really, she delighted in showing off Hyde Park Mansions. She and Miss Grant, who seems a game sort, entertained. She had the services of a cook and maid and in the dining room hung a dreadful pastel portrait of herself, done by an admirer in Paris. She had quite liked it at first, at least until her sister Hazel likened it to the ugliest old maid in Bristol. Seeing the funny side, Clara hung it in a prominent place where she and her friends delighted in poking fun at it. One evening, as the night progressed and the lads

---

\* Both recorded exquisitely by Maggie Teyte

tippled, it became the target for food throwing. When rissoles, which the cook had taken pains to ensure would be to Madame's taste, were served these were lobbed in their entirety at the picture. The behaviour got raucous with screams of laughter. The maid had to clear it up when the party retired, some on all fours (to more laughter), to the withdrawing room. There were compensations for the maid – when Clara was on tour she did not have much to do then and sometimes didn't see her mistress for days on end.

About this time it was reported to Mrs. Butt that the soprano Emma Albani had said Clara's voice was "the most beautiful in England". Mrs. Butt said she thought that was "very nice," perhaps unwilling or unable to fully grasp her daughter's exceptional talent. Clara still regularly visited Bristol and invited her family to Hyde Park Mansions. Two of her sisters, Pauline and Ethel, inspired by her success, wanted to become singers themselves. Both had good voices and went on to have careers. Ethel, a contralto too, made some excellent gramophone records under the name of Ethel Hook. There is a short British Pathé film in existence, made in 1932, where Ethel is singing the lullaby *Brownie a' Dreams* to a young boy of about five who might be her son. He is in his pyjamas getting ready for bed and she stands by the window pointing to the stars and singing. Her voice is glorious and her singing immaculate. Clara's fame undoubtedly helped her along, but she is entitled to remembrance in her own right on the strength of this performance. She speaks a few words and her speaking voice is as beguiling as her looks, dark and elegant. She puts the child in his cot and kisses him goodnight – it is every bit as sentimental as her sister's domain. A charming relic.

All Clara's sisters when they appeared professionally took the name of Hook, their mother's maiden name. This was less in tribute to their mother than a conscious effort not to tread on Clara's toes. For a while Pauline and Ethel worked as duettists. Clara paid for both of them to study under Henry Blower at the Royal College of Music and with Madame Novello Davies. Later her sister Hazel, born in 1889 and the baby of the family, also became a singer, helped by Clara. Her brother Fred, three years younger than she, had a reasonable baritone and he, too, was sent to Madame Novello Davies, with whom he stayed for two years as a boarder. She was generous to all her singing siblings and often invited them to appear with her in concert. After Clara was married, on the rare occasions when her baritone husband could not appear with her, she gave Fred his chance. Announcing him as her brother, he was ensured a round of applause however he sang.

Madame Novello Davies' son, (David) Ivor Novello was born 1893 and was a sweet, talented little tot when Clara moved into Hyde Park Mansions. His mother often brought him to visit Clara. She would stand him on a chair and teach him *Abide with Me*, then considered appropriate fodder for children, pointing out the solemnity of life and a respect for death. Just the thing for a child. He would grab Clara's hand and sigh with delight when his mother came into the room dressed in her finery, whispering "Isn't mam's face lovely" or "Doesn't Mam look beautiful?" He grew up to be quite beautiful himself and was to break a million hearts on stage when he starred, always in a non-singing role, in his record-breaking West End musicals – all of which have absurd books and lush melodies.

Clara's fame was growing and with it grew a commensurate amount of public attention, some of it unwelcome. An example occurred one evening when Clara was getting into her brougham at Victoria Station while a maid sorted out her luggage. A man shoved his face through the carriage window and told her he was determined to marry her. Sometime later, he arrived unannounced at Clara's door, informing the maid that he wanted her to sing at his house, and she could name her fee. Clara, unsurprisingly, refused to see him. Undeterred, he persecuted her friends, swearing that he would marry her. The matter reached a climax when Clara was appearing at the Queen's Hall and he attempted to detain her as she left the stage. Her brother Wilfred intervened, forcibly ejecting him from the hall as he yelled that he would "do her in". Eventually the police had to place a restraining order on him. Clara suffered the attentions of other stalkers, too, but none quite so violent.

Narciso Vert, Clara's agent, organised a tour of America and Canada for the autumn of 1899. With the experience of her continental tour under her belt, Clara felt more prepared for this mammoth venture. She still carried dreams of emulating Jenny Lind's American success. Whereas Jenny had the wizardry of impresario Phineus T. Barnum to guide her, Clara had Vert, certainly Europe's most astute concert agent. This was a tremendous undertaking and her mode of transport reflected her now elevated status. Expenses were not skimped – she was to travel first class in her own flower-filled stateroom. Clara had fitted herself out with a new wardrobe with outfits for every conceivable occasion. A tour manager was hired to sort out any problems. Never again would she find herself unable to pay the fare.

In early October, 1899, her family and a large group of friends came to the dock to see her off amid a flock of well-wishers. Prominent among them was Signor Foli (her rescuer in Paris) and Clara Novello Davies, who was smarting at the Russian pianist Mark Hambourg having ruined Clara's Christmas present to her of a handmade silk quilt. While staying at her house, Home of the Nightingales, he had tipped a cup of tea over it. At the last moment before embarkation, Clara leant over the ship's rail and tossed a little bundle to the Signor. He picked it up and found it was a piece of paper wrapped round a coin to give it ballast. The paper contained a note telling him that she was engaged to be married to Robert Kennerley Rumford.

"Bertie" Kennerley Rumford was a tall, handsome baritone, one year her senior. His baptismal name was Robert Henry Rumford, but he had taken his father's middle name of Kennerley, as it had a better professional ring. Later he was to hyphenate it to Kennerley-Rumford and enrol his children in school under that name – in those days a double-barrelled name was a sign of gentility. He had appeared, as supporting artiste, on a bill with Clara a few years ago and, before this, had seen her in concert – what music lover could have missed her? At his request he had been introduced to her at one of society hostess

Madame Blumenthal's soirees where Clara had been engaged to sing. She must have been smitten for, at her request, Bertie had joined her on a provincial tour of England in both 1898 and early 1899 and had suggested they duet together – this suggestion from a less fascinating man, made directly to her and not through an agent, would have been impertinent. However, handsome Bertie fascinated her and she was delighted to include him in her spotlight. A clandestine romance developed. He was Clara's first and only love, and she fell hard.

Bertie was a ladies' man, and they adored him. Clara's latter-day pianist, Ivor Newton, described him as an "elegant six foot, best dressed and handsomest of singers ... fine golfer and determined to be a gentleman first and a musician afterwards". He had good claim to gentility, his pedigree including, somewhere along the line, Count Rumford, eminent scientist in the field of thermodynamics, and his wealthy parents had educated him at Canterbury, Frankfurt and Paris. He was the only brother of two sisters who doted on him. His career would never have had great impact without his association with Clara and it has been said he only survived professionally by hanging onto her coat tails. This is correct. His agents had a hard time booking solo work for him even after he became Clara's husband. But, as Newton points out, he was not overly ambitious. He revelled in his wife's status, and was quick to defend it. But, unlike Clara, he did not enjoy the circus that went with fame. She could handle it effortlessly but Bertie resented the intrusion. Left to his own devices he would have been a happy amateur, which is not to demean his ability. He could sing well enough and had a pleasant voice, but others could do better. He was not particularly memorable as a singer, whereas his wife-to-be was unforgettable. She seems, on the surface, a most unsuitable wife for him – it must have been love, too, on his part. Few men would relish the idea of a taller and more talented wife, but Bertie supported Clara through both good times and bad, her constant companion during an extraordinary career.

Clara's note to Signor Foli was the first "public" announcement to her friends of her intentions towards Bertie, although she had confided in her family. The Signor looked up in amazement at the giggling Clara, who was leaning over the ship's rail. Really, it was not so surprising. A young, successful woman brimming with confidence, she was bound to get married. Somehow, he had expected she would marry an older, richer man, probably with a title. For a moment he forgot he was shivering with cold. Not for long though. On returning home he could not seem to get warm. His chill intensified and on 20 October he succumbed to double pneumonia and died at his home in Southport. Clara no sooner arrived in New York than she had to cable home for flowers for his funeral. Clara was thrilled to tour America but her heart was still at home with Bertie. All through her adventure she couldn't wait to get back to him.

# CHAPTER TWELVE

## America and Romance

In 1899 Clara crossed the Atlantic in style for the first time, conquering America and Canada. It was not quite the universal fanfare Barnum had whipped up for Jenny Lind, but certainly not without impact. That doyen of publicity merchants, Barnum, had made his reputation by promoting a slave lady he advertised as being 161 years old and whom, he claimed, had nursed the baby George Washington. He presented a "genuine", mermaid, Siamese twins and Tom Thumb (all of who seemed fond of him). He had sold Jenny's tickets by auction, one man paying an astronomical $625 for a single seat. When the practically-minded Jenny was told this she simply shrugged her shoulders and said she thought the man a fool. Mr Vert had been a little more cautious in his promotions. Clara made her debut at New York's Carnegie Hall, prompting critic W. J. Henderson to write in the *New York Times*:

> The debut of Miss Clara Butt was the most important event in the world of music last week. ... Already it is announced that Miss Butt will sing for us again and this will afford the needed opportunity to regain the poise which her impetuous temperament somewhat disturbed on the occasion of her first appearance. But it is not exceeding the bounds of moderation to say, after the calm which succeeded the storm, that a temperament like Miss Butt's is not often so fortunately paired with a voice commensurate with its demands for expression.

But here is a woman who has majestic physical power – a volume of voice which would make her queen of all Kundries if a Parsifal could be found who could stand beside her without being dwarfed. Perhaps it is better she is not suited to the domain of the operatic stage. Such a splendid personality should be permitted to reign alone. She is a magnificent creature of the concert platform and that will be, for her, the finest field. Her voice is the grandest contralto organ that has been heard by the present generation of music lovers in this city, and she sings with an overmastering passion.

Yet, she is not without self-control. She knows what she is doing at all times and her art is singularly well balanced. Faults in voice production she indeed committed at her first appearance, but they will not be noticed by the general hearer.

The main thing to remember about her is that with a wonderful voice she sings most influentially and her delivery of such an air as the *Divinities du Styx* would charm a stone.

Henderson was an influential critic and also present at a later New York appearance. He had mentioned faults in her technique at her New York debut but, indulgently, had let her charm override these. He was not so kind on his second visit, a month later:

> Miss Clara Butt, radiant in a gown that shimmered with the glory of the serpent of the Nile, came back to us to demonstrate that the fires of her temperament had burned the fine edge off her vocal art. Twice within a decade we have heard superb contralto voices marred by vicious technique. One of them is a wreck of what once it was. It seems a pity, but the other must inevitably go the same way if its owner does not reform her methods.

Henderson was among the small minority of dissenters. Audiences loved her as much for her glamorous appearance as her voice. She was dubbed a "majestic English beauty" and "the greatest contralto of the generation". At one venue she sang a dozen additional songs, yet still the audience clamoured for more. Clara appeared at the Waldorf Hotel at the prestigious Morris Bagby Concerts. Bagby was a New

York impresario – a friend of Liszt, with whom he played cards, and Brahms whom he described as playing the piano with ten thumbs – who organised fund raising concerts to aid aspiring musicians. These were invariably morning affairs after which a hefty lunch was served for around sixty people. Morning is not a helpful time for singers, as the voice needs time to warm up, but since singers and musicians were usually working in the afternoons and evenings, there was no choice but the morning. The repertoire was never too highbrow or taxing. Nellie Melba was asked to appear and, when told the time, snapped to the earnest young man who had invited her, "I can't even spit at 11am." She sang though.

At Clara's concert in Toronto pro-British feelings were strong. The Boer War was being fought in South Africa and a Canadian unit was serving with the British Army there. She was introduced by Dr G. R. Parkin, Principal of Upper Canada College. While a portrait of the Queen was projected onto a screen, the doctor confided to his listeners, "It is pleasant to know that we have with us one whom the Queen dearly loves." She sang 'God Save the Queen' and the 4,500 strong audience jumped to its feet, roaring its approval and joining in.

Back home it did not take Clara long to resume contact with Bertie Rumford. They sang together constantly, Mr. Vert hastily re-arranging things to include Bertie in her programmes. Previously Clara had been a solo star and had allowed no one – apart from a choir or musicians – to share the spotlight with her. Now she was half of a double act, albeit the vital half. During concerts, Bertie started flirting, by passing love notes to her; it was customary for performers to sing from scores and he would slip his billets-doux between her pages so, when she turned them, she would unexpectedly find a flattering declaration of affection. Among their most requested duets was Ernest Newton's *The Keys of Heaven*, arranged for them by pianist-composer Samuel Liddle, an ultra-coy song of courtship. With Kennerley's lines, "Madam, will you walk, Madam will you talk, Madam will you walk and talk with me?" he made it abundantly clear that this was not just a song but a personal plea. She would certainly walk and talk with him, and much else, too. The audience quickly twigged what was going on and applauded wildly to her blushing acknowledgement. It gave an extra fillip to a Butt concert.

They recorded the song several times, and whereas he sounds a bit strained at times, he certainly paints his words vividly enough. There's no doubt it is a declaration of love. Clara makes it so too, she is all coyness, and those who expect the trombone-like notes for which she was famous will be disappointed. There is no booming at all, she sings in her "other" soft, gentle voice. Audiences of the day quite liked a dash of the "dainty" and, among her dainty items is the twee *A Fairy Went A-Marketing*, sung by Clara without the faintest touch of a send-up. As her entry in *Grove's* notes, "[it] may well raise a smile, but the smile is tempered by admiration for the magnificent voice and the beautiful articulation of the words".

Rumford had undergone a thorough vocal training by tenor Giovanni Sbriglia in Paris, among whose pupils were the de Reszke brothers, darlings of society and beloved by Nellie Melba. He turned baritone Jean de Reszke into a tenor, and escalated his career in the process. His other pupils included Lillian Nordica and Pol Plançon, to whom Clara had taken such exception when he had attempted a friendly kiss. It was George Henschel who convinced Rumford to become a professional singer, much against the wishes of his parents who, while proud of him as a gifted amateur, thought becoming professional quite beyond the pale. These were sentiments with which Rumford himself almost agreed.

Clara and Bertie retained their friendship with Henschel and Clara grew close to his daughter Georgina, who preferred to be called "George" and bred horses and wrote books on them. Clara was still fond of horses despite her earlier accident. Bertie took further voice lessons from established teacher Alfred Blume and, helped by his society connections, launched himself as a professional. Not least among his helpers was Francesco Tosti, Clara's friend and aide. The two

## 12: AMERICA AND ROMANCE

moved in the same circles. Bertie, too, had sung for Queen Victoria, accompanied by Tosti, but at Osborne House, and, like Clara, was awarded the Diamond Jubilee Medal. Her Majesty had also presented him with an autographed copy of her *Journal of our Life in the Highlands*, which would now be worth a fortune. Among Bertie's many female fans was a now neglected composer, Maude Valérie White. She wrote a cycle for him – *Three Little Songs (While the Swallows Homeward Fly, A Memory* and *Let Us Forget)* – which was published in 1897. He included this in his solo recitals and was to do so in future days, when he sang solo before duetting with Clara in their concert parties. They are rarely sung today. She wrote over 250 songs and was a great influence on the better-remembered Roger Quilter.*

Sir Adrian Boult, in his autobiography *My Own Trumpet* cites an anecdote concerning Bertie when he was courting Clara. Bertie and a friend were on a cycling trip and paused for a rest. Bertie said "I'm going to call my bike Santley (Charles Santley, famous baritone) because it's a Singer" (make of the bike). His friend replied, "I'm going to call mine Clara Butt because it's not." On the way home the first speaker noted a "frosty atmosphere", only later did he realise Bertie was engaged to Clara. Boult was not born until 1889 and was eleven when Clara and Rumford married, but by the time he wrote his memoirs there was a certain snobbery in effete musical circles concerning Clara, who had risen to fame through popular song.

The success of Bertie's *Keys of Heaven* love notes encouraged him in his courtship and, when they toured together, he began sending her different love notes each night. Sometimes, for a change, they were in German, which he understood and which Clara had picked up in Berlin. She would turn a page of manuscript and find, to her fluttering heart's delight, another little billet-doux. She had to compose herself as her rapt audience were hanging on every note. Mr Vert made the

---

\* Sadly blackmailed for his homosexuality; driven to despair by the death of a beloved nephew during World War One, and eventually to die mad in an asylum – leaving a legacy of some exquisite songs, some recorded by Kathleen Ferrier.

most of their engagement and announced it to the press, who paraded the news. It was suggested Westminster Abbey would be a suitable marriage venue. At their first concert after breaking the news, Bertie accompanied Clara at the piano as she sang *When the Nightingale his Mate has Found*. The applause was outrageous.

Another outrageous success was Clara's appearance at the Norwich Festival where she premiered Elgar's only orchestral song cycle *Sea Pictures* on 5 October 1899, with the composer himself conducting. The piece had been specially commissioned for the Festival. As the music critic for *The Times* wrote, "Both singer and composer were recalled over and over again ... the songs have undoubtedly been launched on a prosperous career." But for Elgar's perseverance, *Sea Pictures* might never have happened, at least not with Clara. He had called, unannounced, at Hyde Park Mansions in January 1899, with a sketch of the cycle which he had just completed, excited and eager to show it to her, certain she would love it. Clara was in the bath so Elgar was received by her companion, Miss Snella (Miss Grant had moved to the country). Elgar hurriedly explained about the new cycle, anxious to get it to Clara and try it out with her on the piano. Miss Snella, perhaps confused by Elgar's rapid speech, was not sure what this excitable man was talking about, but went to Clara in the bathroom, explaining there was a man anxious to show her a cycle. Song pluggers drove her mad, everyone wanted Butt to sing their songs, and the bell never stopped ringing with importunate hopefuls. She told Miss Snella, "I don't care if it's a bicycle – if he wants to see me he must call on another day!" Elgar was sent away. He was (understandably) outraged and inclined to offer the cycle to someone else; however, he could not envisage any other voice doing it, so explained the situation to Mr Vert; he, in turn, explained the situation to Clara. Mortified, she sent her apologies and the composer received a warm welcome when he called again. They even laughed about it later.

Clara entered into the aquatic spirit of the songs by wearing a costume designed to make her look like a mermaid, doubtless a revamp of the green shimmering gown designed by Madame Wyatt for Eisteddfod. R. H. Mottram, a Norwich resident, described it as "a wonderful dress, the material of which, it was whispered, indicated appropriately the scales of a mermaid's sinuous form." The dress does not seem to have discomposed Elgar who barely seemed to have noticed her frock, merely mentioning to his friend, architect Troyte Griffiths (inspiration behind the 7th Variation of the *Enigma Variations*) '[she was] dressed like a mermaid". He was, nevertheless, delighted with her performance and enthused to the perspicacious A. J. Jaeger (publishing manager of Novello, inspiration behind the *Nimrod* section of the *Enigma* plus contributor to Elgar's later oratorios *The Dream of Gerontius, The Apostles* and *The Kingdom*): "She sang *really well*." Two days later they gave the first London performance. Then, at Queen Victoria's request, she sang some of the songs for Her Majesty at Balmoral, with Elgar playing his piano arrangement of them. This was a high time for both forty-two-year-old Elgar and twenty-seven-year-old Clara, coming so soon after her North American triumph and bethrothal, and his enormous success with *Enigma Variations* earlier that year, which had catapulted him into the front rank of composers.

Sometime later, in Manchester, Clara was booked for a recital, the first half of which was to be *Sea Pictures* conducted by Elgar. In the second half, she was to sing another song, conducted by her old enemy Stanford, whose recasting of *Orfeo* had caused such contention and who had sworn never to conduct her again. He had endeavoured to keep his word but, unfortunately, they were now confronting each other once more. Neither had realised the other was on the bill until they arrived for rehearsals. Stanford refused to rehearse with Clara. She asked if he were not "sportsman enough" to forget their quarrel. Clearly he was not, and he would not lift his baton. It was an *impasse* and agents had to be contacted and management sent for. Clara, who was prepared to sing, icily pointed out that, as they had both been contracted to perform, Stanford was in breach and she would sue. By then it was too late to rehearse. Ponder tells us a compromise was reached whereby Stanford would conduct but would take his timing from Clara and the initiative of the orchestra leader.

Elgar more or less wrote *Sea Pictures* for Clara. He had written the cycle years earlier for soprano and piano, but orchestrated and transposed it for her. Comparisons with Clara hung like a spectre over all subsequent performers for years, but there have been several decent recordings of it. Janet Baker did a fine version, particularly with one of the longer songs, *The Swimmer*, the orchestra conducted by Sir John Barbirolli. Barbirolli was fond of the cycle and often performed it with Kathleen Ferrier. She loved him and would have done most things for him, which was why she sang it so often. Actually she detested the piece, as she wrote to her accompanist John Newmark, "I'm sure the audience will have had enough by the time I've splashed my way through." Ferrier initially auditioned for Barbirolli with a song from *Sea Pictures*. The venue was the Sheffield City Hall whose acoustics he likened to "playing in a bale of cotton wool." A beautiful woman, she had bought a new dress for the occasion but might as well have been wearing a sack. Barbirolli was in a bad mood and she no sooner started singing than he tore his score from the stand and hurled it, narrowly missing her. The missile was meant for a musician behind, but that was not explained at the time. However, they overcame this incident and became devoted companions, and towards the end of her life he guided her career with a sure hand. Unlike Clara, who exploited her lower register, he actively encouraged Kathleen to lighten her voice, and to expand her higher tessitura. Barbirolli was no lover of low contraltos and referred to their owners as "oratorio contralto – that queer and almost bovine monstrosity so beloved of our grandfathers".*

In contrast to Clara, Kathleen was self-consciously aware of her

---

\*   Strangely Kathleen did sing *Land of Hope and Glory* which Elgar wrote for Clara – strangely because it is out of Kathleen's normal repertoire and might be thought too jingoistic for her voice. In 2003 the Barbirolli Society with the BBC released a previously unknown crackly recording of it, which had been transmitted in 1951 to mark the re-opening of Manchester's Free Trade Hall.

histrionic shortcomings and in her early days was embarrassed singing music she considered overly dramatic. She was to overcome this, with coaching by Bruno Walter, when she introduced Mahler's emotion-drenched *Das Lied von der Erde* to British audiences. She did not welcome comparisons to Clara, although they regularly occurred. The *Nuneaton Observer* noted: "The extraordinary beauty of her *O Rest in the Lord* indicates her as a coming Clara Butt." The *Liverpool Evening Express* followed with, "She is a great contralto ... worthy to be mentioned as a possible successor to Clara Butt." She indignantly wrote to her sister Win, "I don't sound a bit like Clara Butt." The *Hinkley Times* snidely wrote, "She (Ferrier) has what Clara Butt never did have, a grand voice trained over its whole range." This was monstrously unfair to Clara and, had she been alive to read it, would undoubtedly have resulted in a libel charge, or a punch on the nose from Bertie Rumford. He did not take kindly to hostile criticism of his wife (neither did she) and more than one critic had faced his pugilistic wrath for "writing filth" about her. Ferrier in no way resembled Clara, neither vocally nor in manner. Singing styles had changed – what pleased a Victorian and later Edwardian audience did not work in the 1940s.

Clara spent that Christmas with her family in Bristol. Bertie was also invited, as was Mme Novello Davies and young Ivor. According to Madame, Bertie was paying his fiancée "devoted attention". As the Bristol house was not large, albeit large enough for the ten Butt children, the two Claras shared a bedroom. Christmas Eve was a late night and Big Clara, already steeped in a life of performances and late dinners followed by an even later bed, wanted to lie in on Christmas Day. Mrs. Butt would have none of it and kept dashing in the bedroom insisting she help with the dinner, a monumental undertaking with fifteen or so guests to feed. Clara, now with her own cook, was less keen on domesticity that she ever had been, but resigned herself to getting up. Mme Novello Davies tells us, "She maintained what is now an old-fashioned strict obedience to her parents' wishes until the very end." Be that as it may, Little Clara would not hear of her getting up, which was presumptuous given she was a guest. She told Big Clara that Mrs. Butt had more than enough daughters to help her – Big Clara was a professional and needed her rest. Despite Mrs. B's several returns, Clara stayed put. Nicely and sweetly, but she stayed put. It became a standing joke and the girls burst out laughing when Mrs. Butt made yet another entrance. Dazzled and bemused as Mrs. Butt was by her eldest daughter's fame, she was still her child and she believed she should perform her filial duties.

Madame Novello Davies did not have much luck with presents from Clara. The quilt she had been given a few Christmases ago had been ruined by Mark Hambourg. This Christmas, Clara gave her a magnificent string of pearls, mainly to thank her for taking in her brother Fred for two years and giving him singing lessons. These were treasured until one day, alighting from her carriage, she caught them on her reticule and broke the string. The pearls clattered along the gutter and most went down a drain. She was prevented from saving the rest by the public, agog at the obviously expensive jewels running loose, who nearly bowled her over to get at them.

On the 20 January 1900, Clara was again at the Albert Hall with a concert to raise funds for Boer War charities. Among her songs was *The Lost Chord* with an orchestra accompanied by Sir Arthur Sullivan, who had promised he would compose and perform a piece for her wedding. The finale was the Band of the Royal Engineers, with whom she sang *Onward Christian Soldiers,* augmented by the great organ and the audience joining in the second and third verses. This audience was estimated at 10,000 and an uplifted group they were as they teemed into the streets afterwards, knowing their attendance had contributed to the might of the Empire.

When Clara was on tour in Wales with Bertie, as she always was now, they stayed with Mme Novello Davies, who still maintained a property there. Toddler Ivor took to Bertie, who liked children as well as Clara, and rushed between their separate rooms with little messages. Clara would instruct him, "Go into uncle Bertie's room and say 'Boo' to him from Auntie Clara, darling." A faux-surprised Bertie would send him back with "Uncle Bertie says 'Bah' to you." It was a sweet courtship between two decent people and their love held them together through the dreadful trials to come.

# CHAPTER THIRTEEN

# Marriage

Although Clara was not offered Westminster Abbey for the wedding, she *was* offered St Paul's. This she gratefully declined, although it was mightily tempting. She never forgot, throughout her life, the kindness of the people of Bristol who had clubbed together to help finance her Royal College of Music studies. Brushing all other offers aside she decided she would be married in Bristol Cathedral. The ceremony took place at 1.30 p.m. on 26 June 1900 with the Dean of Bristol officiating. It was the first marriage performed there in 100 years, a token of the high regard in which Clara was held by the city. Factories, shops and offices closed down for a half-day holiday to mark the event. On behalf of the Bristolians, the city presented her with an elegant brooch, with "Clara Butt, City of Bristol," engraved on it. It is currently stored in Bristol Museum.

Ever the professional, Clara travelled directly to Bristol from an appearance at the Handel Festival. Crowds turned up in droves, and people had been queuing since 7 a.m. There was no way the cathedral could accommodate them all and hundreds had to stand outside. Special trains from London had been laid on, as were extra police to control the, largely good natured, mob. Clara Novello Davies reported that she had never before seen such "scenes of unprecedented public acclaim for anyone not royal". Sir Arthur Sullivan had composed an anthem for them, and had intended to play it on the organ. Unfortunately, he was too ill to do so, or even to attend the wedding, and died shortly after in the November of that year. He had helped her considerably in the early days and it was a Sullivan composition, *The Golden Legend,* that had started her success. However, there was no shortage of spectacle. Clara looked exotic in a shimmering haze of gushing, jewel-bedecked frills. For those interested in such things, the *Illustrated London News* carried the description: "She wore ivory-white crêpe-de-Chine, the long tunic fringed and falling over a train with full frills of crêpe, while the bodice was fully draped with fine Brussels point. The bridesmaids were in pink gowns made Empress fashion, and carried very tall sticks in which poses of pink flowers were tied. The bridegroom's gifts to the bridesmaids were brooches in the form of a musical stave, on which the notes B and C – their joint initials – were set in pearls, a gold heart-shape enclosing the design."

Bertie was dashingly handsome, fitting Sir Henry Wood's description of him as "A typical English gentleman, whose birthright shone through every bar he sang." The marriage licence bears his baptismal name of Robert Henry Rumford. Pride of place among the wedding gifts was one from Queen Victoria. For all the splendour, the bride herself did not have a single penny in her bank account. Clara had decided she must pay off her father's debts before her marriage; his overdraft alone exceeded £600 (around £50,000 today) and he owed several hundred pounds to various creditors.

Among the guests were Belle Cole, who had been Clara's inspiration to become a contralto, and Australia's premier soprano Nellie Melba. Emma Albani sang *Oh God, Thou Art Worthy to be Praised* and a choir delivered *Onward Christian Soldiers.* Her sisters Pauline, Ethel and Hazel were bridesmaids and there were two pretty golden haired pageboys. One of the pageboys was not, actually, as pretty as he appeared and wore hair extensions. This was seven-year-old Ivor Novello. When being measured for his page boy suit he had noticed that his fellow page, a lad named Bernard Green, had a mass of golden curls, and they were coveted by the dark-haired Ivor. He stamped his foot and raged. He would not be a pageboy unless he, too, had golden curls. Madame Novello Davies was not to be denied the kudos of her darling son at the Bristol wedding of the year. A resourceful woman, she knocked up a home-made wig of golden curls herself, gleaned, it is said, from the sweepings at a local hairdressers. Her delighted son smiled throughout the ceremony. Doubtless at the reception he entertained the guests with his party piece, singing *Poor Wandering One* from *The Pirates of Penzance* to his own accompaniment, golden curls and all. Ivor was lucky to have actually made the ceremony. Ten minutes beforehand he had demanded a raspberry ice-cream, which someone gave him to shut him up. What with the excitement and nerves, he brought it straight back up again, all over his little white satin suit, knickerbockers and lace cuffs. His mother tells us she washed off the mess, then covered the stain with her talcum powder, which she carried in her reticule. It would take more than a dose of vomit to keep the Novellos out of the limelight. Apparently, when he walked down the aisle there were sighs of "That darling little angel." The angel looked even littler standing next to his magnificent "Auntie Clara" as he called her. Bride and groom had to exit via a police cordon through waves of cheering well-wishers.

Almost a decade later the Ivor Novello-Butt friendship suffered a rupture when he presented her with a song he had written specially for her. By this time Ivor was an ambitious teenaged composer. He and his mother, clutching the precious MS of his new song, set out in the carriage, confident of gaining Auntie Clara's patronage. They were in for a shock. Novello's biographer James Harding tells us, "She disliked it and told him so in brutal terms." Madame Novello Davies, when recording the anecdote, says "Although 'Auntie Clara' afterwards sang his songs she did not let her loving friendship with us stand in the way of her criticism ... she was quite candid about it, also in throwing a wet blanket on the smouldering embers we both thought might yet blaze." Despite this setback, they did indeed blaze, right through the West End

## 13: MARRIAGE

of London, where his shows became the hottest tickets in town. Clara was a huge star when he gave her his early song, picture postcards of her selling by the cart loads. She could have been smothered under the weight of songs delivered to her home by hopeful writers, as a performance by Butt automatically gave a piece the seal of success. Novello was an overly ambitious, pushy youngster trying his luck. Generous and fair as she could be, Clara's talent was the overriding element in her life, and she would allow nothing to jeopardise it, as young Ivor discovered. Madame Novello Davies sadly reflects: "If she could have seen him (Ivor) as we drove sadly home, her kind and motherly heart would have made her suspend a judgement that was sadly to be proved in error ... friendship and love does not always pull strings." She should know – there was no more ambitious soul in the world that Ivor's mother.

Ivor had further humiliation piled on him shortly afterwards when his waltz *Spring of the Year*, his first published song, was included at an Albert Hall concert, sung by the popular Evangeline Florence whom he accompanied on the piano. His touch was a little light for the huge auditorium and eluded much of the audience; it also eluded Miss Florence who stomped off hissing, "I couldn't hear a note you were playing." The applause was so thin they left to the sound of their own footsteps. Ivor saw the imperious Clara looking at him from a box.

Ivor's first big hit was during the 1914-18 war when, capitalising on the wave of patriotism flooding the country and encouraged by his mother, he wrote the music to the monumentally successful *Keep the Home Fires Burning* to a lyric by Lena Guilbert Ford. It did more for morale than any politician's speech. Alas Miss Ford did not gain as much enjoyment from her hit as Ivor. Her contract with the publishers omitted a claim for royalties and, sadly, she was one of the many who perished during the war when a Zeppelin fell on her house.

Ivor and Clara resumed communications fully in 1924 when she agreed to sing his new song *The Land of Might Have Been* at an Albert Hall concert. But before doing so she insisted lyricist, Edward Moore, rewrite the words of the second verse "on a note of optimism". This was done and the song had a limited success when later recorded by Maggie Teyte. It reappeared phoenix-like when featured in the 2001 movie *Gosforth Park,* sung by Jeremy Northam in his role as Ivor. This would never have happened in reality as Ivor was renowned for never singing his glorious tunes: "My singing voice finished at the age of 16 and a half. Now it's like the croak of a tired bullfrog, and I would not dream of asking an audience to pay to hear me."

It would be untrue to say that after her marriage Clara never appeared alone on the concert platform, but from then on she and Bertie were a team. If Clara was booked then, nearly always, Bertie had to be booked too. She did not want him from her side and that suited Bertie just fine. When they returned from their honeymoon in Norway she gave up Hyde Park Mansions and moved in with Bertie to his flat in Montagu Mansions. This was only on a temporary basis while the Hampstead house they had decided to buy was decorated. This was to be in great style. Compton Lodge, bought for the considerable sum of £27,000 had almost that sum again spent on its renovations. There was a splendid music room, a ballroom and spacious grounds. The highlight was its magnificent marbled hall with a giant semi-circular staircase down which Clara would descend, dressed exquisitely, to admiring applause from those assembled below. Compton Lodge now bears a blue plaque stating Clara's residency from 1901-1929. As Roland Foster says, it was "as impressive a sight as anything ever staged by Hollywood". Actually the Rumfords were happiest with a few close friends or by themselves, but their status demanded occasions when they had to "entertain". When this happened, celebrities from all walks of life would be gathered in their sumptuous home.

By 1901 they had decided upon the form that was to become their standard method of appearance: the concert party. A collection of artistes would be amassed for the first half and after the interval Clara would appear in one of her magnificent gowns and walk imperiously downstage, to thunderous applause. Later she was to use a spotlight in a darkened auditorium, the first artiste to do so. A pinspot, meticulously positioned beforehand, would hit her face, the light gradually enlarging to encompass her whole figure as she walked to the footlights. Audiences liked Bertie – they would not have got the best out of Clara had they not – and seemed to genuinely care for him. It was like being invited to an intimate house party, a glimpse of the Butt-Rumfords at home. The Butt-Rumford union, however, put paid to one of Clara's long-held dreams – that of appearing in opera. Bertie was fearfully, albeit gallantly, jealous of her and, according to Clara's sister Ethel, he did not want her, as Michael Aspinall puts it "simulating love scenes with other men".

The audience, and Bertie, were greatly alarmed when Clara fainted again during a performance. She had kept reports of her previous fainting fits from him. It happened in Carlisle. But this time it was not her weak heart that was to blame. She found to her, and Bertie's, joy that she was pregnant.

# CHAPTER FOURTEEN

# Australia

Queen Victoria died on 22 January 1901, shaking the nation and Clara, in particular, to the core. A great sense of loss was felt by her people all over the world, many of whom had known no other monarch. It was inconceivable to Clara; she did not expect the Queen would ever die. She had been part of her career, instrumental in her success. It was like losing a parent, and she felt the end of the era keenly. Clara sang the new version of *Abide with Me* at the Queen's memorial service at Kensington Palace Chapel. Her Majesty had loved it. Composer Samuel Liddle, who had been a pupil with Clara at the Royal College of Music, had written the new tune for her and dedicated it to her. It earned him a fortune in royalties.

Liddle was acting as her accompanist at the time and they were arranging a concert programme. As they flipped through the music, which included the customary *Abide with Me* air, Madame Novello Davies, who happened to be with them, suggested it would make a change if he could write a different tune for the piece. Clara off-handedly agreed, not thinking too much about it. A few days later he arrived at her home with his new setting – a far more dramatic affair, with several key changes. As Jeffrey Richards writes in *Imperialism in Music*, it was a "quasi operatic aria" designed especially for her voice. It became the most popular of Clara's songs. Queen Alexandra, wife of Edward VII, who had succeeded Victoria, announced it was her favourite, along with *The Lost Chord*. Clara sang the new *Abide with Me* until the end of her days, and her recordings sold widely. As Richards continues, "It became an integral part of the popular musical consciousness, evoking spiritual feelings and summoning up memories of people and places. It was much played during the Western Front during the War and was a favourite in tuberculosis sanatoriums." The Rev. Lyte, who had written the words, had died of TB.

Clara's biographer, Winifred Ponder, noted in 1928: "No song ... has been quite so identified with a singer in the public mind as *Abide with Me*. ... The percentage of concerts at which she sang it is simply astounding and, even now, over more than 30 years, it is still in the list of public favourites – the sound of the opening chords when the song was given unannounced as an encore was certain to call forth a spontaneous burst of applause from every audience."

It has been written that, "Of all creative voices that of Clara Butt best expresses religious fervour." Sir Arthur Sullivan thought so too, particularly of her singing of *The Lost Chord*. Although first sung by his mistress, Fanny Ronalds, he told Clara, "That's how I always meant it to be sung." It is not known what he told Mrs. Ronalds. Whatever it was, the two ladies must have delivered entirely different accounts, as Mrs. Ronalds had a light (and very fine, it seems) soprano and her version could not have sounded anything like the weighty rendition we have from Clara. It has been said that the original MS of *The Lost Chord* was buried with Mrs. Ronalds at her grave in Brompton Cemetery in 1916. This, however, appears to be apocryphal, as it now reposes in the Guildhall Library of the Worshipful Company of Musicians. It is more probable that the likeable Mrs. Ronalds bequeathed the original to Clara. It went to Bertie at her death and he gave it to the Worshipful Company in 1955.

*Abide with Me* has been a staple of many a singer, male and female. The Wagnerian soprano Kirsten Flagstad regularly featured it during the 1950s, and it suited her to perfection. But she could have made the contents of the telephone directory seem moving. Mme Novello Davies tells us her pupil, actress Lily Hanbury, was so overcome when she heard Clara rehearse the new setting of *Abide With Me* that she fell on her knees in an attitude of prayer.

Clara had her pregnancy for which to pray. A new life stirring inside her. As the baby developed she would lovingly place Bertie's hands on her swelling abdomen while he murmured endearments. She continued working until her pregnancy showed, after which it would have been, in those days, indelicate to appear on the platform. On 1 July 1901 Clara gave birth to a fine healthy daughter who they called Joy, summing up Clara's feelings for her. She was the apple of her parents' eye. A nursery was designed in the Hampstead house and, as soon as was decent, the Rumfords, having engaged and thoroughly researched a nursemaid, took to the road again, taking Joy with them. On 11 June 1902 Clara gave a concert for funds for King's Hospital, a grand affair held in the presence of the Prince of Wales. Nellie Melba was also on the bill and the ladies divided the honour of the National Anthem between them. Melba performed the first verse and, with a dramatic change of key, Clara the second. The Union Jack-waving audience joined in the third.

Clara was a caring mother who adored her children. She was also to have two boys, Roy and Victor, born in 1904 and 1906 respectively. Her small brood was to make foreign trips out of the question for a while. Instead, she and Bertie took a lease on a seafront flat at St Aubyn's Mansions in Hove from 1903 – 1906. Clara had been born just a few miles along the Sussex coast, and had always felt an affection for the area. It was also not far from London and Clara was a great believer in the health-giving properties of sea air, perfect for her children. A plaque now graces the Mansions, commemorating her residency. This was unveiled as recently as 2011 by deputy mayor Geoff Wells, with Brighton's *Argus* newspaper covering the event. Unfortunately, the revealed plaque gave Clara's date of birth as 1848, aging her by twenty-four years. This has now been rectified. These things happen.

Brighton and Hove are proud of the many famous people who have lived in the area and some of their double-decker buses are named after them. The graceful cream-coloured Dame Clara Butt, a dignified and spacious vehicle which will not be hurried, regularly and reliably ferries passengers along the coastal road, its uncompromising fascia impervious to the sometimes inclement weather. Clara was not the only star who lived at St Aubyn's Mansions. The male impersonator Vesta Tilley moved there for her retirement long after Clara had gone.

Clara was anything but dignified in early June of 1905. She and Bertie were staying at a friend's house in Henley for the weekend. It was a lovely evening, so they took out a little rowing boat for a ride on the river at sunset, Bertie at the oars. Their romantic idyll was cruelly shattered when the boat overturned, pitching them both into deep water. Clara could not swim, but, thank goodness, the ever-gallant Bertie managed to get the gasping Clara to a landing stage, where others dragged her up, drenched and panic-stricken. As the *Manchester Guardian* put it: "The shock of the immersion ... proved too much for Madame Butt, and for some time she was in a fainting condition." Fortunately, the ill effects were only temporary, and Clara did at least know she had married the right man in Bertie.

There were no more children after Victor, and it is not known whether this was by design or due to her physical problems. Clara made no appearances for eight months after his birth. She was seriously ill, although the newspapers kept this quiet. There was a code of honour among editors then; they were as keen on a story as today, but decency prevailed and privacy was respected. No artiste wants their public to think performances might be jeopardised due to ill health. Clara kept the details of her illness to herself and it is not mentioned in her biography. But the Ibbs and Tillett correspondence regarding her return to the stage notes that she "has completely recovered from her recent illness and operation after an absence of 8 months".

Clara was often photographed with her children, pushing them in a pram and riding with them in open carriages, like many a proud mother. Unlike most other proud mothers, the photos were made into commercial postcards which sold well, and she would sometimes spend an hour at a time autographing them. But that was the most the children saw of public life. At home they were a tight family unit. There was no press intrusion, and no one was really that interested. Children should be seen and not heard. The Rumfords adored them in private and that was an end to the matter. Clara would often croon to them when they were in their cots and, looking through suitable songs, came across Joan Trevalsa's melody to Matthian Barr's *My Treasure*. She liked it so much she included it in her recitals. It caught on and became another of her hits. Audiences knew, as she knew they would, that she was really singing to her children.

There was another health scare about this time and concerts had to be cancelled. Her agents emphasised that this was only a bout of influenza because "we do not want false rumours flying about". Bertie, of course, could and would have fulfilled the engagements, but the concerts had been predominantly billed with Clara's name. An appearance without her would be unthinkable. His agents constantly sought solo work for him: "May I beg you to bear Mr. Kennerley Rumford's name in mind – he has been doing a great deal of oratorio work[.]" They managed to get him a booking in Cambridge but, as ill luck would have it, on the day he was to sing the area suffered one of the heaviest snowstorms of the year. The box office was disastrous. Clara insisted it was the bad weather that cursed it. There was a further solo appearance booked for Eastbourne and he hoped that would do better.

Clara was up and about by the autumn of 1906. The station master at Bournemouth received a letter of thanks from the Rumfords shortly after their afternoon appearance in that city in November. They were late for the 5.14 back to London, so a messenger was sent to request the train be delayed. This was cheerfully accommodated and an announcement made to the other passengers, who were only too thrilled to think they were travelling on the same train as the famous singer. Clara waved regally as she and her entourage, including the children and the nursemaid, proceeded down the red carpeted platform, preceded by the station master, to their first class compartment. When Clara travelled by train, red carpets were invariably laid for her arrival and departure, the top-hatted station master escorting her to her carriage. On this occasion Bertie wrote to apologise for not having time to thank him personally.

That autumn the Rumfords, and concert party, were in Southend, followed by appearances in Blackpool, the Isle of Man and the Hereford Festival. So it went on. With Clara's fees in the region of 200 guineas per concert, she was making a handsome living. Elgar had wanted her to create the part of The Angel for his oratorio *The Dream of Gerontius* which, as Jaeger told Elgar "requires brains as well as voice". She sang it often, but the first performance was given by Marie Brema as the Festival organisers simply could not afford Clara's fee. It was composed for the Birmingham Festival of 3 October 1900 and Clara had sung *Sea Pictures* there the previous evening, so logistically there would have been no problem. Her artistic sensibilities may have persuaded her to turn down the inaugural *Gerontius* as it was not a particular success, receiving nothing like the rapture accorded *Sea Pictures*. She felt she had done right by refusing it, although she was later to sing it many times. Based on a poem by Cardinal Newman, it tells the story of the journey of a pious soul from death to judgment before God. Kathleen Ferrier, who was later to sing The Angel, called it "Gerry's Nightmare."

Elgar always wanted Clara for the Angel and, in 1903, when he was working on his overture *In the South*, there were plans for *Gerontius* to be included in the Covent Garden Festival. He again requested Madame Butt, as Ibbs and Tillett now insisted she be billed, and again, he could not afford her. Her terms were described as "prohibitive." This difficulty notwithstanding, Clara and Elgar remained friends, although perhaps not as close as Clara might have thought. After the death of his beloved wife Alice in 1920, when he was deciding on the wording for her headstone (it refers to her as Lady Elgar), he wrote to a friend:

"I know quite well that it is incorrect to put Lady – it should be Dame but in these days, polluted by all sorts of awful women now Dames, I would not let myself put the desecrated word. My God! Clara Butt and Melba in the same world, either this or the next, with Alice!"

The Elgar work most associated with Clara is *Land of Hope and Glory*. She says this came about when she was sitting next to Elgar at a performance of his music in the November of 1901, as the *Pomp and Circumstance* marches were being played. Hearing the wonderful melody she whispered to him to "write something like it for me". They continued discussions after the performance and she alleges he told her, "You shall have that one, my dear." Both realised its commercial potential as, indeed, did the publishers Boosey, who snapped it up. The text was provided by A. C. Benson, brother to author E. F. Benson who continues to delight readers with his Mapp and Lucia novels. There were reservations about adapting the sweeping melody to a song, and among the objectors was Elgar's publisher friend, Jaeger, who feared the range and volume required might overpower most singers and also fretted that it might "sound damn vulgar". Vulgar or not, Clara had no problem with the range or volume and sang it for the first time at a concert at the Albert Hall on 24 June 1902. It brought the house down. Like *Abide with Me*, it became an essential part of her repertoire and she always sang it when the occasion called for patriotism. It was one of her most enduring encore items throughout the Empire.

Early in 1907 Clara was singing in Macclesfield. She had appeared in Cardiff the previous week and caught a cold that she could not shake off. She did not feel well for her concert, but carried on regardless. She was in pain throughout the performance, although the audience was unaware of her suffering. She collapsed afterwards in her dressing room. The *Manchester Guardian* reported that "she escaped an attack of rheumatic fever" and that "a doctor found she was suffering from acute tonsillitis, which developed into double quinsy".

Clara had recovered sufficiently by May 1907 to sing in a testimonial concert at the Albert Hall for baritone Charles Santley (elevated to Sir

Charles in the December of that year) who was then seventy-three and had claim to have been the most notable Elijah of his time. She had sung with him often, notably in 1894 at one of music publishers Chappell's Ballad Concerts at the Queen's Hall, with Antoinette Sterling also on the bill. Her co-artistes at the Albert Hall, who included Bertie, of course, were all friends – Emma Albani, who had sung at her wedding, Edouard de Reszke, Fritz Kreisler and cellist W. H. Squire, a personal friend who often toured with her. The London Symphony Orchestra was conducted by composer Landon Ronald, who was often Melba's accompanist. Melba sang several of his songs, including the lovely *Down in the Forest Something Stirred,* part of his *A Cycle of Life*. £10,000 was raised at the Santley concert. This was an enormous amount, considering the average fee for a top-liner was between fifty and seventy guineas. With luck a newcomer might expect ten guineas. The stratospheric Clara, et al were not subject to normal rates.

Clara had learnt a lot from Santley. When they first sang together he was an established artist and she a beginner. He had started in opera but, like her, switched to the more lucrative concert circuit, despite the fact he had headed the cast of the first Wagnerian opera to be performed in London, *Der Fliegende Hollander,* at the Theatre Royal, Drury Lane. Towards the end of his life he taught, his star pupil being Australian baritone Peter Dawson, who was sometimes to sing on the same bill as Clara and was to write poignantly of one of her last concerts in Australia when she was singing, crippled with pain, from a wheelchair. After the Santley benefit Clara appeared in Liverpool. She sang in many "Celebrity Concerts" at Liverpool's Philharmonic Hall where, as was her custom, she would sing six or seven items, leave the stage to applause, only to return to give three or four encores, each one climaxed by a storm of cheers. This is similar to the platform technique practiced by Dame Shirley Bassey today. It was not unknown for Clara to return six times. One critic considered this "a highly inconsiderate demand on the part of the audience". She would have it no other way, it was fully how she intended it to be.

Later in 1907, while the children were still toddlers and baby Victor in nappies – he had just had his first birthday for which his Godmother, the Princess Christian, had sent him a silver bowl and spoon – preparations were completed for a tour of Australasia. This was a massive undertaking for which Ibbs and Tillett had joined forces with the Australian agency J & N Tait. There was now a change in the Butt management. Narciso Vert had died in 1906 and his company reformed by former employees Robert Leigh Ibbs and John Tillett. Clara knew them well, "Bob" Tillett had been groomsman at her wedding. Ibbs and Tillett, as the new company was called, became the dominant concert agency of the twentieth century. Its stellar roster was to include Kreisler, Rachmaninoff, Casals, Segovia, Ferrier and many more. Clara was appreciative of the considerable part Vert had played in her career. He had raised her fees until they were above those of most other singers, ensured she worked in first class venues, and that appropriate conditions were met for her appearances. He had treated her like royalty, taking her and Bertie to Bellini's, just behind St George's Church in Hanover Square, one of her favourite restaurants, when there were matters to discuss. Ibbs and Tillett were based at 19 Hanover Square themselves and the manager of the restaurant adored her.

It was an era of loyalty, agent and client enjoying a symbiotic relationship. The company certainly earned its commission, however, as the Butt-Rumford demands could be draining. Clara, however, was its mainstay, contributing far more than any other client to the coffers. Ibbs and Tillett oversaw fees, contracts and conditions, but it was not necessary to find her work: demand exceeded supply.

Before their departure for Australia, Bertie and Ibbs and Tillett had consultations with the P & O shipping line to ensure every comfort was provided on the voyage. Electric fans were installed in their luxury cabin to modulate the effects of tropical weather, and a separate dinner table was reserved should they chose to eat in public, as they often did. Clara was no hermit. An inveterate traveller, she was keen to tour again. Her pregnancies, and illness, had kept her home far too long. They gave a Farewell Concert at the Albert Hall on 29 June. Edward VII sent his regrets that he could not attend due to a state appointment, but wished them every success. This royal patronage was placed prominently in the programme.

As they would be away for nearly a year, the children went with them. This presented few problems, as their suites of rooms easily accommodated both them and several nursemaids. When the embarkation date was finally confirmed, with several having been pencilled in and changed, there was a hitch. Clara was not normally superstitious, but was alarmed when she realised that their day of departure was a Friday. Salt was in her veins and, like many old-time mariners, she believed this was an unlucky day to start a voyage. She insisted everyone concerned arrive at Tilbury the day before, which would mean, in her eyes, they began the journey on a Thursday. They sailed on the SS Mongolia, which was expected to arrive in Melbourne well in advance of their first concert on 10 September. Bertie announced in the *Evening Post* of 15 August 1907: "I need hardly say how keenly we are looking forward to our tour of the colonies, and particularly so to our visit to New Zealand, of which country we have heard such glowing accounts." Few Britishers had ventured to Australia, even fewer to New Zealand.

Bob Ibbs was travelling with them to smooth out any difficulties. This was a mark of Clara's status. Most artistes did not have the benefit of their agent travelling with them, and had to fend for themselves in what could be difficult conditions. In 1948, when Kathleen Ferrier was touring America, she too was accompanied by an Ibbs and Tillett partner. In Ferrier's case it was the then elderly John Tillett. At times she was impatient with him, finding him a bit doddery. What she couldn't know was that the poor man was, in fact, suffering from cancer, the disease that was to cut her down so viciously at the height of her career, just as it would Clara.

If Bob Ibbs thought the trip would make a nice change, he

Clara aged 14

Clara in her early twenties

Clara shortly after her wedding

The famous grape dress

A typically glamorous pose of Clara wearing in her hair the diamond star brooch given her by Lady Morgan after a soirée

A statuesque Clara, always proud of her magnificent figure. The neat waist, it seems, may have had a little help from airbrushing

Top left: Clara the mother with Bertie and Joy

Top right: Clara, Bertie and Joy

Left: Clara and Joy

Left: Clara and Roy, her eldest son.

Bottom left: Clara, Bertie, Joy and Roy.

Bottom right: Clara and Bertie with Joy.

Louse Kirkby Lunn - (not in Delila costume) who beat Clara to Delila at Covent Garden

Clara at foot of staircase in her (slightly remodelled) wedding gown

Clara and Bertie in their sleigh on tour in Ottawa

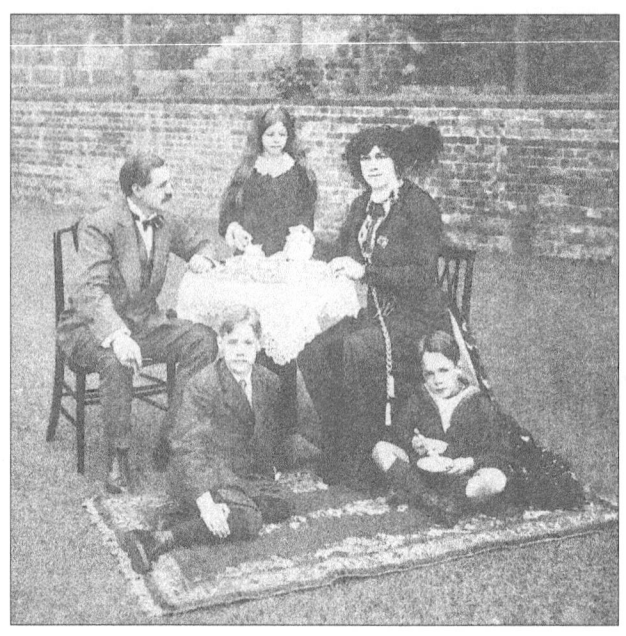

The family at tea in Sydney. Clara knew how to travel in style

A publicity shot of Dame Clara Butt's Day - raising funds for The Three Arts Women's Employment Fund

Ellen Terry, Bertie and Clara

Clara in Orpheus costume for
her Covent Garden appearance
in the title role

Clara with Robin the galah

Clara, Bertie and menagerie

Above: "Madame Will you Walk?" was a recurring phrase in the lyric of one of their most popular duets *The Keys of Heaven*

Left: Clara's headstone in North Stoke, Oxfordshire (with thanks to Julia and Keld Smedegaard)

was in for a rude awakening. It severely tested the Rumford-Ibbs friendship. As Christopher Fifield writes, "Few had greater opinions of themselves that the wife and husband team (note the order) of the contralto Clara Butt and baritone Kennerley Rumford, the latter's career largely dependent on the fame of his wife." This did not make Bertie easier to deal with. He accepted his status as artistically subservient to his wife (although indispensable, she would not be making the trip without him) and could even joke about it at times when critics virtually ignored his performances to concentrate on hers. However, he was still an Edwardian man, nominally head of his family, and with an Edwardian man's pride. He was constantly on the lookout for suspected humiliation. Ibbs and Tillett had managed to secure a few solo concerts for him at music clubs in Melbourne and Sydney, principally because of the curiosity extended to one who was married to such a phenomenon. As always, Clara was pleased when Bertie got solo work. No one dared criticise him, man or musician, in her presence.

Despite the demand to see them off a day in advance, there was a crowd at Tilbury for the leave-taking and, indeed, the travellers themselves constituted a pretty hefty part of it, what with their nursemaids, children, dressers, secretaries, maids, chef and over forty trunks of clothing. They were taking their concert party with them, it would be impossible to augment the programme with local artistes. Clara and Bertie were the only singers and Arthur E. Godfrey was their accompanist; violinist Carl Barre and pianist Frank Merrick would provide spots in the first half. They were fortunate to get twenty-year-old Merrick, who was attracting much attention and had been recommended to them by Mark Hambourg. Merrick was to have a colourful future – he was imprisoned as a conscientious objector during the First World War (which did not go down too well with patriotic Clara), won a competition from the Columbia Gramophone Company for finishing Schubert's Unfinished Symphony, and also wrote songs in Esperanto, of which he was an enthusiast. A Frank

Merrick Society still thrives.

The weather was calm for their first few days at sea but then a monsoon hit them, raging for four days. Mid-voyage Clara gave a concert in aid of nautical charities where autographed programmes were raffled, three reaching seventeen pounds each – more than a month's wages for most men. Their ship docked at Port Melbourne where their reception was positively regal, to the extent that even Clara was taken aback. They were besieged by reporters from both radio and newspapers who rushed at them like a pack of wolves. The Lord Mayor, in full regalia, led a welcome deputation on board, conspicuous for the huge bouquets it presented to Clara. The Rumfords, accompanied by the mayoral party, then took the train to Melbourne itself. Crowds were at the station and more bouquets presented. Their hotel suite was full of flowers and more were constantly arriving. If Clara had suffered from hay fever, like the Australian soprano Joan Hammond, she would have been incapacitated for weeks. Sacks of mail were also waiting for them. Although Bertie set about doggedly answering all letters (he was conscientious on all points of courtesy), he found the attention intrusive and uncomfortable. Showing no sign of fatigue, although the journey, with its temperature fluctuations and changing time zones, had taken its toll, Clara opened bazaars, gave prizes to young musicians and made speeches. She quite enjoyed making a short speech now, and assumed it as one of her public duties.

Lunch was at the Town Hall next day where 700 guests were present, including the Prime Minister. Crowds cheered them in the street. Bob Ibbs informed the London office it was an "extraordinary sight". As yet Clara had not sung a note. The people were determined to adore her, grateful she had taken the trouble to appear for them. Admission prices ranged from five shillings through to a stiff guinea. These had been carefully worked out and were what had been charged for earlier visits by Melba and Paderewski. If they had been a penny less, and Madame Butt found out about it (as she would surely have done), there would have been hell to pay.

But Clara was forced to share the newspaper headlines. It was announced, well before their first concert, that Nellie Melba, who had taken her name in tribute to Melbourne, had arrived for a holiday. It was a holiday, she stressed, and she would not be singing. As Bob Ibbs wrote to London, "she said nothing would induce her to sing, everyone believed she would". He later added, "I don't know what her game is but there must be something going on." Melba, having read of Clara's tour, had decided to see what it was all about for herself. Professional curiosity had been her impetus, but she was, in fact, genuinely in need of a holiday. She was going through a rough patch. 1906 had been a heavy season at Covent Garden, after which she had gone to New York for impresario Oscar Hammerstein, for whom she had an affection, and appeared at the newly opened Manhattan Opera House, which he had set up in opposition to the established Metropolitan Opera House. Hammerstein knew that Melba was his only chance of beating the Met. He paid her a whopping £3,000 per performance and, as John Hetherington says in *Melba* she was "worth every nickel!" The place was packed out and the Met trounced. Back in Britain she caught pneumonia but still somehow managed to sing at Covent Garden. Now she felt unwell and uncharacteristically depressed. She needed a stimulus, to see her beloved father and her own people. She also wanted to keep an eye on Clara, startled by the evident enthusiasm with which her countryfolk were greeting her.

Melba attended Clara's opening night, nothing would have kept her away, with a modest little party of 200 or so of her own friends. She applauded enthusiastically after every item, personally presented her with a magnificent bouquet of snow white flowers and gave a large supper party at the Grand Hotel for her afterwards. Actually, it had been uncertain whether Clara would be at her best for her opening. Shortly beforehand, both she and Bertie had gone down with severe colds. She could not believe her wretched luck. They did not get up until the last possible moment, dreading the worst. She waited nervously in her dressing room for the first half to end then, after the interval, stepped on stage to be met by deafening applause. It was several minutes before she was allowed to sing. She did not let them down. Her experience won through and her singing mechanism sprang into place, despite her chest problems. Her programme included Handel, Bach, Schumann, Schubert, Brahms, Beethoven, Richard Strauss and Gluck, including the latter's *Divinités du Styx*. This blood-curdling aria literally stopped the show and afterwards numerous bouquets were thrown on stage. But, as always, it was her religious songs that brought the house down, especially *Abide with Me* and *The Lost Chord*. Clara gave three encores, the last being *Land of Hope and Glory*, after which the entire audience stood and cheered till they could cheer no more. When eventually she was allowed to leave the stage Clara was ecstatic but, as Ibbs put it, "dead beat." Attendants had to make several trips to the stage to remove the flowers and there were incidents when fans "fought like cats and dogs" to grab a bloom as a souvenir. Ibbs informed London that "success was assured" and there was "little trace of illness about her." Unfortunately Bertie "showed he had a cold towards the end." Amid the nursery of flowers showered on Clara was a Maori shield and laurel wreath for Bertie after he had sung his encore of Handel's *Largo*.

Extra concerts were hastily arranged, as they were to be throughout the whole tour. Everywhere she sang was packed, managers clamouring for more. Thousands were turned away and refused tickets. Abundant as the takings were, press agents made sure the amounts were exaggerated to make for exciting reading. The truth was hardly less exciting. Eight concerts had cleared a staggering £5,000. Ibbs informed the office that concerts throughout were "all crammed. Whole houses standing and shouting themselves hoarse ... hundreds of flowers". At one concert it took two carts to carry the bouquets to the local hospital. Ticket touts and unscrupulous managements took advantage where they could and there were instances of police raids for overcrowding and enforced refunds. Some desperate people paid five shillings each to stand underneath the concert platform where they could see nothing at all, and barely breathe, but could hear most of what was going on.

Clara was presented to everyone of note and seems to have attended almost everything to which she was invited. She was made an honorary member of several clubs and societies. Roses were named after her. At Fremantle they were received by the Governor General and his wife, Lord and Lady Northcliffe. An entertainment had been arranged for them of a 1,300-strong ladies choir, accompanied by a ladies' band. How Madame Novello Davies would have pined for such resources. Clara was congratulated not purely on artistic grounds but as a wife and mother. Handmade toys were given her for her children. She attended an exhibition of women's work where she was awarded a full-sized harp made of flowers. At one concert she seemed unearthily divine as she sang while a thunderstorm raged. Amidst thunder and lightning she delivered *Abide with Me* with great feeling; some said she quelled the storm. The Premier of Victoria made a speech saying he had already met the King of England and now had the honour of meeting the Queen of Song. As always, her royal connections were exploited.

Clara's progress was reported by Bob Ibbs to the international press authorities and he had instructions from the Rumfords to keep them abreast of what was being written about them in the British papers. The *Sydney Mail* for 23 October 1907 noted that their concert "attracted an audience of fully 4,000 ... scores had to be content with standing room, and intense enthusiasm prevailed throughout. The programme was judged from a critical standpoint the best of the season ... Madame Clara Butt was heard in a group of beautiful Brahms songs ... in which she displayed the admirable clearness and tenderness of her lighter tones which delighted the audience almost beyond expression. Considerable interest was manifested in the item *Eastertide* a new composition by Liddle," and she was "literally overwhelmed by floral gifts and designs". After four encores, the paper noted of *Land of Hope and Glory*, "The stirring patriotic song was magnificently rendered, her gloriously rich, full voice in the lines 'God who made thee mighty, Make thee mightier yet' thrilling the vast audience so that the last note was sounded to the accompaniment of a tremendous outburst of cheering." This must have made galling reading for the Canadian Albani who had sung at Clara's wedding. Around twenty-five years Clara's senior, she'd had a distinguished international career, but was now portly and reaching the end. She had recently appeared in Sydney but attendances had been poor and at one recital the entire "take" had amounted to a meagre fifty-one pounds.

At one press call, Clara sang *Abide with Me* to an ancient bushman and reduced him to tears. The oddest tribute of all was the Butt Trophy awarded at a dog show to the "Best bull bitch" – perhaps the epitome of a backhanded compliment. Begging letters came in droves, one reading, "Can I have one of your evening dresses now you've finished with them." The clamour to see her gathered momentum, with some people travelling a week to attend a concert.

For all Melba's lavish treatment of Clara at her opening concert, the news of her unprecedented success right across Australia, with extra concerts packed out all the way, nearly drove the still unwell Melba mad with frustration. She could not stay idle for long, announcing towards the end of December (to no one's great surprise) that, due to public demand, she would sing after all. She could not refuse her countrymen. Despite her indisposition, she would give a single concert in Melbourne. At least this would take the spotlight off Clara for a while. A Melba evening could guarantee a full house, and so it was. But she was in poor voice. This did not stop audiences cheering but Melba was humiliated. A perfectionist, she did not want to short-change her own people by giving less than her best – that defeated the whole point. She felt even worse after the concert and wished she hadn't given it. Delighted as she was to see her father and be back on home soil, her Australian visit had not been the tonic for which Melba had hoped. It was an altogether wretched time and worse was to come. Believing her position at Covent Garden to be unassailable and that the opera house would patiently await her return, she heard the scarcely credible news that a rival had sung one of her coveted roles there, and caused a sensation. Queues for tickets had stretched from the opera house to the Strand. This was the London debut of Italian Luisa Tetrazzini, ten years Melba's junior, a singer at the peak of her powers and possessor of a diamond-bright voice of striking range and clarity, crowned by a dazzling coloratura technique. To make matters worse, in Melba's eyes, she had triumphed in *La Traviata,* which Melba viewed as her own personal property at the Garden. How dare anyone else sing it? She could not wait to get back to London to resolve matters. Which she did, one way or another.

Tetrazzini, a warm-hearted and greatly loved artiste, was not the most prudent of women. Towards the end of her life, when her voice was worn to ruination by her reckless lifestyle, she was forced to tour music halls, trading on her once glorious reputation. By that time not much of her reputation remained and she was playing to half-filled houses. Pianist Ivor Newton accompanied her on some of these dates. One evening, as can happen with singers, the voice inexplicably returned and she sang to the largely uninterested provincial audience like the diva she had once been. Afterwards he rushed to her humble little dressing room to congratulate her, telling her it was wonderful. "Wonderful," she replied, "It was a miracle". She, who had once set the world afire, died in poverty.

Clara continued to march through Australia like a conquering army. In Perth, as everywhere, extra concerts had to be fitted in. The streets were impassable, with crowds fighting to see her, and public transport ground to a halt. An additional 2,500 tickets were sold out in just three hours. At none of these extra concerts did she stint her audiences. The shows, originally designed to last two hours, now extended to three. In Adelaide, where a single concert had been booked, she gave sixteen more. Bob Ibbs was constantly chided by the Rumfords for not providing sufficient coverage in the British papers, which he was obliged to provide for them at every major stop. He did his best, regularly cabling news, but there was a limit as to how many times British editors could run the story. Clara would not accept this entirely reasonable explanation and Ibbs began to dread the times when she was not mentioned. She considered coverage of her Australian successes to be of international importance.

The whole party arrived exhausted in Auckland early 1908. Full houses, cheering crowds and extra dates were now taken for granted and, gratifying as they were, they were also tiring. Everyone was worn out. It was one thing for Clara to be worn out, everyone had to be understanding, she was after all the star and the reason they were there; it was quite another for Bob Ibbs to be worn out. No one was interested in him and he was expected to work even harder to keep everything going. The poor man was at his wit's end. In an attempt to placate his importunate client, he organised a carriage with liveried coachmen to ferry the Rumfords about. Clara barely noticed it, accepting such treatment as her due.

A problem arose with the extra New Zealand dates. As in Australia, these had been booked in advance by J & N Tait, the Australian agents. The Rumfords had agreed terms for additional Australian bookings, but claimed this did not cover New Zealand and they refused to honour them. This was a catastrophe and cables flew to and fro between Auckland and London. They would not budge, although it meant everyone losing a deal of money. Matters were finally resolved when it was pointed out that, although there was nothing in the contract, Bertie had verbally approved the extra New Zealand bookings when they were in Australia. It had been a gentleman's agreement, settled with a handshake. Bertie was honest enough to concede that this was the case, and he had simply forgotten. Bertie's word was his bond and the Rumfords backed down (they would have backed down in any case – cancelled houses would not only mean a loss in revenue but a considerable amount of public bad feeling levelled against them). It was agreed that in future everything would be in black and white – no more gentlemen's agreements. Even so, Bob Ibbs was hurt, informing London that it wouldn't take much for him to "throw in the sponge". The situation was a result of tiredness all round. Under normal circumstances it would not have arisen – everyone would have been delighted with the extra interest.

There was no time for rest. They sang their way through Auckland, Wellington, Christchurch and Dunedin, extra concerts included. Clara performed her full repertoire, including encores, and always left to the cheers of *Land of Hope and Glory*. Such was the spontaneity of her performance, audiences would have sworn it was the first time she had sung it. Even then they were not finished. It was back to Australia for yet more concerts, both scheduled and additions. They finally left for England in early May. It had been quite an undertaking.

## CHAPTER FIFTEEN

## The Recording Star

Clara rested on the voyage back, satisfied with a job well done, but completely exhausted. Ever the consummate professional, this did not stop her giving a charity concert on board. The rigours of the tour were soon forgotten but its stupendous success lived on. It was all the musical world could talk about. Offers flooded in and, within weeks, they were on the road again. This, after all, was their life.

Clara had often been requested to make gramophone records. Patti, Caruso and Melba had all succumbed and done well from them. Clara was reluctant, suspicious that if people could hear her on record they might not bother to turn out to see her – a fear initially shared by other artistes. Clearly, however, it had done no harm to the careers of the aforementioned. In 1909, some four or five years after her contemporaries were already on disc, Clara started recording. She had again been approached by executives of The Gramophone Company and this time agreed to meet them for lunch at the Savoy Hotel to discuss the matter. She had been giving it a great deal of consideration; records seemed to be playing everywhere and she was beginning to feel left out. Over lunch it was decided that she and Bertie (of course) would record a few titles. Should she prove unhappy with the recordings, the idea, and the records, would be scrapped.

It was not, actually, her first introduction to the recording studio.

She had made a recording for The Gramophone Company at its London premises in Maiden Lane in the January of 1899. Originally an American company, it had been founded by Emile Berliner, inventor of the laterally cut record, as opposed to the cylinder. She and Bertie had recorded the duet *Night Hymn at Sea*. Nothing much seemed to have happened to it, which is surprising, for that was the year she had premiered *Sea Pictures* and her name was on everyone's lips. But it was also the year America was being captivated by the wild syncopation of ragtime, the craze for which was to last two decades before being superseded by another new sound – jazz. They went to The Gramophone Company studios, now based in Hayes, Middlesex, to record her items, which would include another version of *Night Hymn at Sea*. She was impressed by the improvement in recording techniques since her previous studio visit. It might have been expected that such a big voice as hers would have been subject to "blast," but once placement had been worked out, and a level of volume agreed, the sound engineers found her voice adapted well. She agreed and is reported to have said at a playback, "My records are in very truth the living voice of Clara Butt." This seems an uncharacteristic statement.

A celebratory lunch was given, again at the Savoy, to launch the records. Somewhat eccentrically, she and Bertie sang the items they had recorded before the records were played so the guests could compare them. A couple of years later, in 1911, a record was issued of Clara singing the national anthem, which she would sing at the Coronation of King George V, accompanied by the band of the Coldstream Guards. This was retailed at half the usual price, at Clara's request, as she said, "To bring it within the scope of a greater number of the King's loyal subjects."

Recording techniques gradually improved during this period, allowing a wider choice of venues beyond the traditional studio. Clara was able to record in a church for its superior acoustics, and even at home where a spare bedroom was converted into a studio with a cable linking it to her music room.

Clara recorded many items in 1909, not all of them released for various reasons, but those that did appear included Handel's *Largo*, Hahn's (who had said she had "une voix obscène") *Si Mes Vers avaient des Ailes*, Thomas Moore's *Believe Me if all those Endearing Young Charms* and *Two Little Duets – Snowdrops* and *The Leaves and the Wind* with Bertie. They heralded a whole avalanche of Butt recordings. They were designed to be played at 78 revolutions per minute, but this was only a guide as to the speed at which they had been recorded and which had, actually, varied from anything between 68 to 80 rpm. Gramophones carried a fast or slow mechanism, so records could be played at a speed to suit the listener, altering the timbre of the voice accordingly, which was not always satisfactory to the artiste. Clara's records, or the catalogues in which they were included, carried details of the keys in which she sang so buyers could tap the notes on their pianos and adjust the turntable speed to match. "Clara Butt may be accompanied on the piano" read one such inducement. These instructions were not infallible, the turntable tended to alter speed towards the centre of the record, where the resistance was less, and if the wind-up mechanism was not fully employed then the whole thing could slowly grind to an ignominious halt. Blunted needles also distorted voices. But most record buyers just loved the novelty of hearing her, and didn't even notice a few revolutions per minute difference either way. The gramophone, then as now, provided hours of joy.

The sales were enormous, in Britain and abroad, making Clara famous in countries in which she had never set foot. She stayed with The Gramophone Company until 1915 when a dispute over royalties caused her to transfer to Columbia. She made her last records in agonising pain from a wheelchair, Bertie hovering concernedly by her side. It is not apparent from her voice that she had suffered a moment's discomfort. Gramophone record royalties augmented her income considerably, as did royalties from sheet music. Any piece of music which carried "As Sung by Madame Clara Butt," or in later years Dame Clara Butt or, in Sam Liddle's version of *Abide With Me*,

"Dedicated to Madame Clara Butt", also carried a royalty for her. Ivor Newton recalled a time when she stopped including one of her most popular songs in her programmes. Asked why, she told him the financial agreement had run out. She would resume singing it when it was renewed. This astonishing business acumen helped build her immense fortune.

Although Clara could, and did, command huge fees through her representatives, her life was by no means ruled by money. She often performed for charity, and not just the fashionable ones, either. Her management was horrified one day when she insisted on turning down a lucrative engagement in favour of a charity gig for a boy's cricket club. Sharing her husband and sons' love of cricket, Clara would not dream of letting them down. She had always been keen on sports, once even taking Nellie Melba to a cricket match.

On 27 November 1909, Clara and Bertie gave a concert for 200 dangerous prisoners at Bagthorpe Jail, Nottingham. Among them was Samuel Atherley, under a death sentence for slitting the throats of his wife and three young children. Clara told the prisoners she considered it a privilege to be able to help cheer the lives of those less fortunate than her. Bertie sang *There is a Green Hill* and Clara sang, "amidst breathless silence," *O Rest in the Lord* and, of course, *Abide with Me*. The *Manchester Guardian* covered the event and noted that the condemned Mr. Atherley "broke down during the singing, burying his head in his hands and sobbing bitterly".

Clara often sang the songs of her friend Liza Lehmann. Formerly a singer, Miss Lehmann, ten years Clara's senior, had taken lessons with Jenny Lind, studied piano with Clara Schumann and dined, as a child, with Verdi. She was forced to stop singing in 1894 after developing Bell's Palsy, a form of facial paralysis. Turning a negative into a positive, Lehmann spent more time in composition. She and Maude Valérie White were the most successful female songwriters of their time. Lehmann's compositions, which are still sung sometimes, include *There Are Fairies at the Bottom of Our Garden* and the four-voice cycle

*In a Persian Garden,* settings of FitzGerald's *Rubaiyat of Omar Khayyam.* She was the President of the Society of Women Musicians and went on long tours of America as accompanist to singers giving recitals of her songs. She would accompany Clara on occasion and Bertie sang her cycle to Tennyson's *In Memoriam.* Clara and Bertie introduced, at the Albert Hall, her *Four Cautionary Tales and a Moral,* set to the words of Hilaire Belloc. The subtitles give an idea of the content – Rebecca who slammed doors for fun and perished miserably; Jim who ran away from his nurse and was eaten by a lion; Matilda who told lies and was burned to death, and Henry King who chewed little bits of string and was cut off in dreadful agonies. The Edwardians found them great fun.

The Rumfords and Bedfords (Miss Lehmann's married name was Bedford) delighted in practical jokes, Clara perhaps inheriting these puckish tendencies from Theodore Hook. In her autobiography Miss Lehmann can scarcely contain her mirth while relating those in which she and Clara had taken part. She tells of a time when she and her husband dined with the Landon Ronalds. During dinner a maid kept spilling food. After hilarious misdemeanours the maid was revealed to be none other than concert pianist Irene Scharrer. To hoots of laughter she then sat down and dined with them and, most hilarious of all, still wearing "cap and apron". In "revenge" a subsequent dinner was given by the Bedfords to which the Rumfords, the Ronalds, Maude Valérie White and Irene Scharrer were invited. During the evening the maid kept smashing plates, eventually dropping a whole pile. The fragments were cleared away and another pile was dropped behind Mrs Ronald, making her jump out of her skin. Clara, apparently incensed although, unknown to Bertie in on the jape, rose from the table with a "wild expression of countenance, her eyes rolling as if her wits had deserted her, and exclaimed, 'This is too much! I can't bear it any longer! Give me plates! Plates!" She tried to throw every plate off the table but was prevented by Ronald. She rushed to the sideboard, grabbed more plates, which she threw into the fireplace. Bertie rose to his feet and thundered, "Sit down Clara! Control yourself and sit down at once!'"By this time Mrs Ronald and Miss White were virtually in tears, so the joke was declared. Cheap plates had been specially bought for the occasion with the maid, and Clara, in cahoots to break them.

This glimpse into how the privileged amused themselves (a contemporary parallel is rock stars trashing hotel rooms) throws light on the relationship between Bertie and Clara. She was Empress of the Concert Platform but it was he who was master at home. He had ordered her to behave. It was how they wanted it. It also shows they had fun together, not just lovers but friends. Nor were jokes confined to social occasions, they also took place on stage. Clara and Bertie delighted in leaving foreign objects – such as bananas or miscellaneous toys – on the keyboards of their accompanists. Once when Johannes Wolff was accompanying them on the piano, Bertie moved across the stage and dropped a box of liver pills on the keyboard. Wolff left his seat and bowed to Bertie as he returned them. The prankster was then obliged to spend the rest of the concert holding them. Elsewhere, while the cellist Leo Stern was playing, Bertie and some friends lurked backstage and rolled coins across the platform to him. Another favourite was for Bertie to paste out certain bars of music so the accompanist would have to improvise. The accompanists did manage to get their own back, usually by weaving in other songs while Clara and Bertie were singing. This happened during a performance of *Night Hymn at Sea* – instead of it being a duet, it became a solo for a while, as Clara could not sing for laughing. Tours could be long and arduous, so something had to be done to enliven them.

In 1911, the Butt-Rumfords were off again, this time to South Africa, a trip that would bring Clara into contact with even more of her growing international audience.

# CHAPTER SIXTEEN

## South Africa

The Festival of Empire at the Crystal Palace, spreading over 250 acres of Sydenham, opened on 12 May 1911 and ran through till 28 October. This was a grand affair attended by the King and Queen, who entered to a trumpeted fanfare, accompanied by so many members of the royal family that the royal box had to be enlarged. Its purpose was to celebrate the achievements of the Empire in all walks of life. There were sporting contests, pageants and cultural and military exhibitions, plus a fabled display of South African diamonds valued at £2 million. As *The Times* put it, it was the most "elaborate advertisement of the resources of the British Empire that has ever been devised". The opening concert featured a choir of 4,000, the Queen's Hall and London Symphony Orchestras, and the Festival of Empire Brass Band, with various well known conductors, climaxing in the public singing the national anthem. This was not sung as well as could be hoped. There was confusion about the tune, which was only rectified, as a last resort, by the organ booming out the correct melody. Following this debacle, Sir Henry Wood conducted a suite of Purcell themes which was all but drowned by the noise of the crowd who preferred the attractions of the sideshows. "However," as Jeffrey Richards points out, "where an orchestra failed to subdue the crowds, the commanding figure of Clara Butt succeeded," as she performed J. L. Hatton's song *The Enchantress*.

*The Times* remarked, "She is so well able to command the masses that ... she could be heard without effort." There was more confusion as people rushed back to hear her. She returned to the bandstand later in the day to sing what everyone really wanted – *Land of Hope and Glory*. This was a mixed blessing as far as the organisers were concerned, for as soon as she had finished many got up and left. It had been hoped they would stay for further delights. Clara performed *Land of Hope and Glory* again on 22 June 1911, this time accompanied by the band of the Coldstream Guards, to celebrate the coronation of George V at Westminster Abbey.

That year the promoters, J & N Tait, with the backing of the British government, organised a South African tour for the Rumfords. The Union of South Africa had been created in 1910, a self-governing dominion of the British Empire, and Clara's visit, it was hoped, would strengthen ties. It was only necessary to think back to her first Canadian tour and the patriotic enthusiasm she had aroused with *Land of Hope and Glory* to realise her strength as a goodwill ambassador. It would be an unhurried trip, combining business with pleasure, and with leisurely breaks between engagements. The children, and their retinue of staff and employees, would be travelling with them, plus accompanist Harold Craxton. They were to give several concerts in Cape Town where they stayed with Major General Sir Henry Scobell, Commander of the British Garrison in South Africa, at his luxurious estate in Rondebosch. Among the many letters awaiting Clara was a request from a member of the public that she sing "No foreign songs". One emotional lady, at the end of the first concert, grabbed her hand and told her, "I think that if nature could speak she'd have a voice like you." The more Clara thought of it, the more she agreed with the woman. The Governor of Cape Town presented her with a gorgeous bedspread which she used for years at home.

Concerts followed in Johannesburg where they were guests at Hohenheim, the extravagant home of gold mining millionaire Lionel Phillips. A ceremonial war dance was performed in their honour.

South African estates were like palaces. Phillips' estate employed ninety gardeners and eventually became the site of the Johannesburg General Hospital. They luxuriated there for weeks. One concert was enlivened by packs of dogs which wandered in and out through the doors, left open to quell the heat. In Pretoria, though frequent guests of Lord and Lady Methuen, they actually stayed in a hotel. A batch of Clara's records had been ordered to coincide with her arrival. To Clara's consternation they were being played outside the concert venue as she arrived as a form of trailer for the coming event. Her fear that records would deprive her of an audience flared up and she muttered to Bertie, "I don't suppose they'll bother to come if they can hear me outside." Her fear was unfounded.

Back at the hotel, after the packed concert, Clara was staggered as she walked into the foyer to hear her records again being played, this time for an audience. The hotel had organised a Clara Butt recital evening, despite the fact she was singing elsewhere. Strong words were delivered to the management. For all her reluctance to record, records became a part of her life. She displayed the same initial reluctance to broadcast, and for the same reason. If people could hear her on the radio why should they pay to see her? But, once in the radio studios, she was seduced by the grandeur of an institution that could reach the furthermost corners of the world. She saw radio as a means of spreading her gift in the service of international harmony. Song, she believed, could do this: "Someday one voice will do it. I want, above all things, that voice shall be mine."

South Africa is a magnificent country. For five-year-old Victor it was a memory that never left him, and he would return to Africa. Not South Africa, but Rhodesia (now Zimbabwe), a country that was to form the backdrop to a horrific episode in the lives of the Butt-Rumfords.

## CHAPTER SEVENTEEN

## Australia Again

Near midnight on 14 April 1912 the world's most famous liner, *Titanic*, hit an iceberg and sank. Among the 1,500 killed was William T. Stead, campaigner against child prostitution and author of *Hymns that have Helped*. Clara often sang hymns and they had, indeed, helped, but she had another reason for being aware of Stead. He was an ardent Spiritualist and had written copiously on the subject, much of which she had read. Believing he was inspired from the Other Side by the spirit of a dead journalist called Julia A. Ames, he had founded *Julia's Bureau*, in an attempt to forge communication between the Two Worlds. In life he had often drawn pictures of a sinking ship and predicted, accurately, that it was how he would meet his end. If the stories of his death are true then, clearly, death held no terrors for him. After helping women and children to lifeboats on the sinking *Titanic*, survivors allege that he entered the first-class smoking room, where he was seen sitting in an armchair, lighting up a cigar and reading.

Despite the horror of the *Titanic*, by 1912 the Rumfords were ready to again sign up and face the ocean for a tour of America, Canada, Australia, Tasmania and New Zealand – grandly announced as a World Tour – to commence the following year. J & N Tait had been besieged with requests for a further tour ever since Clara had left Australia. Bob Ibbs had still not recovered from the rigours of the previous trip, so, as gracefully as he could, begged to be excused. While Clara was still fully represented by Ibbs & Tillett, Roland Foster, who had previously arranged concerts on behalf of Rhyl council, was to be their new tour manager. Seduced by the glamour of his new charges, he jumped in head first.

Clara had less than pleasant memories of Wales. As a student, she had gone on holiday to Llandudno with friends. Ladies bathed from a bathing machine in those days, a hut on wheels which actually entered the ocean. The swimmer emerged from this contraption, descending steps into the sea, draped in a voluminous garment, rather like a burqa, which must have made swimming difficult. An athletic girl, Clara waded too far from the machine and got into difficulties. She was saved by a friend hoisting her out by an umbrella. Discounting her misadventure when a baby, this was the second time she had nearly drowned, having been fished out of the Thames by Bertie. Given her propensity to end up in the water, it is a wonder that Clara never learned to swim – her nautical heritage did not imbue her with natural buoyancy.

Tour-managing the Rumfords was a triumph for Foster, for earlier, on behalf of Rhyl council, he had tried to book them for a concert, only to be felled, like Elgar and others, by their fees. When he mentioned the figure Rhyl was prepared to pay, Ibbs "refused point blank". Refusing to give up, Foster bypassed Ibbs and Tillett and went to see Bertie when the Rumfords were singing at Queen's Hall. It must have been a good day as, explaining how Rhyl would be bereft without their visit, and buttering them up as much as possible, he managed to secure one of Bertie's "gentleman's agreements," sealed with a handshake. The Rumfords would get seventy percent of the net profit with a guarantee of £250, plus Rhyl would finance two supporting artistes. The council, which had budgeted one hundred pounds for the Rumfords, was horrified at this extravagance but had to go along with it, fearing a dreadful loss. Despite there being a rail strike on the concert day the hall was packed and, as Foster puts it, "the takings were not far short of £400. Marvellous!!" He impressed not only Rhyl but also the Rumfords.

Influenced by this successful arrangement, and learning that Bob Ibbs was unavailable, Bertie had written to Foster during a European tour he and Clara were undertaking. If he was interested in becoming their world tour manager, he was to come to Paris for discussions with them and their American impresario Loudon Charlton. Foster describes the letter as "the biggest surprise that ever came my way". Charlton, who was to marry American opera singer Helen Stanley, had made waves in New York by holding Sunday concerts in defiance of the wishes of the Brooklyn Sunday Observance Association. Clara had no truck with the hoped-for ban and was pleased to go along with Charlton. She frequently sang at Sunday concerts. For her, singing was akin to praying. Among Charlton's clients was contralto Clara Clemens, daughter of Samuel Clemens, better known as author Mark Twain. She was to be his only surviving daughter and astutely managed his estate, living in great style in Hollywood. In his discussions with Charlton, Foster was horrified to find he could not fit in the foreign dates with his existing Rhyl commitments. He received another offer increasing his fee by one hundred pounds and delaying his starting time by two months, allowing him to complete his Welsh commitments. This settled the matter.

Back home, Clara mentioned her new tour to Nellie Melba and, with Foster and Bertie, spoke of managers in general. Foster recalls, "I shall never forget the look of horror on Dame (sic) Clara Butt's face when a well-known Australian soprano used the expression 'He's done the dirty on me'." Like Her Majesty Queen Victoria, Clara detested vulgarity in any form and had a strong distaste for slang and expletives. The same could not be said for Melba.

One of Foster's first duties was to settle a dressmaker's bill for £500; Clara was one of the few who paid promptly. He was horrified at the amount she spent on clothes and shocked, when party to a telephone conversation between her and her dressmaker, to hear her order "a neat costume for walking, about 30 or 40 guineas". In his world around eight guineas was the norm for a good quality costume. He was to become accustomed to her extravagance. She ordered seventy new gowns for the world tour, each costing between sixty to one-hundred guineas apiece, some from Paquin but most from Lucile, the highly fashionable shop owned by Britain's leading designer Lady Duff Gordon. Most of the designs were Clara's own. She was fascinated by fashion and had the figure and wherewithal to display it.

Before leaving on their world tour, the Rumfords had to give more British concerts, at London's Alexandra Palace, Dundee, Sheffield, Bournemouth, Liverpool and Brighton. They also appeared at the centenary concert of the Philharmonic Society and the Handel Triennial Festival. Their regular pianist, Harold Craxton, was travelling with them. Ever keen to promote his own songs, he was always pressing them onto Clara who would, on occasion, sing one. They must have been good otherwise, friendship or not, she would not have done so, as Ivor Novello could have told him. He was later to write songs for soprano Isobel Baillie and baritone Roy Henderson, Kathleen Ferrier's coach. Most of the travel was by train but Clara, and Bertie especially, were keen motorists, to such an extent that they would ferry their car and chauffeur to Europe on occasion. They decided it would be pleasant to drive to the Alexandra Palace engagement. Never ones to travel light, this entailed two cars with chauffeurs. It was a disaster. Fog came down and, although they arrived safely, both cars were involved in accidents on the way home. The Rumford car actually left the road and tumbled down a flight of stairs. Fortunately, no one was hurt but they decided the risk too great to continue by car and, abandoning the chauffeurs to fend for themselves with their luggage and the cars, fumbled their way by foot, in an undignified and dishevelled manner, to the nearest railway station. There was no red carpet and top-hatted station master to greet them that night, and they finally reached home in the small hours, glad to be alive.

A continental tour followed. By now Foster was in harness and travelled with them as a sort of rehearsal for the world tour. Apparently for their concert at the Salle Gaveau all Paris high society was present. Bertie was in poor voice due to a cold and had difficulty being heard above the heavy accompaniment of the Lamoureux Orchestra. From Paris they went to Budapest, where Clara's repertoire included lieder and *Sea Pictures*. After a rehearsal the orchestra stood and applauded for several minutes. A reviewer, in translation, noted: "Her splendidly trained voice poured forth with thrilling effect"; elsewhere it was recorded: "To her Valkyrie-like appearance the voice corresponds. Her manner of delivery is of great elegance and reveals exceptional musical taste." Her name was spelled Klary Buttoue. They sang in Prague, Berlin and Cologne, where Clara sighed at the beauty of the cathedral. In Vienna, according to the *Neue Freie Presse* "she entranced every ear". Other ears she entranced were the heroic members of Captain Robert Falcon Scott's ill-fated Antarctic expedition. All the explorers were found dead on 12 November 1912, including Dr Adrian Wilson. He had loved Clara's record of *Abide with Me*. In the 1948 movie *Scott of the Antarctic* this song was played over his dying body.

The Rumfords arrived in New York on the *SS Campania* just before New Year 1913. Clara was able to visit her brother, Wilfred Lawson Butt, now living in Long Island with his American wife. Roland Foster, who had travelled in advance of the Rumfords to ensure everything was in order, had spent Christmas with them. Lawson, as he was known, had made a career on the stage, including two Broadway productions, *The Wanderer* and *Merry Wives of Windsor,* under the name of W. Lawson Butt. He was 6' 2", with the brooding dark looks that made him ideal for the part of villains. Naturally the Rumford children were with their parents – Joy now eleven, a willowy girl who promised to grow as tall as her mother, Roy eight and Victor six. The Rumfords were pleased to show them off to Lawson, but there were too many of them, not to mention their retinue of staff, to make staying with him a possibility. This was a relief to them all, really. Lawson told them of his interest in the blossoming film industry, which he was soon to join.

For a while it seemed his fame might even match Clara's after he moved to Hollywood in 1915. He broke into the movies with the pioneering Kalem Company, one of the first to make movies on location as opposed to the confines of a studio. He appeared in thirty-six silent movies, including Cecil B. de Mille's *Ten Commandments; Male and Female* with Gloria Swanson, and *The Beloved Rogue* with John Barrymore, about whom *Twentieth Century* cautioned he was "an awful warning of what can happen to a star who becomes too sure that the world is his oyster". If Lawson thought the world his oyster, it was soon to snap shut. Despite his stage career, his voice did not record well and he was one of the many actor casualties who did not survive the transition to sound during the early 1930s, a transition that was to enhance the career of Greta Garbo, who sounded as huskily gorgeous as she looked. It was ironic that his sister made her career with her voice, and he lost his for the same reason. He returned to London and even directed a movie or two before dying there in 1956. The Butts really were an adventurous family. Another of her brothers, Warwick, had gone to Argentina, working on a project mining for precious metals. He married and had two children, a girl named Clara, in honour of his famous sister, and a boy Warwick.

Clara's first concert was on 7 January 1913 at Carnegie Hall where she would be accompanied by the Volpe Symphony Orchestra, the orchestra that had given the world premiere, in 1910, at the Metropolitan Opera House, of Puccini's *La Fanciulla del West*. As usual she caused a sensation in the packed house, by her appearance as much as her voice: "Heroic in stature and regal as an Empress". She could hardly give *Land of Hope and Glory* as her finale in New York, so made it *Where Corals Lie*, part of *Sea Pictures* which had, of course, been written for her. The *New York Sun* wrote, "In an emerald green gown with flying buttresses of gauze like great sails attached to a bracelet at her wrist, a gold girdle and gold filet in the dark hair set off by two large cameos at the temples, Clara Butt at her full height of 6' 2" was a regal figure worth going miles to see." Her seventy-five gown investment with Lucile had been worth the money. The press hype was enormous, with extravagant claims made as to her earnings. Flames, it might be said, fanned by her representatives. It was written she earned $6,000 for a single concert, received $1,500 for an At Home, had refused $10,000 to appear in vaudeville, and received $4,000 each time she appeared at London's Albert Hall. It was known she was appearing in Australia after America, and it was said that her previous Australian tour had netted $160,000. One unidentified paper wrote, "Consider the sad case of Madame Clara Butt ... whose voice is just what the operatic stage needs but whose height bars her from that land of promise." She had made a pretty good compromise.

Foster, rather gently, tells us that Bertie "did not make an equal impression on audiences," although his "artistry" was mentioned. He took it well, jocularly remarking, "To be described as an artistic singer is one way of saying you haven't got much voice." It stung deep down, however.

It was unusual for an artiste to undertake a world tour with three children of school age – a tutor travelled with them – and this, too, was written about, much to Bertie's indignation. He was protective of his family and could barely contain himself when journalists asked him personal questions. Neither was he mad on travelling, apart from an academic interest, preferring instead Sunday lunches and cricket matches at home. She and Bertie were engaged for a fee of $500 to appear at the Bagby Morning Musicales at the Waldorf Astoria. She sang Handel's *Rend' il sereno* and some English songs, which the Americans loved. Bertie sang Irish songs which, again, the Americans loved and their finale was their duet *Night Hymn at Sea*. Geraldine Farrar, the Metropolitan Opera's favourite soprano and, incidentally, a film star, was also on the bill. Farrar had so many youngsters following her they formed a cult known as "Gerryflappers".

The Rumfords also accepted two private, well-paid, bookings to sing at the mansions of millionaires. From then on it was their usual exultant march through America, after which they made the 1,000-mile journey to Vancouver, Canada. What an education for the children.

There were numerous functions along the way, most of which poor Bertie had to manage. If Clara was singing that day she returned to the hotel for an afternoon rest and he had to deal with everything. She was inundated with fan mail and he felt obligated to answer each letter personally in his neat handwriting. He was never finished. Extra concerts were regularly fitted in and then the repertoire had to be amended. Many of the same people would come again, so the programmes could not be merely duplicated. Clara saved the more popular songs, which went down best, for the end of the show, a tip she later passed onto the Irish tenor John McCormack. They played to sell-out houses all through, yet there was still a demand for tickets. It was hastily arranged that Clara would travel back along the same route and give encore concerts.

They arrived in Sydney on 10 May 1913. Clara gave in all seventy-eight concerts in Australia, *Land of Hope and Glory* restored to its customary finale position which, as on the previous tour, brought the house down. It was known Clara still enjoyed royal patronage from George V, and this went down well with the Australians. She was treated with great pomp and ceremony, as though she were royalty herself. Clara was cheered, even in the tiny outposts through which her train passed, where audiences were too small to warrant a performance. But the news of her entourage passing had somehow reached them and, gracious to a fault, she ordered the conductor to slow down, back up if necessary, and stop so that she could ascend the platform and give the royal wave.

Clara gave fourteen concerts in Sydney alone. As always with a Butt tour, there were several charity concerts included. Again the streets were lined and traffic stopped. One confused elderly lady was heard to murmur to a theatre commissionaire "Is something on tonight?" When told it was Clara Butt she replied, "And will she be singing?" In Melbourne it was reported, "When Clara Butt appeared there was a demonstration that seemed to shake the building." Bertie lovingly cut out every mention of her in the papers which he pasted into albums.

Clara presented prizes at schools and music colleges and sometimes "adopted" promising pupils, including them in the first half of her bills. Roland Foster did not always think this a good idea, a case in point being a young soprano, Ethel Osborn. Clara signed her up as part of the first half of her concert party and employed her for years. He was convinced that because of this patronage Osborn did not bother to try for other work, thereby missing the chance of appearing at Covent Garden.

Due to her connection with Saint-Saëns and his coaching of her in the role of Delila, Clara considered *Mon Coeur s'ouvre à ta Voix* (or *Softly Awakes my Heart*), to be her personal property, despite the fact she had never publicly sung the complete Delila. She had studied the work with the composer and her version was, as she saw it, definitive. Therefore Clara was outraged, after a performance in Adelaide, when a critic had the temerity to accuse her of taking breaths in the wrong places. Furthermore, he suggested that by singing it the way she did she set students a bad example. The ill-starred man was pointed out to her in the green room after a subsequent concert. Without waiting for an introduction, she pointed her finger and, following its direction, verbally attacked: "You're the man who said I set students a bad example by breathing in the wrong place. Allow me to inform you the composer himself told me where to breathe and next time you criticise me adversely make sure you know what you're talking about!" There was a dreadful silence, then he fled, but had the gumption to send a fulsome letter of apology. That was necessary if he wanted to attend any future Butt concerts.

That wasn't the only time Clara was criticised for her version of the aria – it happened on yet another Australian tour when the Sydney Symphony Orchestra was accompanying her, under its feisty conductor William Arundel Orchard. In his memoir *The Distant View*, Orchard recalls rehearsing Clara with the orchestra when she "came in too early – looked at me and called out in that Amazonian voice 'That's wrong!' 'Yes,' I said, 'You were too soon.' 'Rubbish!' she replied. 'I've sung this with the composer, we'll have it again.'" They repeated the aria and it was wrong again. Orchard pointed out it was she who was at fault. "Nonsense, I can't be," she said. Orchard showed her the score, and by this time the orchestra was getting restless as the musicians could see, clearly, her timing was out. She conceded to sing it again with the score in front of her and things went right. "She was most ungracious about it," Orchard writes. There were other examples to suggest that adoration of Clara was not entirely universal. She would usually warm up by performing a few vocal exercises at the hotel before leaving for a concert. One fellow guest rang to complain he could stand it no longer and "had had enough."

In Coolgardie, well off the beaten track, Bertie was singing his solo *Eyes that used to gaze in mine* when a stray dog wandered in and sat in the aisle staring at him. As in Africa, doors had been left open to allow a breeze. Ever the professional, Bertie finished the song but then, with the audience, dissolved into laughter. Clara regretted she had not been in the wings to see it.

Although Bob Ibbs had had more than enough of the Rumfords on their first Australian tour and cried off this one, Roland Foster had nothing but praise for them. Having no work waiting for him in England, and trading on the enormous publicity the Butt tour had generated, Clara advised him to cash in on it and remain in Australia as a singing teacher, something he was qualified to do. "If you go away," she told him, "people will forget you." He saw the wisdom of this suggestion and, liking Australia and having built up contacts, decided to take her advice. He was contracted, however, to stay with the Rumfords until they were safely back in London which would not only have made it an expensive and protracted business, but would have meant a loss of momentum. When this was pointed out, Clara instantly and chivalrously released him, saying they would fend for themselves on the trip home. "So ended my connection with two of the most generous, gracious, unaffected and altogether loveable people the world of music has ever known," he writes. Elsewhere, he adds,

"This was the most easy-going and untroubled period I had known ... generous terms ... and Taits had organized well. Checking details was merely a formality ... not the case in America where dodgy dealing had taken place."

So successful was the Australasia trip that receipts exceeded £30,000. Requests for a follow-up tour were already in the offing. On the voyage home the ship docked at Hawaii and they gave an unscheduled concert at Honolulu, although the ship was only in port a matter of hours. Foster had arranged matters by wire beforehand. It seems that half the ship's passengers disembarked to join the locals for this occasion. Afterwards Clara was showered with garlands of hibiscus. They met Rupert Brooke on the way to a sight-seeing trip to Haiti. Clara tells us that her son Roy spotted him first, telling her "I've just seen the most beautiful man." This seems an unusual comment for a ten-year-old cricket-mad son to say to his mother, a lad who was described by Foster, together with Victor, as "splendid specimens of manhood". Brooke, however, was certainly beautiful. Yeats dubbed him "The most handsome man in Britain" and Frances Cornford thought him "A young Apollo, golden haired". The beautiful Brooke and the Rumfords struck up a friendship and saw Haiti together, where Brooke fell in love with a local girl. News of Clara's presence spread through Haiti and she was persuaded to sing. Unlike many professionals, it did not take much persuasion for Clara to perform. As Craxton was with them they found somewhere with a piano and she and Bertie gave an impromptu performance of *Night Hymn at Sea*.

They arrived in London at the beginning of July 1914. A London that was deeply troubled. On 28 June 1914 Archduke Franz Ferdinand of Austria had been assassinated, the repercussions of which threw the major European powers into a state of conflict which soon spread internationally, involving 70 million military personnel and over 15 million fatalities. Europe was on the brink of the First World War. As for thousands of others, Clara's world would never be the same again.

## CHAPTER EIGHTEEN

## War

It has been said jestingly that Dame Vera Lynn's agent started the Second World War due to the huge popularity of her patriotic songs. The same could be said of Clara and the First World War. Maintaining morale through that terrible conflict was what she had been designed for, and all that had happened before just a prelude to her real life's work. Clara was as frightened as the rest of the country by the impending war, but it was not a complete shock. Although she had been well received in Germany, she had noticed anti-British sentiments on her latest visits. Before the war she had been asked by the Kaiser to sing with the Stuttgart Choir, but was unable to do so, due to prior engagements. This had been a royal request and she felt she had behaved badly by refusing, even though there was nothing she could do about it. But she had maintained her contact with the German royal family which, after all, was closely related to British royalty.

In 1912, when her health had broken down again, probably due to the stress of preparations for her world tour, Bertie felt Clara had needed a break and arranged an incognito holiday in Berlin, where she could take some lessons from Etelka Gerster and freshen her much-used voice for the forthcoming trip. They would leisurely motor there and stay at the Adlon Hotel. Although it was an incognito visit she had felt she must pay her respects to the royal family, and explain her disappointment at not being able to perform with the Stuttgart Choir. She did not want them to learn of her visit and think she had snubbed them. Clara sent her chauffeur with her card which read "Clara Butt-Rumford" to the royal residence at Potsdam. The reply invited her to join members of the royal family there.

The conversation avoided politics, as ever, and revolved around children. Clara explained she was worried about Joy who was reluctant to eat certain foods. The royal party sympathised, one of them had the same problem with her grandchild. Clara said she couldn't wait to be a grandmother and spoil her grandchildren. She sang *The Lost Chord* and left with a present of a diamond brooch and gentle regrets from her hosts about the deteriorating political situation. She appeared in concert again in Berlin before the war, but the delicate situation would not permit a royal visit. Her last meeting with the Kaiser was after her return to England in 1914 when he attended the unveiling of a statue of Queen Victoria.

As soon as they had got their breath back, shortly after that meeting with the Kaiser, the Rumfords gave a Welcome Back concert at the Albert Hall. Clara was to sing there many times while war raged, but this was the last occasion until after the war that she appeared on her own behalf. During the war she sang there mainly to raise funds for charity, mostly the Red Cross, and her efforts were tireless.

She and Bertie would be separated during the war. They had discussed matters and agreed that their duties left them no alternative. He had volunteered his services, and that of his new Wolseley car, as a despatch rider and would be posted to the Front. As a sort of farewell honeymoon, they leased Slaines Castle, Aberdeenshire, for the autumn to enjoy what time was left them as a family. The holiday was almost ruined when Clara nearly drowned, yet again. On 2 September, Bertie's birthday, Clara decided to take a dip in the sea, accompanied by her petite French maid. Considerably taller than the maid, Clara left her in the shallows and waded far out of her depth. She was carried out by the tide, but managed to drag herself back the shore, where she promptly fainted. Guests carried her to her bedroom where they revived her with the aid of smelling salts and burnt feathers. Clara gradually composed herself and was able to join in the dancing and *tableaux* arranged for the evening.

War was declared while they were there, cutting short the holiday. They gave fund-raising concerts in Scotland and other cities on their way back south, culminating in a benefit concert for the Red Cross at the Albert Hall. At the end of the evening, when it was announced Bertie would be leaving for the Front, he received some of the greatest applause of his career, Clara standing to one side so he could bask alone in it.

This would be the first time they had been parted for any length of time and it was a terrific wrench. As Foster wrote, "They were genuinely devoted to each other, their domestic life was harmony itself." Nonetheless, neither queried for a moment that Bertie's decision was the right one. Their country needed them and that overrode personal happiness. Clara had a flair for organisation and immediately set about placing herself at the head of several war committees. Few would refuse a Butt appeal, and she would flatter, plead, cajole, or coerce, if necessary. She organised and starred in concert parties all over Britain. She did not, however, expect supporting artistes to work for nothing and ensured they were each paid ten guineas a week plus expenses. She had not forgotten what it was like to be without money. One tour alone raised £14,000 which was used to create the Clara Butt Committee to distribute funds. Committee members included Elgar, Sir Henry Wood, Fred H. Cowen, Landon Ronald and cellist W. H. Squire. Her secretary was Gertrude Blower, daughter of her Royal College of Music teacher.

This committee of grandees was found to be top-heavy, comprising too many people who liked the sound of their own voices. It was dissolved and the Clara Butt-Rumford Fund formed, co-trusted by W. H. Squire. Money was distributed to hospitals, work houses, asylums and homes for incurables. Clara and Bertie missed each other dreadfully, and grabbed what news they could. This was not always easy as Bertie had to keep his whereabouts secret. But there were hurried, unexpected phone calls at times and, of course, letters. Sometimes Clara could be seen snivelling after he called. There was the terrifying threat of Zeppelins, rumours of which swept the country. These vast airships, pioneered by Count Ferdinand von Zeppelin, had been used as luxury liners before the war but were now feared as bombers, their range and capacity eclipsing anything else in the air. This threat was never fully realised due to their vulnerability to fire. If incendiary ammunition hit them, or came near, they erupted into flames.

Clara would not allow herself to give in to depression, it was not in her nature and also it would be letting down the side. There were also three children for whom she must care. She knew she was better off than many other wives and mothers bereft of their husbands. But she could not restrain her pride when she spoke of Bertie's war work. Winifred Ponder wrote: "No other woman could have done what she did, because the place she had made in the hearts of the British public was unique and gave her a power and an influence which she used to the hilt." There was satisfaction, even a happiness of a sort, in the comradeship of service, and that mighty voice never stopped. People cheered, wept, prayed and were inspired. Jeffrey Richards writes in *Imperialism and Music* that she provided "pleasure for thousands whose anxieties and worries the concerts she organized helped to alleviate". Clara also provided work in a depleted economy. Concerts required servicing, and she hired many who would otherwise have been unemployed. She plunged into war work like Esther Williams was to plunge into swimming pools; energetically and with grace. From 1914 to 1918 her life was a kaleidoscope of fund-raising.

Clara organised another great Red Cross fund raiser at the Queen's Hall. For a solid week in May 1916, with the London Symphony Orchestra conducted by Elgar, she, dressed from head to foot in white lace, sang his new composition *For the Fallen*, his setting of Laurence Binyon's poems. *For the Fallen*, as Jeffrey Richards writes was "a work which struck an extraordinary chord with people". Included in the evenings were full performances of *The Dream of Gerontius* in which she sang the part of the Angel. This was then performed at Leeds with the Leeds Choral Society. Elgar had written the Angel with her in mind but couldn't afford her; in this time of need she did it for her country for nothing. *The Times* wrote: "one could not for a moment lose sight of the serious intention of all concerned. The dominant idea was not the making of music for pleasure or profit. It was an act of commemoration for the dead with a message of comfort for 'all tormented souls'."

After *Gerontius* Clara made a speech outlining her Spiritualist views: "in this tremendous upheaval when youth is dying for us, I want to give people a week of beautiful thoughts for I am convinced that no nation can be great that is not truly religious. I believe the war has given us a new attitude towards death, that many who had no faith before are now hungering to believe that after death there is life." Together with Spiritualism, she believed in personal responsibility. Her health was still precarious, but she refused to give in. Sometimes it was simply will power that kept her going, that and the belief in the divine power of her voice. Neither would let her down. As Winifred Ponder says, she had "a religious motive ... [she] felt people experiencing the horror of war should hear music that was spiritual ... [her] art should try to express life in death." What was heaven, about which she so often sang, if not life in death? A critic has written she was "one of the greatest missionaries of our time." That was her impetus.

Later that May, Clara organised another mammoth Albert Hall Red Cross concert. The King, Queen and Princess Mary attended, the King requesting she sing the national anthem with her "deep chest notes in it" and the Queen asking for Liddle's *Abide with Me*. She was backed by a choir of 250 and the massed Bands of the Brigade of Guards. Both Albani and Edward Lloyd came out of retirement for the occasion. Every audience member was provided with a flag to wave during the King's entrance to *Rule Britannia*. The atmosphere was electric, compounded when Bertie made an unadvertised appearance, having been granted special dispensation by the War Office. He wore his army uniform and sang to unprecedented applause. Clara's joy at working with him again, albeit for a brief period, was a tonic for everyone. Much of the audience consisted of wounded men in uniform and nurses. Clara paid all expenses herself, making a profit of £9,000 for the fund.

While this highly publicised event was taking place, burglars broke into her home and, among other valuables, stole a pile of cheques and monies that had been sent for funds. The papers next day notified banks to stop payment of the cheques. Bertie lost his beloved meerschaum pipe. Not everyone was behind the war effort. Money and morale were desperately needed, as the carnage was horrifying. On 1 July 1916, the first day of the Battle of the Somme, there were over 57,000 British casualties, a third of them fatal. Officers on the front line were given a six-week survival rate. The trenches, ghastly in themselves, were full of rotting corpses, with huge rats constantly nibbling away at the dead and wounded. As Juliet Nicolson writes in *The Great Silence*, "These ghostly creatures would move swiftly towards sleeping men, waking them with a start as they dragged their tails across the men's faces in the constant search for another meal."

Clara sang at another two concerts for wounded servicemen at which servicemen themselves were admitted free. These were arranged by agent Lionel Powell and The Columbia Gramophone Company, for which she recorded. Clara organised, with composer Frederick Bridge, a Westminster Abbey evening in aid of funds for the blinded soldiers at St Dunstan's Institute, a hospital for wounded military personnel. Someone described her as singing with tears in her voice. They were in her eyes too when she saw her rapt audience. She sang Sullivan's *God Shall Wipe Away all Tears from their Eyes* from *Light of the World*. Clara ended the concert with *Abide With Me*, in the middle of which, as she took a breath, she inadvertently inhaled a fly (referred to by Ponder as "the enemy within"). This could have been a total disaster, and not just for the fly. Ever the professional, Clara maintained her composure, avoided choking, and finished the hymn. Any slight break in her production was ascribed to an excess of pathos on this moving occasion. It was just as well Signor Foli was not with her.

Clara also toured the colliery towns, travelling with a helper and driver in one of her beloved huge cars, for which she got a special petrol allowance. If there was nowhere to eat she stopped to buy food where she could and ate it in the car. Food was not always available but she had no scruples about scrounging. Clara had many helpers and sometimes Sir Herbert Beerbohm Tree's wife, the distinguished actress who worked under the equally distinguished name of Lady Tree, went with her. "Are you going to hear Clara Butt?" she asked one stunned shopkeeper, who was still recovering from the sight of the limousine parked outside his shop, with a fur-wrapped Clara on the backseat. When he nodded in reply she told him, sweetly, "Well, she'll not be at her best if she's hungry ... can't you spare a little more?" Neither was Clara above bribing with free tickets if it helped. On other trips to Wales, in aid of nurses, she travelled by train with her faithful pianist Harold Craxton, cellist W. H. Squire and soprano Carrie Tubb. Because of the similarities in their names, and the fact they worked together, there was a false rumour Miss Tubb was one of her sisters. If there were no hotels in some of the out of the way places, they slept on the train. After an evening concert at the Blackpool Tower, Clara returned tired to her hotel looking forward to her dinner. No sooner had she entered the dining room than was asked if she would sing to raise funds for the Red Cross. With the loyal, equally tired, Harold Craxton at the piano, she sang in the ballroom and made a further one hundred pounds.

On 8th May 1917 Clara organised and took part in the spectacular *Pageant of Fair Women* at the Queen's Hall. Written by pageant master Louis N. Parker, it starred many female stars – singers, actresses and socialites, each costumed to depict a part of the Empire. The Queen sent a message of good wishes which was read out. All proceeds were to go to war charities. Clara's daughter Joy, by then a fourteen-year-old schoolgirl, was Sudan, but the climax was Clara herself, arrayed in helmet, shield, Union Jack and brandishing a trident. She was the British Empire. Joan of Arc was to be portrayed in a *tableau*, although some objected on grounds of blasphemy. Clara put pen to paper, defending this decision in a letter to The Times on 26 April 1917: "Joan of Arc has frequently been presented on stage, without giving offence, both in France and England, nor can I easily believe that her impersonation in a pageant is more likely to offend either our French allies or the Roman Catholic community than that of the Madonna in recent Charity Tableaux." It went ahead.

The pageant raised thousands of pounds and was repeated shortly after and then given another two performances in Chiswick specifically for funds to build flats for disabled soldiers, one flat to be named after Clara. Horrifying as it was at the Front, it was harrowing for those left at home, those whose lives now seemed futile and who could only wait and pray. Clara's job was to give meaning to that ghastly waiting, to prove there was a purpose to it, and her audiences could pray with her as she sang. Her spiritual songs were prayers. But she, above most others, could actually do something practical for the troops, she could raise money for things and services they needed, and help provide medication and comfort for those sent home badly damaged, some beyond repair. Her voice could achieve this and she would sing herself into the grave for her country.

On the rare occasion that Clara did get a few moments to herself, she studied Russian. The country and its singers fascinated her and she regretted she had not appeared there. She still hoped to do so. Clara was always interested in learning foreign languages. Her patriotism was certainly not motivated by xenophobia.

Clara felt the need for a patriotic naval song as there did not seem to be one that suited her. She approached Rudyard Kipling, no less loyal a subject than she, to write a suitable lyric. He didn't think he could come up with anything. A little later she read in a newspaper his poem *My Boy Jack*. It was written after Kipling's teenaged son died in

1915 in the Battle of Loos. That, she told Kipling, would do the trick. She persuaded Edward German to set it to music, explaining exactly what she wanted. *Have You News of My Boy Jack?* became a poignant item in her programmes.

Clara held charity auctions, selling her own possessions, one such being a much cherished jade bracelet. She felt there was no point in selling unwanted things; unless there was a degree of personal sacrifice, the point, in her eyes, was lost. With so much suffering around she felt the need for personal forfeit. The bracelet had been given her in 1907, when she had been leaving for Australasia, by her friend, actress Lily Hanbury, who had since died giving birth to a stillborn child. She had been wearing it when saying goodbye to Clara and spontaneously given it her for luck. Clara treasured it. Unknown to Clara, Bertie, knowing how she loved the bracelet, tried to buy it back for her. He was too late, it had already been bought. But the successful bidder was Mr Herbert Guedalla, husband of Lily Hanbury, who reunited the bracelet with its previous owner. By the time war was over, Clara had raised hundreds of thousands of pounds and been a beacon of hope for thousands.

Bertie had been no less industrious, albeit in a less spectacular way. After a period at the Front with the Red Cross, driving his by then battered Wolseley he had been moved to Army Head Quarters and from there to the Secret Service. He had been mentioned in despatches twice and promoted to Captain, a rank he was allowed to retain in civilian life. He had also sung for the troops and organised concerts. Clara's voice had been with him throughout the war. Her record of *Abide with Me* was played wherever it was possible to carry a gramophone, in messes and hospitals, and he had heard it even in the trenches.

Post-war Britain in 1918, with the battered, grief stricken country staggering to its knees, was a less discriminatory place than the pre-war class-conscious society in which Clara had grown up. George V was still on the throne but in 1917 he had changed the royal family's name from the Teutonic Saxe-Coburg-Gotha to the very English-sounding

Windsor, a patriotic emblem of the social changes to come. Britain had fought for its right to exist, but that existence had been altered. Crowds had gathered in Trafalgar Square to celebrate victory, but the euphoria was short lived. In addition to the social adjustments, the country was engulfed in political and economic problems. It was in debt to the hilt, unemployment was high and industrial strikes were soon to wreak havoc. Industries that had mushroomed during the war shrunk, and women (some of them reluctantly) had to give up their jobs to the returning men.

Nearly everyone had lost somebody, husband, sweetheart, son, father, or brother. Moreover, there were 41,000 amputees, many of whom had lost more than one limb in the fighting. These were among the lucky; others had had part of their faces blown away, leaving them hideously disfigured. Some hospitals were asked to keep these patients inside as the sight of them wandering about was too upsetting for people. Divorce was common. The nation's shock was epitomised by an advertisement for Kensitas cigarettes, *You've seen it through. You don't want to talk about it.* On the plus side the working class could now move up the social scale; many blue-collar workers could take white-collar jobs, opportunities they could only have dreamed of before. Women over thirty had the vote and there was universal male suffrage. Britain was altogether more democratic.

London was a changed city, more egalitarian, but the classier sections were shabbier. As were certain members of Clara's audience. During the war she had wholeheartedly sung to all stations of life and that policy was to remain. On grand occasions she still looked out from the stage onto tiaras and dinner jackets, but scattered among them were lounge suits and tweeds. At Homes were fewer. Many of society's famed hostesses were dead. Of those that survived some had suffered reversals of fortune and were considerably poorer. Some of the huge country estates had been converted into hospitals and would never return into what they had been.

Some artistes, such as Nellie Melba, predominantly an opera singer, could not get used to this violation of protocol, as they saw it. Pre-war Melba nights at Covent Garden (which had been used to store furniture during the war) had been glittering occasions, evening dress *de rigueur*. Clara, as a concert singer, felt this less so – she had always had the popular touch, accustomed to less formality. She did not necessarily welcome the change but it was a fact of life, and she accepted it with pragmatism. Also, she had been in London throughout the hostilities, and had gradually absorbed the changes. Melba had been in her home country and when she returned to England after the war the changes had shocked her.

One of these changes was Clara's status. She was now a heroine. She had stuck by her public, sung herself hoarse for them, and Bertie had volunteered for the Front. People had not forgotten their sacrifices and effort. Her very presence mirrored the courage of the British, and this was reflected in her record sales and box office takings. The conductor, Sir Adrian Boult, who had provided the "cyclists" anecdote in his memoirs, was now a conductor himself, making his debut at the outbreak of war. Unfit for military service, he was able to continue his career during the conflict. At one point he had worked with Clara and remarked, in amazement, how during rehearsals she was able to sing through four B flats with ease: a full three octaves.

Clara's voice had taken a real battering during the war, and she was never one to hold back – her public was always waiting for the great thundering organ tones. That she could still demonstrate such a range in her mid-forties, and after such usage, shows both the hardiness of her instrument and her mastery of it. Now, with Bertie at her side, she continued the patriotic tours. Despite national poverty, patriotism was still strong and they travelled with the Band of the Coldstream Guards.

The summer of 1919 saw another tour of Canada, America, New Zealand and Australia, where they were cheered for their war work. *Land of Hope and Glory* was sung everywhere. Some of her Vancouver concerts were held at 12.15 in the morning which meant they did not finish until the very small hours. This initially came about because the

10,000-seater Horse Show Building where she was due to appear burnt down. The only other suitable venue – although smaller – was a cinema, and this was available only after the films had finished. Nevertheless, the place was packed out and the audience demanded encores, as was usual with Clara's performances. Such was the demand for tickets, this practice was happily employed elsewhere. None of the cast and crew, not to mention the star herself, was unduly put out. Many fans made arrangements to sleep for what was left of the night with friends or at their offices.

Upon her return to England, Clara gave another charity concert to a packed Albert Hall. All four professional Butt sisters took part in this event, each singing individually, with Ethel, Pauline and Hazel then joining Clara in Liza Lehmann's *The Birth of Flowers*. Liza Lehmann had been another of war's casualties. She had lost her beloved soldier son to pneumonia in 1914, and died herself, still missing him dreadfully, in 1918.

Clara's repertoire did not change. It would take a long time for war memories to subside. There were now even more ballads, a few novelty songs like *A Little Bird* – "Out of the ivy hopped a wee small bird and that was me!" – acted as well as sung, by a 6' 2" bejewelled, feathered and buttressed Clara, hopping about like a bird. There were, understandably, fewer lieder and oratorio appearances. The world might have changed, but Clara Butt was reassuringly consistent.

## CHAPTER NINETEEN

## Opera at Last

Clara's longing to sing opera had never died. She still cast an envious eye on those denizens of Convent Garden. In 1920 she decided to return to the opera stage, riding the crest of her success. It was, after all, now or never. She was not confident enough to try something new, and since Kirkby Lunn had stolen Delila from her, there was no point in competing. Sir Thomas Beecham invited her to sing Orpheus at Covent Garden under his conductorship, and she decided this would be her operatic return. It was, of course, the only opera she had ever sung. She knew the music suited her voice, and the character suited her height. She had enjoyed a success with it at the Lyceum eighteen years earlier, but the Lyceum was not Covent Garden, and she would now be competing with herself. There would be many who remembered her earlier, younger performance.

Beecham was at least as charismatic as Clara, it was he who had quipped: "On a clear day, you could hear her across the English channel." He had spent the entire family fortune, derived from Beecham Pills, on music by diverting it into the Beecham Opera Company, which was to go bankrupt later that year. As unorthodox in his approach as Clara, he had brought some exciting works to Covent Garden, including *Meistersinger, Elektra* and *Salome*. He also had championed the now seldom performed works of Ethel Smyth (most famous for her suffragette anthem, *The March of the Women*), mounting her opera *The Boatswain's Mate* at the Shaftesbury Theatre in 1916.

Clara looked magnificent in her Orpheus costume and Bertie was not offended by her making love to another on stage, as Euridice was, of course, a woman. This was English soprano and Beecham favourite Miriam Licette, twenty years younger than Clara and owner of a particularly beautiful voice, a Marchesi and Jean de Reske pupil. Madeline Collins was Amor. Licette studied the role with her friend, tenor Jean de Reszke, and while doing so, American soprano Marguerite Valdi came into an adjoining rehearsal room and noticed a pile of luxuriant sables carelessly slung on a chair. She exclaimed that she had never seen such furs and was told their owner was Clara, who soon hove into view, leaning on de Reszke's arm, wearing green velvet and casting a regal nod at the onlookers. Someone whispered irreverently that she was the biggest crème de menthe ever seen.

Beecham was not the easiest conductor to work with, as Clara was to discover. For years she had merely told conductors what she wanted without consulting their opinions. This time she was faced with a man of definite views. Clara had been her own boss for far too long to take direction from anyone. There were disagreements as to tempo and these were never resolved, continuing throughout all four performances of the opera which, at times, made it resemble a wrestling match. *The Times* noted that "she played fast and loose with the timing and spoilt the phrasing," the *Musical Times* adding, "Butt went through her work with great seriousness and no small effect," writing of the other performers that "neither distinguished herself". Despite this, all houses were sold out and Clara received sixteen curtain calls after her last performance. Unknown to the audience, this triumph was soured by a tragedy backstage. While scenery was being prepared a stagehand had fallen to his death through a trap door. His lifeless body had to remain there until the scenery move was completed and help could be summoned.

This was one of the rare occasions on which Clara was involved with a production that was not an unqualified success. She concluded that ensemble work didn't suit her and returned to being a soloist. Opera would have to manage without her. Her audiences would stick by her. They certainly did. As Jeffrey Richards writes, "She was, in fact, a national figure, almost as well known to the people of the Empire as the Queen or Prince of Wales." Clara was rewarded accordingly. That year she received an accolade from the country she had served so well. In recognition of her war work she was created Dame Commander of the Order of the British Empire (DBE) in the civilian honours list, which meant she should be addressed as Dame Clara. A title that seemed tailor-made for her. Dame and Clara went together like bread and butter. Whereas other singers who were accorded titles, Melba for instance, who also became a Dame, were still primarily known by their surnames, Clara was not – it was and is always Dame Clara. It would seem wrong to designate her otherwise.

In fact, several had been clamouring for Clara's rank to be elevated, even before the war had begun. Among them was the suffrage group the Women's Freedom League, who had in 1914 written to both the Prime Minister and the King, pointing out that the birthday and New Year's honours lists never included the names of women who had rendered distinguished service. Clara's name featured prominently among their roll call of notable omissions, alongside Ellen Terry, the superb Ethel Smyth, and socialist reformer Annie Besant, a woman who was to heavily influence and, indeed, comfort Clara towards the end of her life.

In the September of 1920 Dame Clara recorded *Where Corals Lie* from *Sea Pictures*.* As the *Oxford Dictionary of National Biography* notes, it is "an example of the lightness of touch she could command, and explains why the composer valued her artistry so highly in his works – when managements could afford her high fees".

That autumn she and Bertie managed a trip to one of her favourite haunts, Monte Carlo. She had become a fan of the tables and Dame

---

\* She had also recorded it in 1912.

Clara was known to enjoy a flutter, sometimes with her friend, actress Constance Collier. She had actually been introduced to Monte by pianist Benno Moiseiwitsch. It would take her as long to dress for an appearance at the casino as it did for a royal command performance.

On 22 July 1921, Clara was back in the world of light entertainment, a world to which she would not completely capitulate but always had a soft spot. This was the star-studded last night of *Chu Chin Chow*, the record-breaking musical at His Majesty's Theatre. An oriental fantasy based on the *Ali Baba* tales, it opened in 1916, running throughout the terrible war years, surviving slumps, and kept going for five years, playing 2,238 performances to over three million people. This was almost double the number of performances of any other musical at the time, an astonishing record that was maintained for nearly forty years until the advent of *Salad Days*. *Chu Chin Chow* had done almost as much for morale as Clara.

Actor-manager Oscar Asche, who starred in the show, made a speech at curtain call and Clara who, twenty-four years ago had sung at the opening of His Majesty's was now, as Dame Clara, invited from her box to lead the audience in the national anthem. It was a sweltering evening, the theatre was humid and it was late, but this did not dampen the crowd's enthusiasm. The rafters rang. There was a New York production and two screen versions of *Chu Chin Chow*, one silent, the other a talkie, made in 1934 and starring George Robey and Chinese-American star Anna May Wong. But it was the His Majesty's version that stayed in everyone's hearts.

In 1921 Clara was in Bristol, unveiling a memorial to lyricist Frederic E. Weatherly. A lawyer by profession, he had written lyrics to some hugely popular songs, some of which, like *Roses of Picardy* (one of the First World War's most requested items), *The Holy City* and *Danny Boy*, are still thriving. His *Danny Boy* lyric is just one, albeit among the most popular, of the hundred or so lyrics arranged to fit this poignant folk tune. It was actually a case of third time lucky, as he had already used the *Danny Boy* words in two other tunes, both of which failed to take off. Then his sister sent him the Irish air and he transferred the words to it and success followed. Sung lovingly by Irish people the world over, it is doubtful Weatherly ever set foot in Ireland.

In June 1922 Clara's daughter Joy was presented at court – not bad for the grand-daughter of a dredger boat captain. Her frock from Handley Seymour was featured in the *Illustrated London News*, who described it as: "white moiré, richly embroidered with seed pearls. The chiffon train was edged with silver tissue and trimmed in the centre with silver lace". The caption announced she was Clara's daughter, but made no mention of Bertie.

Up until the 1920s Clara had led a charmed life – loving parents, her prodigious gift recognised, spectacular career yielding a hefty remuneration, excellent marriage and three healthy children. She had experienced bouts of ill health but had battled through and kept them private. Her sterling war work was acknowledged and rewarded by the loyalty of the nation. But from 1920 onwards it seemed as though the Fates turned mean and were determined to get even with her and extort payment for their largesse. It was reckoning time. A great equalisation process began which brought her luck right down to rock bottom.

## CHAPTER TWENTY

# Family Tragedy

Plans were soon being made for another coast-to-coast tour of Canada and America to take place in 1923 and Clara needed an accompanist. Harold Craxton was unavailable. As well as a pianist he was a composer and wanted to spend more time on composition. He was also a family man. He had met a violinist when on tour, married her and they went on to have five children. He'd had enough of travelling the world. A replacement was needed and for that only the best would do. This was Ivor Newton.

Born in 1892, twenty years after Clara, Newton was an accompanist of the first rank who was to work with some of the finest singers in the world, including Melba, Flagstad, Gigli, McCormack and, in 1973, with Callas herself. He had a robust sense of humour which had kept him sane in a life filled with megalomaniacs. When he was with Callas he was in his eighties and suffered from dizzy spells. He told his page-turner, Robert Sutherland, that if he had a heart attack while Callas was taking a high note, he was simply to shove him off the stool and take over "as though nothing had happened". Apparently, she was quite fond of him and, although his memory could play tricks, would not hear of replacing him. In his 1966 book *At the Piano* he has a section on Clara entitled 'Britannia in Song' which is how he viewed her. He perspicaciously points out that, nowadays, many are inclined "to think of her with amusement. They would be wrong to do so."

He was summoned to the Hampstead mansion in the summer of 1923, greeted by the butler, questioned by the secretary and, having given a satisfactory account of himself, finally led into the drawing room to face their regal presences. Clara was modern when it came to decor. There was little of the Empire about her mansion. Art Deco was to arrive in 1925 with the advent of the Paris *Exposition Internationale des Arts Decoratifs et Industriels Modernes* but its advance guard had already arrived, notably in the Rumford drawing room, whose deep blue ceiling and black walls bespoke of the influence of Diaghileff and the Russian Ballet. The Empire was not entirely banished though. Amidst this modernity, clashing somewhat, were signed photographs of royalty, including those of Queen Victoria and Edward VII.

Newton, to his surprise, was required to audition, something he had not done for years, his illustrious clients vouching for his reputation. However, the party moved to the music room and he was accepted on the basis of his performance, not just for the tour, but to immediately start work in England. One of his engagements was to accompany them in concert at Eton College, probably the most famous public school in the world, where they were to sing to raise funds for the Eton Mission. Her son Roy (her favourite son, it was whispered), was now at Eton. A handsome, strapping nineteen-year-old, with enormous hands and feet – clearly he took after his mother – he had been enrolled there in January 1918 in Mr Lubbock's house and, after college, was to go up to Oxford. Roy excelled in sports and was a member of the select Eton Society known as Pop. Clara and Bertie revelled in his success and gave several concerts in support of Eton. After the concert, in which she was accompanied by Newton, she was presented with her customary bouquet and Bertie a cricket bat, with which he was enormously pleased.

Roy was a superb cricketer, and he had shone in the Eton XI in both 1922 and 1923. Sir James Barrie, better known as J. M. Barrie, creator of *Peter Pan* and much else, had organised a cricket match at

Lords in which Roy played. Like Bertie, and indeed Roy, Barrie was fanatical about cricket, although by all accounts a poor player. He organised his own team called the 'Allahakbarries' (Allah as in God, linked to his own name – i.e. God help the Barries) of which his friend Sir Arthur Conan Doyle was also a member. Music lovers both, they had actually collaborated on the libretto of an opera, *Jane Annie*, which has sunk without trace.

Roy played in the match and was to stay the night with the Barries, but he developed a crushing headache which only got worse. He was rushed to hospital, diagnosed with meningitis and operated on. He was brought home but his condition worsened, necessitating his removal to a nursing home in Park Lane. He died three days later on 23 August 1923. The King and Queen sent sympathetic messages to Clara and Bertie. For once royal messages did not mean much.

The funeral took place on 27 August, officiated over by the Revs F. H. Gillingham and H. R. L. Sheppard. Among the large congregation were Dr Allingham, headmaster of Eton, along with many cricketing and schoolfriends, and some Old Etonians. The show business world was represented by Lady Tree and Constance Collier, a staunch friend of Clara. Herbert Guedalla, who had bought and returned to Clara his wife's bracelet, also attended.

For all his splendid physique, Roy, like his mother, had not enjoyed robust health. To his pride, the previous autumn he had been chosen as a member of the Free Foresters cricket team to tour Canada, but had been obliged to decline due to illness. More recently he had suffered head pains when on a school camping holiday, but, like his mother, had shrugged them off. She had encouraged him to do so. The symptoms of meningitis are notoriously hard to diagnose – more often than not they are mistaken for 'flu – and sometimes there are no symptoms. When Roy was dying, all that medical science could provide had been administered.

*Wisden Cricketers' Almanack* for 1923 noted, "His early death, which was much deplored, removed a young and promising cricketer."

The *Eton College Chronicle* wrote that his death "came with a shock of amazement and grief to all of us who remembered him, at the end of the first Half, the picture of health and strength ... he was well known by sight to hundreds of Etonians, old and young, the great figure at coverpoint, with his great hands that moved so swiftly and so unerringly, and with such a complete absence of flourish or self-consciousness. He was supremely modest about it all. ... One who knew him intimately writes 'He was the most unselfish person I have ever known, generous to a fault, marvellously good tempered, a most amusing companion, possessed of a singular personal charm which endeared him to everybody ... no words can do justice to him.'"

Roy died a week before the Rumfords were due to leave for their transatlantic tour. For a son to predecease loving parents is dreadful. What made their loss even more cruel was the fact that Roy was to have sailed to Canada before them to play cricket with the Free Foresters against a Canadian team, then join his parents for the rest of their tour. Many of the Rumfords' acquaintances and friends had lost sons during the war, Liza Lehmann for one, but this had been a sacrifice to what they perceived to be a just cause, none the less painful but there was some sense to it. For Roy to die senselessly on the threshold of manhood seemed, somehow, worse. Clara and Bertie were grief-stricken beyond measure. But they were not destroyed. Clara's faith saw her through and gave Bertie strength. During the war she had become attracted to the teachings of Mary Baker Eddy, the founder of Christian Science. Mrs. Eddy advocated Christian Science as a spiritual and practical solution to health and moral issues. Although subscribing to Spiritualist beliefs, Clara was Christian to the core, and grateful to God for her voice, yet a believer in personal responsibility. The doctrine of mind over matter resonated for her. To Ivor Newton's incredulity Clara refused to cancel the tour or to wear mourning. For her, Roy's life had been a celebration and a blessing; nothing would be achieved by giving in to her grief. This was unquestionably true. But how did she, and Bertie, feel when alone without the need to maintain a public façade? Whatever she felt, the world would never know and she would never show it a tear-stained face. This approach was also adopted by Clara when her own health declined.

The tour party left on schedule on the White Star liner *Pittsburgh*, bound for Halifax, Nova Scotia. Unsurprisingly, given her grief at Roy's death, Clara was furious when she realised, just as she was boarding the train at Waterloo, that all her music had been left behind. A message was despatched to her home and a car sped to Croydon airport with the music, whereupon a plane was chartered to deliver it to the *Pittsburgh*. It arrived moments before the ship departed. Although there was an unspoken depth of grief, which friends knew better than to commiserate with, there was a defiant air emanating from the Rumfords, particularly Clara, amid the subdued circus of goodbyes. It all seemed rather hollow, but it had to be done. Servants, supporting artistes, company manager, crates of dresses, hat boxes, flowers, presentations of bonbons and bon voyage wishes were all loaded onto the steamer. Among the support acts was cellist W. H. Squire, to whom Fauré had dedicated one of his works. Bertie sometimes included Squire's song *For Me Alone* in his concerts. Squire and his wife, who was a painter, had often travelled with them and Clara immediately commandeered Mrs. Squire to act as what Ivor Newton calls her "lady in waiting". She would personally supervise the star's wishes, act as intermediary between Clara and her party, and also run errands.

In America the Rumfords travelled in what had been the recently deceased President Harding's private railway coach, equipped with three additional servants, along with a personal cook. The President had died three weeks before Roy, which must have struck them as eerie. Harding had been in office just over two years. At one of their overnight hotels, Newton was a little discomposed to be proudly told by an hotel employee that he would be sleeping in what had been the President's pre-burial room.

Clara concentrated on the job at hand, keeping the show on the road, which only she could do. In fact, the tour was a blessing in that it concentrated her mind on practical matters. The more Newton worked with her the greater his respect grew. He noted that she had a "tremendous sense of theatre and concerts," enhancing her appeal with magnificent jewels, many of which, it was murmured, had been presented to her by royalty. She was the first "classical" artiste to make her entrance from the back of the stage, lit by her pinspot, taking care to wear a shining dress that reflected the light, making her look iridescent, and truly one of the Gods.

Clara was often presented on stage with a posy by a child. She was greatly affected by this act, being a mother herself. There was an occasion when something went wrong and the child fumbled the presentation and ran off in tears. A little later she was allowed to re-present the flowers and Clara was just as overcome the second time. Had the bouquet been presented a dozen times she would have been equally affected. For all her mastery of stage technique, Newton noted, as had tour manager Roland Foster, that off stage there was "no pose or unkindness about her".

Clara's speaking voice was so deep that there were embarrassments at the hotels when she would telephone down for something. She was often addressed as "Sir," to which she and Bertie grew accustomed, but she was quite piqued on an occasion when her back was troubling her and she rang for a masseuse. The woman, mistaking her for a man, refused to come to her suite.

In Canada it was discovered that Melba was also touring the country and, due to some monumental oversight on someone's part, both divas were booked to sing on the same night in the same town, Calgary, Alberta. When this was reported to Dame Clara by the company manager she barely looked up, airily waving her hand as though flapping away a fly, and told him to get Melba's manager to change her date. Dame Nellie, for she, too, had been honoured by this time, gave a similar instruction to her people. Neither would budge. Melba, too, was travelling by private railway coach and, as luck would have it, both trains pulled in together on the same night to park in the same siding. The ladies received each other, exchanged greetings and were civil.

Both concerts were held as scheduled and both sold out, although it was noted that there were empty seats at times. Some of the audience had booked for both concerts, seeing half of one then rushing off to the other. The civic authorities sought to diffuse the situation by holding a joint reception for both divas. This was full to bursting, attended by every notable in the state. Both were impressive in their own right, together they were overwhelming, and there were moments of confusion. The overwrought mayor called Clara the "greatest of all Australian singers" and then referred to her as Dame Nellie Butt. Melba was buttonholed by one lady who told her she'd heard Galli-Curci sing and Melba was next best.

Melba hated Galli-Curci, who was a friend of Clara's, with a passion. Amelita Galli-Curci was a rival coloratura soprano, drawing enormous audiences and, most spitefully of all, was a good twenty years younger than Melba. She did have a tendency to sing off the note, which the pitch perfect Melba would delight in pointing out to anyone who would listen. In return, Galli-Curci is on record as having said, "To hear Melba sing *Lo, Here the Gentle Lark,* when she has finished you would think it was a turkey." Dismissing Galli-Curci, Melba categorically stated, "I know I have the most beautiful voice in the world." Where sopranos are concerned, plenty would have agreed with her. Melba and Clara crossed paths a few times during the tour and remained on civil terms. When Clara was in Australia she was invited to call on Melba's family. Ivor Newton writes that Clara very much preferred to sing to English speaking audiences "where the Union Jack flew". Although she certainly had a European following, Clara's programmes became more and more English as she became older.

Recalling those Canadian dates, Newton writes: "amongst my memories of her are those of the women in the artistes room of halls in lonely Canadian prairie towns, who dissolved in tears, as they told her that they had heard her in Birmingham or Leicester many years before; she brought England back to them". In the larger cities Clara abandoned the Presidential train and decamped to hotels into which she would sweep straight from the street, commissionaires bowing and managers escorting her to her suite – runners having been despatched to herald her arrival. Once settled she would condescend to sign the register. Newton wrote that when she took his hand to acknowledge applause "friends told me I looked like an infant prodigy".*

Clara's applauded, cheered, bouquet bedecked procession climaxed triumphantly at Carnegie Hall. Few were aware of the trauma she had experienced before leaving, the pain of which did not lessen one iota.

---

\*   I know exactly what he means. I saw contralto Marian Anderson at the end of her career in recital at the Albert Hall, accompanied by Fritz Rupp. In her flowing ivory dress she looked twice his size. The fact she held his hand made him seem even tinier.

## CHAPTER TWENTY ONE

## Enter Mrs Ponder

Clara was heard by probably her largest audience to date on the night of 21 July 1924. The Chelmsford High-Power BBC radio station was officially opened, and what better way to celebrate it than a broadcast by Dame Clara? The range of the station for "reasonable reception" was reckoned to be 1,000 miles, making all of Britain and much of Europe within earshot of her voice. She sang Handel's *Largo*, *Softly Awakes my Heart*, *Kathleen Mavourneen*, *The Little Silver Ring* and *The Lost Chord*. *The Times* thought them "exquisitely rendered".

By 1925 Bertie and Clara had been married for twenty-five years, reaching their silver wedding anniversary. She had never forgotten the support her fellow Bristolians had given her at the start of her career, and decided, since she had been married in Bristol she would give a celebratory concert there to mark the occasion. This took place at the Colston Hall, where she had sung many times. The Bristolians responded enthusiastically, packing the place and providing a warm, congenial atmosphere. She wore her original wedding dress – remodelled slightly, after all it was twenty-five years later and, good though her figure was, she had gained a pound or two. Bertie wore his original buttonhole which he had pressed immediately after the wedding and which he had managed to keep intact. It was an unabashedly sentimental occasion. The Lord Mayor attended and thirty-year-old Malcolm Sargent conducted the orchestra. Both Joy and Victor were with her.

Clara had enjoyed the anniversary concert but was harshly jolted back to reality on her journey home the next day when her car accidentally caused the death of a nineteen-year-old motorcyclist, Francis Willis, near Swindon. According to reports, the motorbike suddenly turned into the car's path and Clara's chauffeur, Albert, could not avoid him. He was not killed instantly and Clara and her friend, Miss Lock, tried to help him while they waited for help to arrive. He died the next day of a fractured skull. An inquest was held, returning a verdict of "accidental death". Having lost her own son so recently, Clara could empathise with the victim's mother.

There was another tour of Australasia that year – the Australians could not get enough of her. In Sydney she was asked to present the Verbrugghen scholarship; violinist Henri Verbrugghen was the sometime director of the New South Wales State Conservatorium, although he was then working in America. He had played extensively in England, notably with Sir Frederic Cowen, composer of many songs that Clara sang, and had toured with Tasmanian opera singer Frances Sherwin and Eugene Ysaye. Clara was actually suffering acute back pain throughout the tour, and had experienced intermittent problems beforehand. Although her Christian Science precepts helped, they also prevented her from seeking medical attention. But now the pain seemed to be interfering with her work, although she was determined it would not. Her morale was not helped when Clara learned of the death of her beloved mother back home. Her father died later the same year.

William Orchard conducted the orchestra in Sydney and had already encountered problems with Clara on earlier visits, notably during her mistiming in *Softly Awakes my Heart*. He was unaware of her health problems but, even so, her attitude towards him did not endear her. He compared her austerity to the "friendly" demeanour of his fellow Australian Melba. Dame Nellie, he says, often called to see him at the conservatoire, wrapped in sables in her limousine, with the car radiator protecting her against the chill. She did not choose to enter the conservatoire unless she was presenting something, or giving a prize, so as not to cause unnecessary excitement amongst the students, but she graciously invited Orchard to sit with her in the car. According to him, she would listen most attentively to what he had to say, proffering gentle advice on promising students and the running of the establishment.

The Rumford family circle was depleted even more in 1926 when Victor, now twenty-one, chose to leave England to take up farming in Rhodesia. He had never forgotten the beautiful continent he visited as a child when his parents had toured there. Having considered many ways to earn his living, he now decided farming was for him. With his parents help he bought a large acreage near Salisbury, hired staff and hoped to make his fortune on the land. They were sad to see him go and would miss him, but neither thought to stand in his way. He was a young man keen to prove himself. He could not live in their shade forever, feeling it incumbent upon him to prove his own worth. Both made it clear they were there for him if needed.

Bertie was always there for Clara. He proved himself so, drastically, when she sang in a Sir Henry Wood concert, the first half of which was a Sibelius symphony. She sang *Sea Pictures* in the second half. The event was covered by H. C. Colles, music critic for *The Times*, who wrote, somewhat disparagingly, that the Sibelius was "above the heads of the audience, which consisted almost entirely of Clara Butt admirers". That was too much for Bertie who saw red, refusing to allow any man to insult his wife. It was as well he hadn't been around during Clara's first New York appearance when W. J. Henderson had implied in the *New York Times* that her technique was less than perfect; he might otherwise have been guilty of murder.

Unbeknownst to Clara, he presented himself at *The Times* offices, asking for Colles. "Are you the man who wrote that filth about my wife?" he demanded. "Any question of that nature should be addressed to the editor," Colles responded. "You'll do," said Bertie, and punched him. He was sued for assault, forced to apologise, settled out of court and paid all legal costs. But what woman could resist such a gesture? He was everything she desired. *The Times,* for its part, in conciliation, wrote that it was "second to none in admiration for the beautiful voice of Clara Butt".

Despite the more egalitarian nature of post-war Britain, Clara was still enamoured of the aristocracy and delighted to accept a dinner invitation from the Duke and Duchess of York. She was performing that night and her concert was not due to end until after the designated arrival time. She, a commoner, could hardly expect royalty to wait for her. The problem was solved by Clara and Bertie cramming all their items into an extended first half, then bolting and leaving the supporting acts to fill the second.

While in Australia Clara had happened upon a former pupil of Henry Blower's who had studied at the Royal College of Music. This was Winifred Ponder, who had had a minor career as a contralto herself in England but gave that up to get married and settle in Australia. She was younger than Clara, who had been her idol and inspiration, although she despaired that she could ever attain such heights herself. Ponder was now pursuing a career as a writer, having published a travel book, *An Idler in the Islands,* which she proudly presented, gift-wrapped, to her idol. The women formed a friendship and Mrs. Ponder was shortly to play a far more dramatic part in Clara's life than either of them anticipated or, indeed, would welcome.

## CHAPTER TWENTY TWO

# The Mystic East and Empire Day

The mystic side of Clara's nature, that which responded to Spiritualism, made her warm to the numinous side of India. She was fascinated by the subcontinent, with its traditions of holy men, reincarnation and spiritual retreats, and longed to visit. Towards the end of 1927, after a provincial tour, Clara felt the Call of the East even more strongly and decided to answer it. For reasons unknown, Bertie did not accompany her, even though she would be away over Christmas. There seems to have been no marital problems, so perhaps he just didn't fancy it. In any case, Clara set sail for Calcutta with a lady friend and her secretary, arriving in time for the Christmas races. Of course, she attended, dressed resplendently, and enjoyed a flutter or two.

Sometimes Clara betted quite heavily (but then she was earning quite heavily, too) and she was not always punctilious about taking care of her winnings. Once, after a rampantly successful evening in Monte Carlo, she left the casino for dinner in her hotel restaurant with £3,500 in notes stuffed into her evening bag. £2,000 of this was her initial stake and the remainder was her winnings. During the meal, Clara placed the bulging bag under the table and rested her feet on it for safety. After she had dined, and also enjoyed a few celebratory drinks, she went to bed, forgetting all about the bag. Fortunately, a waiter brought it safely to her room. Another time, returning from a concert with various family members, Clara changed trains, only to realise that her bag had not accompanied her. The bag contained all their return tickets, plus her fees in cash for two concerts she had given. In a panic, Clara despatched her brother Herbert to the previous train that was still in the station. He hared along the platform, managing to retrieve the bag, just as another passenger was about to pick it up.

Clara was similarly afflicted with her jewellery, losing several pieces when they became unclipped. The little brooch she had bought with the money Queen Victoria sent her for her first royal concert was among them. Fortunately, this was found when she retraced her steps and spotted it lying on the ground. She was not so lucky with other items.

No such disasters befell Clara at the Calcutta races. Since this was a holiday, she was not booked to sing. However, word soon got round and she sang at three hastily-arranged concerts, all of them sell-outs. Cables bounced between continents to make the necessary arrangements, much to the consternation of her harassed secretary. Clara never needed much prompting to sing. Princes and maharajas attended, along with prominent members of the Raj.

Being Clara, she also gave a huge charity concert. This was at the Calcutta Cathedral and was in aid of a children's home in the far-away Himalayan region of Kalimpong. She was always responsive when it came to children's charities. Travelling in style through the country she met many illustrious people, including Mahatma Gandhi, who had been imprisoned by the British from 1922-1924 but was then having a temporary respite from active politics. Another was Annie Besant. Mrs. Besant, best known as the leader of the London Match Girls' Strike of 1888, was a follower of the mystical Madame Blavatsky. Indeed, she had been her lieutenant and, after Blavatsky's death in 1891, became head of the Theosophical Society which Blavatsky had co-founded. Annie was an advocate of Hinduism, while in no way disparaging Christianity (she had been married to a clergyman) – Clara would not have stood for that.

## 22: THE MYSTIC EAST AND EMPIRE DAY

Annie was one of the most gifted public speakers of her time, and she and Clara had several intense conversations. Clara found that Annie's Theosophical teachings filled some inexpressible need deep within her. The theories of reincarnation made sense of the back pain with which she now constantly lived. She realised her karma must be worked out. Meditation helped. Annie propounded that we are never given any burden which, by extending our full capabilities, it is impossible to bear.

The Theosophical headquarters were (and still are) in Adyar, a then sunny suburb through which the lotus-decked Adyar river flowed. It is now a part of Chennai (formerly Madras). India caught Clara in its mystical spell. She listened intently as Annie, seated next to her on the river bank and wearing a sari, expounded on the unexplained laws of nature and the powers latent in the human psyche, which fitted in with Christian Science teachings. This was the path to Nirvana – or to heaven. Clara's talent could be attributed to work she had put in through previous incarnations. Now, in its full flowering, it was her duty to share it with others, as she had done, to help them on the path. This was the reason for her existence. The Theosophical motto "There is no religion higher than Truth" made sense to her. With these mystic teachings pounding through her head, Clara just had time to meet Nobel Prize-winner Rabindranath Tagore, famed for his good looks, flowing locks and exotic robes, as much as for his poetry and teachings, which she had been studying for years. Many of these were based on old Sanskrit texts. Then it was on to the former Burmese capital Rangoon, where Clara gave another charity concert for children and took a trip down the Irrawaddy. Back in India Clara paid another visit to Gandhi, singing *Abide With Me* at evening prayers. For this she abandoned Liddle's arrangement, instead using the traditional melody. Visiting various governors, Clara sang the national anthem several times at the close of functions.

Clara also wanted to visit Japan but this had to be postponed after she received a telegram from Bertie summoning her back home.

There was no emergency this time, rather the exciting news that their daughter Joy was engaged and wanted to be married in June, on her parent's wedding anniversary. Her betrothed was Major Claude Cross, late of the Indian Medical Service. There was much to be arranged, and Bertie sailed to Bombay to accompany Clara on the voyage home.

On 24 May 1928 Clara could not have found herself in a more contrasting setting. The Himalayas had vanished as she was firmly back amid the familiar territory of Hyde Park, taking part in at the Empire Day Festival, presided over by the Duke of Gloucester. On Empire Day the previous year she had captured national attention by wearing a flamboyant red, white and blue Union Jack dress, leading the community singing in *Land of Hope and Glory* and *Rule Britannia*, accompanied by the Band of His Majesty's Grenadier Guards and the 10,000-strong Daily Express Community Choir. This was broadcast on radio although, to her regret, not internationally as the technology was too unreliable. Empire Day 1928 was also attended by thousands. Accompanied by the inspiringly uniformed massed bands of the Coldstream Guards, she sang *Onward Christian Soldiers, Jerusalem, Land of Hope and Glory* and *Rule Britannia*, exactly what her audience wanted to hear. People amassed 300-deep around the grandstand and lustily joined in the choruses, inspired by Clara.

The novelty of the day was intended to be another broadcast, a "live" telephone call from MacKenzie King, Prime Minister of Canada. Unfortunately this failed, due to atmospheric conditions, but his intended message was read aloud by the Canadian High Commissioner. Mr King stated that Canada was proud to be associated with the British Isles and pledged his country's allegiance to His Majesty the King, eliciting huge cheers from the crowds. This was a message of which Clara would approve. As Roland Foster noted, "It may truthfully be said that the Clara Butt-Kennerley Rumford tours played no small part in cementing the bonds of fellowship and strengthening the ties which bind South Africa, Canada, Australia and New Zealand to the motherland." Or, as Ivor Newton put it, "Her success was equally great wherever the Union Jack flew."

Clara and Bertie were soon touring Britain again, accompanied by Ivor Newton. In the green room of the Liverpool venue where they waited before Clara went on, Newton noticed the walls were hung with framed, signed photographs of artistes who had played there. Knowing full well what would happen, he, seemingly innocently, remarked it was odd there was no picture of her. Clara took the bait and told him to remind her secretary to send a large framed photograph which she would sign. The manager of the venue was sent for and informed of the honour he was about to receive. He thanked her profusely, but Newton, still mischievous, asked where it would hang, given the walls were already crammed. "It can go in place of that one, over the fireplace," Clara remarked, pointing to a central picture of another reigning diva.

While singing with the Liverpool Philharmonic Clara was asked to sign the register of the Philharmonic Society. She did so with pleasure, her signature sprawling right across the page. Sir Frederic Cowen, who was with her, was also asked to sign and fitted his entire signature into the C of Clara. Bertie took exception to this to this perceived slight.

Joy and Major Cross were married on 11 June 1928. The Bishop of London, Canon Monroe and Prebendary Gough officiated at the Holy Trinity Church, Brompton, and the bride was given away by Bertie. As at any function attended by Clara, the crowd was enormous and the police had difficulty controlling the livelier elements. After the bride had entered the church, a large number of women rushed the door, even kicking chairs out of the way to get a better view. In the ensuing disruption a guest's handbag was stolen. Doubtless many were glad to get away to the calm of Claridges, where the reception was held.

After the wedding, Newton recalled accompanying Clara to an intimate recital by a once celebrated diva, now past her best and reduced to singing esoteric, but vocally unspectacular, lieder in smallish halls. Noting the sparse attendance, Clara hissed at him, "I don't think I'm so silly to go on singing what people want to hear while I can fill the

Albert Hall." Sometimes he would drive with her to recording studios, noting, "The red carpet was always rolled down for her." He also noted the care technicians took with her voice. She had been recording for twenty years or so, and techniques had improved, but placement was still paramount. The strength of the voice was now the problem with the more sensitive equipment. Although she could rein it in when required, the studio did not want to sacrifice its timbre. Whatever the techniques of those primitive days, a fine job was done. Her voice still sounds magnificent.

Another recording star with whom she was friends was the Irish Count John McCormack. Both larded their recitals with a mixture of the classical and popular. He had enjoyed an international opera career but gave this up as he was, at his own admission, no actor. He now commanded vast audiences as a recitalist. He, Bertie and Clara would exchange anecdotes, laughing long into the night over a brandy or two. He, too, made a speciality of *The Lost Chord,* as did Caruso and others. Limpid as his voice is, with its seamless legato, he does not match the pathos of Clara. But a singer who comes near this, nowadays, is the America soprano Alicia Berneche whose 2008 version on YouTube proves that the old warhorse (the song not the singer) is still awe-inspiring today, even in modern concert halls.

At a recital where Clara was singing Dvořàk's Biblical Songs, she made a mistake during rehearsals which the young conductor pointed out. Arrogant to the end, she refused to admit it and snapped "Don't talk nonsense. I studied these songs with the composer before you were born." There were shades of her behaviour over *Softly Awakes my Heart* in Australia. Dvořàk, who died in 1904, did visit England many times, so it is possible they met, but there is no record of her studying with him. Clara had, however, recently recorded two of the Biblical Songs, *Clouds and Darkness are Round Him* and *Lord, Thou Art My Refuge and My Shield* on March of 1927 at London's Christ Church, with organ accompaniment, so had the music firmly implanted in her mind.

At this time, Clara was also conspicuous in her support of

Commander Locker-Lampson at his anti-communist rallies. The usually apolitical Clara, in keeping with many fellow citizens, had a dread of communism, frightened it might undermine British tradition and all she held dear. The Commander, a soldier and right-wing politician, valued her support and went on, in 1931, to found his famous blue-shirts, the "Sentinels of Empire" whose aim was to "peacefully fight Bolshivism and clear out the Reds". The Sentinels motto was "Fear God! Fear Naught", a slogan that could easily have come from Clara.

# CHAPTER TWENTY THREE

# Scandal

Whether it was that Clara had a foreboding of her impending mortality or, more likely, that she had received a substantial offer from the publishers, Harrap, but she had decided, around 1927, to work on her memoirs. She felt she ought to be consigned to print – it was a duty she owed her public. Perhaps another, more pertinent, factor was she was conscious that her star was starting to wane. She would not admit this to anybody else, and nobody would dare suggest it to her face. Christopher Fifield notes that, at this time, stars of the pre-war years were losing their lustre and that Clara and Bertie were no longer afforded sole representation, in fact, their names did not appear in the 1923-4 Ibbs and Tillett brochure. That was ominous. No sole representation meant they were available to anyone. A decade earlier Ibbs and Tillett were jealously guarding their property, now it was available to the highest bidder.

When Clara had made her first Australasia tour in 1907, she was such a prized asset that Bob Ibbs had gone with her to ensure things went smoothly and that she was not poached by a rival management. Those halcyon days had gone. Now she had to appoint her own tour manager and pay for his services. A biography might draw attention to her again, bringing her once more into prominence. Clara was in her mid-fifties, no age for a singer to think of retiring, of course, and the thought would not have crossed her mind. Nevertheless, she had sung consistently for years using the full range of her voice and had not held back. She was not an economical singer, and at times, particularly during her spectacular register changes, or "gear changes" as they were affectionately called by her adoring public, had almost abused her instrument. Had that great, hardy voice lost a little of its brilliance?

There was no way Clara was going to write the book herself. For one thing she couldn't. She admits in the Foreword that she didn't keep a diary and never made notes, not even of what she had sung and where, which is basic discipline for a concert singer. A great deal of research would be required to find out what had happened, which she had neither the time, nor inclination to do. The answer came in the form of Winifred Ponder, the Englishwoman she had met in Australia, who was now a writer.

When it was suggested to Mrs. Ponder that she might write a book on her idol she seized upon the opportunity with alacrity. Not only could she bask in the aura of her goddess, be with her daily and experience a vicarious thrill out of talking about her career, but it would be a terrific boost to her own career as a writer. Ponder travelled to England, and she, Clara and Bertie took up residence for a month in Rhyl, where Clara had enjoyed such earlier successes, away from the hurly-burly of London to concentrate on the book. Ponder was assiduous in her vocation and managed to unearth much material Clara had almost forgotten about until reminded. The women worked amicably together, mistress and chela, Clara providing what she could remember and Ponder jolting her memory and eliciting more. Ponder diligently interviewed contacts and ploughed through piles of programmes, papers, archives and whatever else she had to do to paste the great ramshackle career together. She was once or twice complimented for "digging things out" of Clara and eventually the draft MS was presented to Harrap.

George Bernard Shaw was a champion of Clara's, giving her glowing reviews right from his days of writing music criticism under the nom de plume of Corno di Bassetto, and her days of *The Golden Legend,* when he had enthused that she had exceeded all possible expectation. He had recommended her to his friends, the actresses Mrs Patrick Campbell and Ellen Terry. Whereas Clara and GBS did not socialise – their friendship might not have withstood that – they were warm when they met. Shaw, Clara decided, was the man to preface her book. She wrote him a gushing, coy letter, asking "Would you be an angel and write the foreword?" He responded equally coyly, "Good Gracious! I'd never dare." Turning a negative into a positive, Clara published both letters as a foreword (see p.212).

George W. Harrap, director of the publishing house, was disappointed when the draft was delivered. Mrs. Ponder had been overprotective in her deference to Clara's reputation. As John Hetherington writes, "Clara Butt, in the best tradition of eminent women singers incubating their memoirs and supported by her husband, forbade the inclusion of any anecdote implying that this is not the best of all possible worlds populated by the best of all possible people." Harrap craved "spicy" stories. This drew a blank, there were no spicy stories, or none that Clara, let alone Bertie, would permit. Then her old friend W. H. Squire came to lunch.

Hearing of the need for gossipy tales, reminiscences started tumbling out. He recalled Clara telling him an anecdote about Melba. It had happened years ago when Clara's first Australian tour had been mooted. Both singers, with Fritz Kreisler and Tosti, had taken part in a command performance at Windsor Castle. On the way back to London, the Rumfords had mentioned the forthcoming Australian tour. Clara alleged that Melba, being Australian, had pricked up her ears and announced, "I made £20,000 on my tour there, but of course *that* will never be done again." There was silence then she continued "What are you going to sing? All I can say is – sing 'em muck! It's all they understand." Everyone laughed, it was so typical of Melba, and Ponder thought it exactly the thing for the book. She excitedly included it and sent it to Harrap, who was delighted. Harrap's manager is alleged to have exclaimed "That's the thing! That will make headlines." No one seems to have considered what Melba might have thought. An unwise proceeding.

By 1928, when the book came out – *Clara Butt: Her Life Story* by Winifred Ponder – Melba was back in Australia, a respected doyenne, regularly wheeled out for prestigious functions. An Australian reporter unexpectedly called on her and pointed out the "muck" passage. She was mortified and, after a pause to still her beating heart, denied ever having made the remark, adding she had nothing but the highest regard for Australia's musical taste. She would telegraph Clara at once and demand an explanation for this blatant falsehood. She did so but not before the world's press carried the story. As the manager of Harrap's predicted, it made headlines. Clara panicked when she received Melba's cable, fearing not only damage to her reputation but also a hefty libel suit. She was in her limousine in a trice and bustled up to Harrap's offices, begging them to extricate her from this dreadful predicament.

Harrap's had printed 3,000 books and 1,000 had already been exported to Australia due to Clara's popularity there. One hundred and fifty of these had already been sold, so nothing could be done about those. 1,000 had also been sold in England and nothing could be done about those, either. The unsold remainder, in both countries, was recalled and the offending passages removed, amounting to a four-page edit, an expensive process. It had to be done, it was one thing to claim Melba had said it, quite another to prove it. While the amendments were being made, Clara called a press conference, explaining the difficulties of working with an inexperienced co-writer. Mrs. Ponder had entirely misconstrued her meaning. She had intended no such imputation and had been far too busy to read the proofs. She was horrified at this slight to her dear friend.

In fact, Melba did not press charges, the removal of the offending passages and Clara's admission of a misunderstanding pacified her. It may also have been something to do with the fact that everyone who knew her, and plenty who didn't, felt this was exactly the sort of thing the blunt-speaking Melba would come out with and in that very idiom. But if the remark had been made, and it probably had, it had been made in private; she did not expect it to swing round and hit her, like a boomerang, twenty-seven years later. Melba, for all her formidable reputation, was a fair-minded lady. Clara had certainly breached a confidence, a professional confidence at that, but perhaps Melba thought it best not to stir up what could become a hornet's nest.

The publicity did wonders for the book sales but, unfortunately, no one wanted the expurgated version. The unedited book was in great demand and fetched a high price, as it still does, on the second-hand market. All through the upheaval there had been silence from Winifred Ponder. She was blissfully unaware of the pandemonium, researching another travel book in a remote Malayan rubber plantation. She had left for the plantation before the furore, giving a Singapore hotel as a forwarding address. The last she had heard was that a presentation copy of her book had been gratefully received by the King, a confessed admirer of Clara's. Ponder happily returned to Singapore to find a barrage of messages awaiting her to explain the appalling situation. Gone were her hopes of making the big time. She recalled exactly the circumstances in which the anecdote had been related and that there had been no misconstruction.

To Clara's credit, if it can be called that, she did write a letter explaining it had been necessary for her to make her face-saving statement to a largely incredulous press. She knew her "dear friend" would understand. As John Hetherington writes, "Her dear friend must have understood many things, notably that great singers will behave as meanly as any other human being when they find themselves in a corner with an action for damages hanging over them." Winifred Ponder wisely chose to author no more music books, instead confining herself to travel writing.

In 1929 the Rumfords moved to Brooke Lodge, North Stoke, Oxfordshire, an expansive, delightful country home on the Thames. An Art Deco theme soon pervaded, which must have enlivened rural

Oxfordshire. Clara adored animals and had an aviary of exotic birds which she would delight in feeding, letting them perch on her shoulders. Many of them had been brought back from Australia, among them were a couple of gorgeous parrots and a galah called Robin. But her favourite had been Joey, a bullfinch she had tamed while living at Hyde Park Mansions. He was never kept in a cage and had been allowed to fly all over the flat, where he would perch on pictures, dado rails, and even Clara's plate while she was eating. She was truly saddened when Joey finally made a successful dash for freedom. There were also several big dogs and some monkeys. Sometimes she and Bertie would indulge in a little do-it-yourself and once, when they were assembling a new bed, he dropped a hammer on her head, which quite stunned her, in fact concussed her for a while. But she soon recovered and they fell about laughing.

The couple entered into the community spirit, Bertie becoming a church warden and Clara leading the singing in the local choir, which must have been rather intimidating for the others. Clara was thrilled with the thought of filling Brooke Lodge with grandchildren. Victor was in Rhodesia and they had heard no news of weddings or children there, but Joy had set up home with her new husband in Bristol. Clara couldn't wait to have children tearing round the place. In fact Joy soon gave birth to a son, Oliver, and Clara took great pleasure in nursing him.

In February 1931, far from well, Clara went on a tour of the East, including Japan, and then Australia, with Bertie and pianist Cecily Murray. She tried to learn some Japanese and practiced it on the locals, and was proud when they told her that her accent was better than that of other foreigners. At Yokohama, disaster struck when Clara fell badly, injuring her already painful back. She was urged to return to England, but refused. "No," she said, "I must get well to return home, and if I get well I may as well get on." Nor would she cancel her Yokohama concert, but did, however, permit an injection of morphine to dull the pain. She had to sing while seated, which was unavoidable if she was to carry on. In this condition she made some recordings which she was contractually obliged to do. She told the papers that she had expected to make some classical records, but "I found they only wanted 'Old Sweet Homes and Annie Lauries'." She added, "Japanese music sounds dreadful to Western ears. Sometimes it hurts you almost and sometimes you want to laugh. Sometimes it's like a dogfight." It was arranged for Japanese translations of Clara's items to be printed in the programmes but there was some resistance from the Japanese. They wanted to study the songs in their original language. "They take their pleasures seriously," Clara noted. "They were keenly interested in Western music."

Clara arrived at Central Station, Sydney on the morning of 23 March 1931 after a gruelling all-night train journey from Brisbane. She had wanted to take the aeroplane but Bertie had put his foot down, nervous that it might upset her. She would actually have been thrilled by this novel mode of transport. She hastily breakfasted, slept for an hour or so, then went to the town hall for a rehearsal. Sitting on a chair, protected by her furs against the morning chill, she went through her repertoire with the conductor. As the reporter for the *Sydney Morning Herald* put it, "Above the organ's booming, the harmony of the piano, cello and violin, her great voice rose." She must have been in a good mood for, despite her travails, she seemed remarkably cheerful, "directing, encouraging and praising her accompanists". But Clara loved to work. While the organist was going through his paces for her finale of *Land of Hope and Glory*, she propped herself on the organ steps and, although the sound must have been deafening, spoke of her sorrow at Melba's death. Dame Nellie had died just over a month before and they had long since patched up their misremembering of the famous alleged Melba quote. "It was a terrible blow," Clara said. "I had looked forward so much to meeting her again." She told of their last meeting in London when they'd had lunch together with Bertie and then gone to Lords for the test match. "I don't believe she's gone", she added. "I don't believe in death. I am sorry that physically we will not meet, but I feel she is very near." Doubtless, she was keeping a careful eye on Clara's concerts.

Clara continued by telling them that each time she visited Sydney she found its musical taste had improved, then spoke of the wireless and the marvels it had accomplished. There was a brief pause while she and Bertie posed for photographers and she had a few words with her manager. Then she was back on the platform, "That last line again, please." The concert was a huge, jam-packed success and repeated two days later, reviewed by the *Sydney Morning Herald*:

> The concerts of Dame Clara Butt and Mr. Kennerley Rumford are in immensely popular favour – indeed gazing at the vast audience at The Town Hall last night, it was difficult to realize that these were times of depression. Every part of the hall was filled, including the organ gallery, and the note of enthusiasm which was sounded with the first concert on Saturday night was emphatically maintained. ... Again, remaining seated while singing, as on Saturday night, she began her programme with Beethoven's *Creation Hymn*.

Also included was Rachmaninov's *In the Silent Night* sung in Russian. The review continued:

> In these two songs Dame Clara sets a high standard for these concerts and revealed how extensively her powers of interpretation have been developed and how completely her voice is under control. ... It was obvious that the people had come to hear the famous contralto sing the favourite songs associated with her name and this was tremendously apparent towards the end of the concert for *Abide With Me* and demonstrably repeated even more emphatically when Dame Clara sang *Land of Hope and Glory*. In these two songs her tones resounded with thrilling effect above the ensemble of the organ.

During this song someone in the audience handed her a Union Jack which she took and enthusiastically waved. The roof nearly came off. Also included in her programme were Brahms' *Von Ewiger Liebe*,

Besley's *For a Birthday*, Broeck's *My Country*, Leoni's *Leaves and the Wind* (which she repeated, turned round to face the organ gallery, for those who, presumably, were sitting behind her), *The Lost Chord* and a Japanese song she had picked up called *Chinkoro*. Bertie also received a good hand and "showed artistic judgment with his reading of Hugo Wolf's *Verborgenheit*". He also sang Ireland's *Sea Fever*, a song of the Irish famine called *Over Here* and *Billy Boy* which "increased his popularity".

After Sydney it was Melbourne and the tour terminated in Fremantle, after which "with a smile of anticipation she said she and her husband were going to Africa ... to meet their son and going to England with him". Victor, an imposing man of 6' 7", was still farming in Inyazura, Southern Rhodesia. It is not known whether they did in fact meet him. It is to be fervently hoped that they did, in view of the ghastly events that were to follow.

Back home, and although somewhat recovered from her fall, Ivor Newton noticed that Clara's back pain seemed worse to him. She still made her dramatic entrances from the back of the stage, lit by her pinspot, and gave encore after encore. But both before and after performances she had to lie on an unyielding couch specially provided for her dressing room. Trying to be careful in her moves, she had another fall and was admitted to Guy's Hospital. She underwent a painful operation to try to ease her pain but internal exploration revealed advanced spinal cancer, widespread and untreatable. All that could be offered were painkillers which, with reluctance, the pain forced her to take. Clara was now in pain most of the time, Bertie often pushing her around in a wheelchair. This was terrible indignity for a proud woman, famed for her statuesque beauty and imperious bearing.

Clara was still receiving offers to make records and, astoundingly, still taking them up. In June 1933 she drove to the London studios to record *The Company of Heaven* and *I Shall Not Pass This Way Again*. A few curious bystanders pausing to watch as the chauffeur and Bertie helped manoeuvre her massive and partially helpless frame from the car into her wheelchair. She managed a feeble wave but hated people to see her like that. She was unhappy with the recordings and refused permission for their release. *I Shall Not Pass This Way Again* did appear much later, after her death, on a CD entitled *The Unknown Clara Butt*. Ivor Newton wrote, "I never ceased to admire the control of herself, and of her voice, on these occasions." Another Australian tour loomed and was accepted. It might as well have been her death knell.

# CHAPTER TWENTY FOUR

## Refusing to Give In

Following the Yokohama accident, Clara was obliged to use her wheelchair if she wanted to stand or move for any length of time, but she forced herself to stand for as long as she could at concerts. Although her face betrayed signs of the strain she was under, few managers, or audiences for that matter, appreciated how unwell she really was. It was never publicly spoken about; not in her presence anyway. She continued with her concerts and would allow no one to commiserate with her. Despite her medical treatment she refused to fully acknowledge the severity of her illness. It was her belief that it would be a weakness to do so. She was not in the wheelchair all the time and forced herself to behave like the fit person she was determined to be. Her will power was indomitable. Where others would have given in, some might think sensibly so, she would not.

Bertie must have known how serious her condition was but he also knew how important her faith was. Destroy that and you would destroy Clara. It was her duty to sing, her reason for existence. By turning down the Australian tour – Clara loved touring and particularly Australia where she was joyously welcomed – would have been an admission she was doomed. It would have done more harm than good. And what good could be done? In any event the question never arose as she would never have entertained it. They were going, and he loved her enough to allow it. To do otherwise would break her heart and, more importantly, her extraordinary spirit which urged her on to survival.

The journey might, in fact, be beneficial to her health. They travelled in such style that it could be considered recuperative. Many of the rich took such journeys to convalesce. True, the concerts might prove an ordeal, but it was an ordeal Clara was determined to undertake. And she loved to sing. Desperately weak and with her voice showing signs of strain, and no one was more aware of that than she, she set out in 1934 for what was to be her final performances. Tait's, who couldn't have known how ill she was, were more than happy to handle arrangements. No one was more dependable at the Antipodean box office than Dame Clara Butt.

Clara was exhausted most of the time and, as in England, forced to lay on her couch in her dressing room before, and after, going on stage. She had no option other than to let her audience know she was unwell. She sang several of her songs from her wheelchair, still magnificently dressed, even though merely getting into her frock was an ordeal. Still they triumphed, although not in quite the same way as on previous visits. Charles Buttrose wrote: "I heard them on their final tour: the once statuesque Dame Clara, getting old, singing most of her concert seated but still with Kennerley Rumford who, in the chilly Adelaide Town Hall, looked as though he should have been home by the fire with his slippers on, bringing down the house with the duet they made famous, *The Keys of Heaven.* They were elegant old-time ballad singers who catered perfectly for Australian musical taste of the times."

Clara believed her Englishness contributed greatly to her success and did not miss the opportunity to make barbed comments about opera singers: "I wish to emphasise the fact that the true English style is that of the minstrel school, which I take to mean the ability to render a simple song or ballad with directness and simplicity, an ability distinct and very different from that of the average opera singer, to whom the art that conceals is not of much use." With age the idiosyncrasies which had always been a part of her singing intensified. Many purists criticised these traits, the very things that had made her such a character. Her old tour manager, Roland Foster, resented censure: "Clara Butt had to endure her share of captious criticism and envious detraction...by those "superior persons" who blamed her for singing popular songs". Critic Neville Cardus was one such detractor, throwing his hands in the air and deploring the effect her singing may have had on students. Students who should be so lucky as to have such a career. But this was a critic who thought Melba uninteresting.

The *Oxford Dictionary of National Biography* notes, "The warm heartedness of her singing later came to be thought excessive, but undoubtedly it met the taste of the time." Consistently full houses endorsed this view. The Australian baritone Peter Dawson, a decade Clara's junior, sometimes appeared on the same bills. His career had paralleled hers in that he, too, was possessed of a glorious voice and technique and, like her, had appeared in opera just once at Covent Garden (*Meistersinger*). He then declined further operatic appearances, restricting himself to the concert platform. Like her, his record sales were prodigious. He was booked to appear with them for some of the Australian concerts and was appalled at how ill Clara was: "I appeared ... with Clara Butt in Australia when she was a very sick woman and had to travel about in a bath chair ... what a tragedy for such a great person! She can be described as a real singer of the people. Faultless diction, glorious quality – in fact, she possessed a voice unequalled before or, as far as I can find, since."

Clara tried to arrive at venues early to avoid people seeing her turn up in such a sorry condition. In her dressing room she would try to will away the pain. She would calm her mind and think of the lotus-scented banks of the Adyar where Annie Besant had spoken of exalted states of being. Sometimes she would crochet, her tapering fingers flicking through the yarn, trying to offset the agonising thuds of pain. In the midst of a Sydney concert she collapsed and plans were made to rush her back home, or as much of a rush as could be managed from so

## 24: REFUSING TO GIVE IN

far-flung a place as Australia. She was fortunate it was Sydney and not some remote outpost in the wilderness. This time there was no question of her getting better and carrying on. She was too far gone. That pain-wracked body which had seen such sterling service refused to continue without treatment. Even Clara had to accept that.

Roland Foster, now living in Australia with a teaching career, helped by his early release from contract by the Rumfords, heard the tragic news. He couldn't miss it, it was all over the world, and called at her hotel to see her. She was sitting in her drawing room, high on medication and singing softly to herself, her fingers frantically working her crochet hook. He was appalled at the deterioration in her:

> She bore her last long illness with the patience of an angel. I was the last person to say goodbye on her final departure from Sydney ... the victim of an incurable bone disease that had reduced her to a pale shadow of her splendid self. What extraordinary courage and wonderful fortitude had she gone through on that last tour, suffering intense pain, yet refusing to break faith with her managers and her beloved public. Only a little while before her death she sent me a Christmas card "I am getting better" in her characteristic handwriting. A false hope.

When Clara eventually arrived back in England, on a stretcher, she was taken, at her insistence, to her Oxfordshire home rather than to hospital. Rest did not help, and her doctor could do little but administer palliative care. She was readmitted to Guy's Hospital, drifting in and out of a coma. The Gods were not finished with her yet. Worse was to come. Shortly after her collapse in Australia the *Sydney Morning Herald* for 13 June 1934 carried the ghastly news: "Mr. Victor Kennerley Rumford ... was found dead on the floor of his room, the cause of his death being a gunshot wound in the head. Medical opinion is that the wound was accidentally self-inflicted. He had recovered from an attack of fever and when last seen was normal and cheerful." This was followed up the next day by an unidentified Capetown newspaper:

"Victor Rumford, son of Dame Clara Butt, was found dead on a farm in Salisbury, Southern Rhodesia, with a gunshot wound in the head. He had been in ill health." Poor Victor had not been at all happy. Evidence was given that he had suffered a severe attack of influenza, leaving him depressed.

An inquest was held in Cape Town, which soon returned the verdict of suicide while of unsound mind. He had shot himself. Victor had been farming in Rhodesia for eight years and who knows what problems he had encountered there? There was no way Clara could be told in her fragile condition so Bertie kept the news secret. Not only was his wife critically ill, but both his sons had died horribly. A terrible burden for him to bear alone. Clara was not told of Victor's death until the August. How can one gently break news to a hospitalised mother than her beloved second and only surviving son had killed himself? To soften the blow Bertie told her at first that he had been killed in a farming accident, the lie another burden for him to bear. Clara, who had spent much of her life conquering pain by will power, was eventually told the truth. Outwardly she was composed, but her mental agony now matched the physical.

The pain was relentless for the remaining two years left to her. When it seemed insurmountable she returned to Guy's Hospital, which did its best for her. In reality, however, nothing could be done. Clara returned home to Bertie, her animals and birds. The illness affected her legs but she insisted on trying to walk with the aid of a walking stick. But she could not go far before she was obliged to return to the hated wheelchair. There were internal problems and bouts of incontinence which were particularly gruelling for a woman of such dignity. All of this had a profound effect on Bertie, too, who had suffered the loss of his sons and supported her throughout her illness. There was a nurse to look after her, of course, but he was with her, often twenty-four hours a day, turning into a nurse himself. His social life dwindled. Mme Novello Davies wrote that, "The greatest of all God's blessings was bestowed on Clara in her long and happy wedded life." Bertie was certainly a stalwart and, hopefully, she never heard the rumours in those last years that he had developed not only a wandering eye but also a mistress. It would have broken her great heart, as Bertie was the only man she had ever loved and she still adored him. The humiliation would have destroyed what part of her was still intact. But whatever he did in the few hours he had to himself in what had now become a wretched life, he devotedly supported her to the end.

Clara was visited by friends, notably the actress Constance Collier, who had sometimes accompanied her to Monte Carlo. Miss Collier spent the last years of her life in Hollywood bringing to the screen upper-class, caustically-tongued eccentrics. She would need all the wit she could muster to cut through Clara's carapace of pain and make her laugh. But at times she succeeded. Another friend was music hall queen Gracie Fields. Born in Rochdale of working-class parents, Gracie had become a national treasure. Her Christmas Day broadcast was listened to by every loyal citizen. She and Clara had met during their many charity concerts. For all she appreciated her friends, Clara's pets were her greatest comfort – the birds and the great dogs which she had loved to walk, but could no longer do so. They would walk behind as Bertie pushed her in her chair through the garden. Clara had taught one of her dogs to sing. This was a Pekinese called Mr. Smee. He would follow her up and down the scales, a party trick they would demonstrate to callers when Clara was feeling up to it. Mr. Smee became quite famous in his own right and even had an article on him published in the *Daily Mail*.

Roland Foster tells of another comfort: "[Clara's] singing of everyday songs brought happiness and delight to countless thousands, the grateful letters she constantly received during her last, long illness being evidence of the substantial contribution to human happiness over a period of many years." For an artiste so long accustomed to adoration those letters meant a surprising amount. She knew she was near the end and could have peace of mind that she had carried out her creator's intentions. The letters proved it. Tales of her high-handedness abound but, once that had been overcome and colleagues got to know her, she inspired great loyalty. Foster continued: "Her kindness of heart and deep sincerity made her as popular in private life as she was on the platform." In 1949, well after her death, he added, "Young people of the present generation who heard Clara Butt only during her last Australian tour, when ill-health had sapped her vitality and sadly impaired her wonderful voice would have no idea of the effect her singing created when she was in her prime."

In desperation, in 1935, Clara sought help from a clinic in Germany which specialised in an unspecified radical new treatment. No one was sure of the outcome but there was not much to lose. It did, mercifully, bring her some relief. In a spirit of optimism that year she wrote, in her characteristic bold handwriting, her Christmas cards to her friends, telling them she was on the mend. As Roland Foster said, it was a false hope. On 20 January 1936 King George V died. Clara followed him three days later, dying at North Stoke, on 23 January. She had been a great royalist so it is cruel that the enormous publicity surrounding the monarch's death robbed Clara of the headlines which might have otherwise been anticipated at her passing. Certainly she would have expected it. Many opined that had she not died so soon after the King, she might have had a state funeral. Rudyard Kipling had died a few days earlier. All three deaths were linked in the minds of many: they had epitomised an era, their passing symbolising the demise of the Empire.

Clara was buried in the local church and her friend, W. H. Squire, played the cello at her funeral. Her grave still stands in its pretty cemetery, the stone mellowed to a rich consistency, befitting for its inhabitant, whose legendary voice could, when its owner decided, produce the mellowest of sounds. Later, Bertie, in her honour, had electric light installed in the church. He did not sing much after her death. He had never really enjoyed the stardom to which Clara had been addicted. Truth to tell, he thought it all rather vulgar, not the life for a gentleman, but he had done it for his wife. Bertie knew he would not have had much of a career without her, yet he had held on to what integrity he could. He had staunchly sung his solos while she watched proudly from the wings; he knew full well the public were just waiting for him to be done so Clara could come on. But then, it is doubtful Clara would have performed nearly so frequently without her beloved Bertie at her side. Those mammoth international tours would not have been nearly so fulfilling had she been alone. He was as indispensable as the piano accompanying her, and the power behind her throne.

Bertie took her death hard. Mme Novello Davies tells us he did not leave North Stoke for years, refusing all invitations. She tells us, however, that she managed to inveigle him out for the first night of Ivor Novello's *The Dancing Years* on 23 March 1939 at the Theatre Royal, Drury Lane. It became the most successful play of the Second World War, a similar cachet to that earned by *Chu Chin Chow* in the First World War, for which Clara had sung on its closing night. It was a glamorous occasion, as all Novello openings were. Bertie couldn't wait to get away. Retirement was a relief. He had his golfing and cricket pals and church duties and, hopefully, a girlfriend or two to while away the loneliness. The ladies always loved Bertie. But none so greatly as his wife.

Probate was declared on 1 May 1936 and Clara's wealth at death estimated as £39,517 6s 11d. Out of this she left a bequest of £3,000 to the Royal College of Music. Her effigy was placed in Madame Tussaud's. There was another bequest, albeit made unknowingly. Michael Aspinall tells us that while Clara was on tour in Australia, an eight-year-old girl had been among her Sydney audience. That little girl later said that she had never heard such a big voice. She never forgot it. She grew up to become "La Stupenda," Dame Joan Sutherland.

# EPILOGUE

Ivor Newton wrote of Clara that, nowadays, many are inclined "to think of her with amusement. They would be wrong to do so." I suppose the nearest to her today is Shirley Bassey, or Barbra Streisand. Concert performers of superior talent and hauteur with years of experience, who sing their own repertoire to a loyal and adoring audience, can guarantee full houses, no matter how large the venue; and they excite fans to frenzies.

The great Maria Callas gave concerts with Giuseppe Di Stefano at the end of her career. Her top register shot to pieces, she sang mostly in mezzo, crashing her way through to her always formidable chest register with a gear change every bit as dramatic as Clara's. It was every bit as exciting, too, as proved by the deafening applause she earned from the capacity houses she had attracted.

The similarity does not end there; she was accompanied by Ivor Newton who accompanied Clara in earlier days. His career lasted over sixty years. I used to know him, and he helped me considerably with my book on Oda Slobodskaya, for whom he also played, and I wished I'd asked him about Clara then. Alas, in those Slobodskaya days, Clara was not in my life.

Bertie retained his attraction for the ladies right until the end and married again on 11 October 1941, at Henley, Oxfordshire, five years after Clara's death. This time the ceremony was more in keeping with his nature – no garish cathedral panoply but a simple ceremony in the

Register Office. He was seventy-one and his bride, Dorothy, thirty-nine. She was a divorcée who was previously married to biographer (Frank) Malcolm Elwin.

Bertie died on 9 March 1957, a dignified and elegant octogenarian, getting on for ninety. His obituary appeared in *The Times* and was followed up by a letter to that paper from someone signing himself simply "TNFW," who wrote, "No one who met him ... could fail to be endeared by his modesty and wonderful courtesy nor to come under the spell of his charm. He never said an unkind word and in his manner and dress he remained one of the old guard of Victorians."

TNFW, clearly a cricket enthusiast, goes on to enthuse over Bertie's love of the game which, of course, he passed on to his two sporty but doomed sons. He was a member of the MCC for years and also the I Zingari cricket club. He enjoyed his honorary position there as "Principal Post Prandial Precentor" where he would sing the official IZ song. Then he could be gently prevailed upon, over the brandies, to give his off the cuff reminiscences of his touring days with Clara and their performances for Queen Victoria. Clara would have loved to have been there with him, glowing with pride.

Compton Lodge, their Hampstead home for many years, became an old people's home; some of its earliest residents had seen her perform and would proudly tell visitors of their connection to her. At time of writing it is still flourishing in this capacity. In Brighton, near where she was born, the Dame Clara Butt bus still winds its stately route down the sometimes blustery coast road. A regular and welcome sight.

The same cannot be said for the Clara Butt tulip, this once popular bloom, whose soft pink image has graced many a catalogue over the years, became "commercially extinct". However, it seems to have been rescued from the brink and is, hopefully, gradually becoming more available.

Clara delighted in her daughter Joy – her only surviving child – and Joy's son Oliver, Clara's only grandchild. She loved to hold him in her arms, and his scampering around her Oxfordshire home brought much solace through her last, agonising, days of pain. But Joy's life seems as disfigured with tragedy as her mother's. She and her husband Claude were living in Bristol, the city that had done so much for Clara, when he predeceased her during the Second World War, in the January of 1944.

Joy moved to Camberley in Surrey and, three years later, on 17 July 1947 Oliver died of pulmonary tuberculosis at the age of eighteen at the London Chest Hospital. Bertie registered his death, thus marking the end of the Butt-Rumford direct descendents. Oliver was cremated at Woking Crematorium and Joy instructed there was to be no mourning. Sentiments Clara would have endorsed. Joy died in Chichester in the June of 1976.

Clara's voice is widely featured on YouTube and compilations of her recordings regularly reissued. Among them is the Marsden 2-CD set *A Critical Survey* which came out in 2000, comprising forty-eight tracks. A bonus are the wittily knowing liner notes by Michael Aspinall – could this be the same Michael Aspinall who gave memorable performances as a soprano? He quotes Clara's 1928 biographer Winifred Ponder: "Her voice is only a means to express something greater than any voice – greater even than music herself – a spiritual force that must have found expression through her by some means even if she had no voice at all."

As far as Clara was concerned her voice was a divine gift, a mystic channel to use in the Almighty's service – and her own, of course. Singing was a duty, a sacred flame, it would have been inconceivable to let die. She viewed herself as God's messenger. If God can be epitomised as Hope then, she was, exactly that. Her singing brought hope to millions.

Dame Clara the recording star. With thanks to the EMI Group Archive Trust for permission to reproduce this image. The Trust is dedicated to "the advancement of education and research and, in particular, to foster and promote the study and appreciation of the art techniques and development of sound recording and the history of the sound recording industry". For more information and images, see www.soundofthehound.com

Dame Clara getting ready for a performance. With thanks to the EMI Group Archive Trust

# SOURCES

## Newspapers and Journals

*Bristol Evening Post*
*Bristol Times and Mirror*
*Daily Mail*
*The Era*
*The Eton College Chronicle*
*Evening News*
*Evening Post*
*Hinkley Times*
*Illustrated London News*
*Liverpool Evening Express*
*The Manchester Guardian*
*Musical News*
*Neue Freie Presse*
*Newcastle Daily Journal*
*New York Sun*
*Nuneaton Observer*
*Pall Mall Gazette*
*Sydney Morning Herald*
*The Times*
*The World*

## Books

*Arthur Sullivan and the Royal Society of Musicians of Great Britain: Proceedings of the Society's 145th Anniversary Festival Dinner and Other Papers Relating to Arthur Sullivan and the Society* (London: The Royal Society of Musicians of Great Britain, 2005)

Basu, Shrabani, *Victoria & Abdul: The True Story of the Queen's Closest Confidant* (Stroud, Gloucestershire: History Press, 2010)

Boult, Adrian, *My Own Trumpet* (London: Hamilton, 1973)

Bulman, Joan, *Jenny Lind: A Biography* (London: J Barrie, 1956)

Buttrose, Charles, *Playing for Australia: A Story About ABC Orchestras and Music in Australia* (Sydney: Australian Broadcasting Commission, 1982)

Cline, Sally, *Radclyffe Hall: A Woman Called John* (London: John Murray, 1997)

Davies, Clara Novello, *The Life I Have Loved* (London: William Heinemann, 1940)

Dawson, Peter, *Fifty Years of Song* (London: Hutchinson, 1951)

Fifield, Christopher, *Ibbs and Tillett: The Rise and Fall of a Musical Empire* (Aldershot, Hants: Ashgate, 2005)

FitzLyon, April, *The Price of Genius: A Life of Pauline Viardot* (London: John Calder, 1964)

Foster, Roland, *Come Listen to My Song: Reminiscences of Music and Travel in Two Worlds and Two Eras* (London: Collins, 1949)

Grove, George, and H C Colles, eds., *Grove's Dictionary of Music and Musicians* (London: Macmillan, 1940)

Harding, James, *Ivor Novello* (Cardiff: Welsh Academic Press, 1997)

Hetherington, John, *Melba: A Biography* (London: Faber, 1967)

Kennedy, Michael, *Portrait of Elgar* (London: Oxford University Press, 1968)

Lehmann, Liza, *The Life of Liza Lehmann:* By Herself (London: Unwin, 1919)

Leonard, Maurice, *Kathleen: The Life of Kathleen Ferrier* (London: Hutchinson, 1988)

Mottram, R H, and James Mottram, *Portrait of an Unknown Victorian* (London: R Hale & Company, 1936)

Newton, Ivor, *At the Piano: The World of an Accompanist* (London: Hamish Hamilton, 1966)

Nicolson, Juliet, *The Great Silence: 1918-1920 Living in the Shadow of the Great War* (London: John Murray, 2009)

Orchard, William Arundel, *The Distant View* (Sydney: Currawong, 1943)

Pearl, Cora, and William Blatchford, *The Memoirs of Cora Pearl* (London: Granada, 1983)

Ponder, Winifred, *Clara Butt: Her Life Story* (London: George G Harrap, 1928)

Richards, Jeffrey, *Imperialism and Music: Britain, 1876-1953* (Manchester: Manchester University Press, 2001)

Rosenthal, Harold, and John Warrack, eds., *Concise Oxford Dictionary of Opera* (London: Oxford University Press, 1974)

Scholes, Percy Alfred, ed., *The Oxford Companion to Music* (London: Oxford University Press, 1970)

*Wisden Cricketers' Almanack*

## Websites

Trevor Midgely's website includes the only full discography of Dame Clara's recordings:

www.trevormidgley.com/ClaraButt/

YouTube includes dozens of recordings by Dame Clara:

www.youtube.com/results?search_query=Clara+Butt

# APPENDIX A

# Dame Clara and George Bernard Shaw

Clara was keen to have the great George Bernard Shaw write a Foreword to Winifred Ponder's 1928 biography of her, as he had favourably reviewed her concerts. She included their correspondence in a postscript:

Before I wrote my own little Foreword—as I was assured that an introduction of the kind was indispensable to a book such as this—I decided to appeal to my friend Bernard Shaw, and wrote him the following note:

Dear Bernard Shaw,

Will you be an angel and write a Foreword to the story of my life? I know I am asking a terrific thing, and I shall quite understand if you refuse.

>   Your sincere and always admiring
>
>   Clara Butt-Rumford

And this is what he wrote in reply:

Whitehall Court
21st October, 1927

My Dear Clara Butt

Goodness gracious, I'd never dare! You are a much bigger person than I. I should look like a ridiculous little busybody making a pretentious bow in *your* limelight. I cannot imagine anything on earth more insufferably superfluous than an introduction of Clara Butt to the British public. I simply WON'T.

And, anyhow, what could I say? "Witnessed her début as Orfeo. Loved her. Would have married her if she'd asked me. She didn't. Might actually have chosen Bernard Shaw, and chose a Mr Rumford instead! What a woman!"

Don't let anybody touch your book except yourself. If you find anyone impertinent to venture, burn his Foreword and drop him into the dustbin.

Ever and ever,

G. Bernard Shaw

He says he WON'T. But surely there was never request more gracefully granted? So I wrote and thanked him warmly—and proudly print his acquiescent refusal as the preface to my life-story!

*Correspondence reproduced by kind permission from the Society of Authors, on behalf of the Bernard Shaw Estate.*

# APPENDIX B

## The Lost Chord

by Adelaide Anne Procter (1825-1864)

Adelaide Anne Procter's poem set to music by Sir Arthur Sullivan was one of Clara's most requested items. He wrote the melody at the bedside of his dying brother, Fred, who had appeared in several Gilbert and Sullivan operas, and specifically requested the song never be parodied.

The poem had first been published in *The English Woman's Journal* twenty years earlier in 1858. Miss Procter, who could list Charles Dickens among her admirers, was as popular as Tennyson and a favourite of Queen Victoria. The song was first sung, with Sullivan at the piano, by his long term mistress and Society favourite, Fanny Ronalds. Mrs Ronalds had a fine voice and was known in Paris, where she had lived, as the Patti des Salons. Her light soprano, however, must have delivered something very different from the weighty version delivered by Clara. According to Clara, after one of her performances of it, Sullivan confided "That's how I always meant it to be sung." It was the favourite song of Queen Alexandra who would specifically request Clara to sing it if she was present at one of her concerts, as she frequently was.

Sullivan wrote "I have composed much music since then, but I have never written a second Lost Chord". After singing it for a lifetime Clara would complain of contemporary music, "What we need now are more songs like *The Lost Chord*, there is something of the grandeur of Beethoven about it."

The original MS went to Mrs Ronalds at Sullivan's death but now reposes in the archives of the Guildhall Library of the Worshipful Company of Musicians. It seems that Mrs Ronalds gave the MS to Clara and it went to Bertie at Clara's death who subsequently presented it to the Guildhall Library.

Seated one day at the organ, I was weary and ill at ease,
And my fingers wander'd idly over the noisy keys;
I knew not what I was playing, or what I was dreaming then,
But I struck one chord of music like the sound of a great Amen.

It flooded the crimson twilight like the close of an Angel's Psalm,
And it lay on my fever'd spirit with a touch of infinite calm.
It quieted pain and sorrow like love overcoming strife,
It seem'd the harmonious echo from our discordant life.

It link'd all perplexed meanings into one perfect peace
And trembled away into silence as if it were loth to cease;
I have sought, but I seek it vainly, that one lost chord divine,
Which came from the soul of the organ and enter'd into mine.

It may be that Death's bright Angel will speak in that chord again;
It may be that only in Heav'n I shall hear that grand Amen!

# APPENDIX C

## DISCOGRAPHY

Special thanks to Trevor Midgley for the discography. Unfortunately, space does not permit us to include the full details of his comprehensive work, but the full version is available on the website – www.trevormidgley.com/ClaraButt/. As he points out, new recordings are still coming to light and the information is constantly changing. Trevor first heard Clara, on the radio, in the 1960s, and says, "She was the first contralto I heard who seemed to truly justify the description" adding that she sang with an "unashamed sentimentality that I never heard in the 1960s...when you listen to Clara Butt recordings you have a direct line to a world long gone – the British Empire upon which the sun never set. She was unmatched by any of her contemporaries."

### Released Recordings

| Title | Recording Date | First issued on | Original Format |
|---|---|---|---|
| A Fairy Went A-Marketing | December 31, 1918? | Columbia | 78 |
| A Fairy Went A-Marketing | August 7, 1930 | Columbia | 78 |

| | | | |
|---|---|---|---|
| A Hymn For Aviators | August 7, 1919? | Columbia | 78 |
| A Page's Road Song | April 3, 1924 | Columbia | 78 |
| A Perfect Day | December 31, 1918? | Columbia | 78 |
| A Perfect Day | May 28, 1925 | Columbia | 78 |
| A Perfect Day | June 24, 1930 | Columbia | 78 |
| A Song Of Praise | September 12, 1930 | Columbia | 78 |
| A Summer Night | 1915-1916 | Columbia | 78 |
| A Summer Night | July 9, 1925 | Columbia | 78 |
| A Summer Night | October 29, 1910 | Gramophone Co. Ltd. | 78 |
| A Youth Once Loved & The Tears That Night | July 25, 1912 | Gramophone Co. Ltd. | 78 |
| Abide With Me | 1915-1916 | Columbia | 78 |
| Abide With Me | Feb/March, 1917? | Columbia | 78 |
| Abide With Me | August 31, 1922 | Columbia | 78 |
| Abide With Me | March 19, 1924? | Columbia | 78 |
| Abide With Me | September 12, 1927 | Columbia | 78 |
| Abide With Me | August 8, 1930 | Columbia | 78 |
| Abide With Me | February 7, 1910 | Gramophone Co. Ltd. | 78 |
| Absent | September 15, 1927 | Columbia | 78 |
| Ame Nescriri & En Prière | July 20, 1909 | Gramophone Co. Ltd. (Label: Gramophone Monarch Record). | 78 |

| | | | |
|---|---|---|---|
| An Idle Poet | June 5, 1925 | Columbia | 78 |
| Annie Laurie | 1917-1921 | Columbia | 78 |
| Annie Laurie | November 15, 1927 | Columbia | 78 |
| Annie Laurie | February 7, 1931 | Columbia Japan | 78 |
| Barbara Allen | August, 1922? | Columbia | 78 |
| Barbara Allen | February 7, 1910 | Gramophone Co. Ltd. | 78 |
| Believe Me If All Those Endearing... | July 20, 1909 | Gramophone Co. Ltd. | 78 |
| Bugeilio'r Gwenith Gwyn | 1917-1921 | Columbia | 78 |
| Caro Mio Ben | December 19, 1910 | Gramophone Co. Ltd. | 78 |
| Chinkoro Koinu | February 7, 1931 | Columbia Japan | 78 |
| Cleansing Fires | June 4, 1925 | Columbia | 78 |
| Clouds And Darkness Are Round About Him | March 21, 1927 | Columbia | 78 |
| Creation's Hymn | August 29, 1922 | Columbia | 78 |
| Creation's Hymn | July 11, 1929 | Columbia | 78 |
| Creation's Hymn | September 12, 1930 | Columbia | 78 |
| Creation's Hymn | (almost certainly) February 7, 1931 | Greenhorn Records | CD |
| Daddy | August 7, 1919? | Columbia | 78 |
| Daddy | May 27, 1925 | Columbia | 78 |
| Daddy | April 7, 1927 | Columbia | 78 |
| Daddy | November 15, 1927 | Columbia | 78 |

| | | | |
|---|---|---|---|
| Dear Love Of Mine | June 18, 1925 | Columbia | 78 |
| Deep River | April 12, 1927 | Columbia | 78 |
| Deep River | (almost certainly) February 7, 1931 | Greenhorn Records | CD |
| Down By The Riverside I Stray | June 10, 1925 | Columbia | 78 |
| Down Here | 1917-1921 | Columbia | 78 |
| Down Here | August 11, 1930 | Columbia | 78 |
| Dream Faces | September 20, 1919? | Columbia | 78 |
| Eileen Alannah | August, 1922? | Columbia | 78 |
| Eileen Alannah | July 12, 1929 | Columbia | 78 |
| Entreat Me Not To Leave You | August 29, 1919? | Columbia | 78 |
| Eternal Father | November 11, 1931 | Columbia | 78 |
| For A Birthday | September 12, 1930 | Columbia | 78 |
| For A Dream's Sake | May, 1925 | Columbia | 78 |
| Four Years Old | July 9, 1909 | Gramophone Co. Ltd. | 78 |
| Friendship | April 25, 1923 | Columbia | 78 |
| Friendship | July 2, 1925 | Columbia | 78 |
| Genevieve | March 23, 1921 | Columbia | 78 |
| Genevieve | May 27, 1925 | Columbia | 78 |
| Gibt's Ein Land | October 26, 1932 | Greenhorn Records | CD |
| God Is My Shepherd | March 21, 1927 | Columbia | 78 |
| God Save The King | April 3, 1924 | Columbia | 78 |

| | | | |
|---|---|---|---|
| God Save The King | June 25, 1930 | Columbia | 78 |
| God Save The King | April 24, 1911 | Gramophone Co. Ltd. (Label: HMV) | 78 |
| God Save The King | August 7, 1919? | Columbia | 78 |
| God Shall Wipe Away All Tears | 1915-1916 | Columbia | 78 |
| God Shall Wipe Away All Tears | June 3, 1925 | Columbia | 78 |
| God Shall Wipe Away All Tears | September 12, 1927 | Columbia | 78 |
| God Shall Wipe Away All Tears | March 2, 1915 | Gramophone Co. Ltd. | 78 |
| Hatikvah | October 26, 1932 | Greenhorn Records | CD |
| Have You News Of My Boy Jack? | Feb/March, 1917? | Columbia | 78 |
| He Shall Feed His Flock | 1915-1916 | Columbia | 78 |
| He Shall Feed His Flock | July 11, 1929 | Columbia | 78 |
| Hear My Prayer, O Lord My God | March 21, 1927 | Columbia | 78 |
| Home, Sweet Home | September 15, 1927 | Columbia | 78 |
| Husheen | 1915-1916 | Columbia | 78 |
| Husheen | May 27, 1925 | Columbia | 78 |
| Husheen | September 11, 1930 | Columbia | 78 |

| | | | |
|---|---|---|---|
| Husheen | July 20, 1909 | Gramophone Co. Ltd. (Label: Gramophone Monarch Record) | 78 |
| I See Not Those False Spirits | 1915-1916 | Columbia | 78 |
| I Shall Not Pass This Way Again | June 29, 1933 | Greenhorn Records | CD |
| If I Might Only Come To You | October 27, 1932 | Greenhorn Records | CD |
| Il Segreto | 1915-1916 | Columbia | 78 |
| Il Segreto | August 1, 1924 | Columbia | 78 |
| Il Segreto | July 16, 1909 | Gramophone Co. Ltd. | 78 |
| Il Segreto | December 19, 1910 | Gramophone Co. Ltd. | 78 |
| In Questa Tomba Oscura | August 30, 1922 | Columbia | 78 |
| In Questa Tomba Oscura | August 1, 1924 | Columbia | 78 |
| In The Chimney Corner | April 25, 1923 | Columbia | 78 |
| Just A Ray Of Sunlight | March 25, 1924 | Columbia | 78 |
| Kashmiri Song | September 16, 1920? | Columbia | 78 |
| Kathleen Mavourneen | 1917-1921 | Columbia | 78 |
| Kathleen Mavourneen | June 24, 1930 | Columbia | 78 |
| Kathleen Mavourneen | February 7, 1910 | Gramophone Co. Ltd. | 78 |
| Kathleen Mavourneen | July 20, 1909 | Olympus | LP |

| | | | |
|---|---|---|---|
| Land Of Hope and Glory | 1916-1921 | Columbia | 78 |
| Land Of Hope and Glory | Feb/March, 1917? | Columbia | 78 |
| Land Of Hope and Glory | August 31, 1922 | Columbia | 78 |
| Land Of Hope and Glory | April 1, 1924 | Columbia | 78 |
| Land Of Hope and Glory | May 24, 1927 | Columbia | 78 |
| Land Of Hope and Glory | June 25, 1930 | Columbia | 78 |
| Land Of Hope and Glory | July 16, 1909 | Gramophone Co. Ltd. | 78 |
| Land Of Hope and Glory | April 24, 1911 | Gramophone Co. Ltd. | 78 |
| Land Of Hope and Glory | March 2, 1915 | Gramophone Co. Ltd. (Label: HMV) | 78 |
| Land Of Hope and Glory | April 24, 1911 | Historic Masters | 78 |
| L'Angelus | August 7, 1930 | Columbia | 78 |
| Less Than The Dust | 1917-1921 | Columbia | 78 |
| Little 'Fleur-De-Lys' | July 9, 1925 | Columbia | 78 |
| Lord, Thou Art My Refuge And My Shield | March 21, 1927 | Columbia | 78 |
| Love Has Come To Stay | (almost certainly) February 7, 1931 | Greenhorn Records | CD |
| Love's Old Sweet Song | August 7, 1919? | Columbia | 78 |

# DISCOGRAPHY 223

| | | | |
|---|---|---|---|
| Love's Old Sweet Song | April 25, 1923 | Columbia | 78 |
| Love's Old Sweet Song | July 9, 1925 | Columbia | 78 |
| Love's Old Sweet Song | September 14, 1927 | Columbia | 78 |
| Lusinghe Più Care | July 24, 1912 | Gramophone Co. Ltd. | 78 |
| Mon Coeur S'Ouvre à Ta Voix | 1915-1916 | Columbia | 78 |
| Mon Coeur S'Ouvre à Ta Voix | (almost certainly) February 7, 1931 | Greenhorn Records | CD |
| My Ain Folk | July 6, 1921 | Columbia | 78 |
| My Ain Folk | July 12, 1929 | Columbia | 78 |
| My Ain Folk | July 16, 1912 | Gramophone Co. Ltd. | 78 |
| My Country | September 23, 1929 | Columbia | 78 |
| My Dear Soul | July 6, 1921 | Columbia | 78 |
| My Prayer | September 30, 1919? | Columbia | 78 |
| My Son | 1917-1921 | Columbia | 78 |
| My Son | November 11, 1914 | Gramophone Co. Ltd. | 78 |
| My Treasure | 1917-1921 | Columbia | 78 |
| My Treasure | September 12, 1930 | Columbia | 78 |
| My Work Is Done, My Task Is O'er | 1915-1916 | Columbia | 78 |
| Myle Charaine | 1917-1921 | Columbia | 78 |
| Night Hymn At Sea | 26 Jan 1899 | Gramophone Co. Ltd. | 78 |

| | | | |
|---|---|---|---|
| Night Hymn At Sea | July 20, 1909 | Gramophone Co. Ltd. | 78 |
| O Divine Redeemer | 1915-1916 | Columbia | 78 |
| O Divine Redeemer | July 29, 1924 | Columbia | 78 |
| O Divine Redeemer | July 11, 1929 | Columbia | 78 |
| O Divine Redeemer | November 10, 1914 | Gramophone Co. Ltd. | LP |
| O Divine Redeemer | March 2, 1915 | Gramophone Co. Ltd. (Label: HMV) | 78 |
| O Don Fatale | 1915-1916 | Columbia | 78 |
| O Don Fatale | December 19, 1910 | Historic Masters | 78 |
| O Lovely Night | 1915-1916 | Columbia | 78 |
| O Lovely Night | July 29, 1924 | Columbia | 78 |
| O Lovely Night | June 23, 1930 | Columbia | 78 |
| O Lovely Night | (almost certainly) February 7, 1931 | Greenhorn Records | CD |
| O Mio Fernando | 1915-1916 | Columbia | 78 |
| O Rest In The Lord | 1915-1916 | Columbia | 78 |
| O Rest In The Lord | March 25, 1924 | Columbia | 78 |
| O Rest In The Lord | July 11, 1929 | Columbia | 78 |
| O Rest In The Lord | February 7, 1910 | Gramophone Co. Ltd. | 78 |
| O That We Two Were Maying | June 18, 1925 | Columbia | 78 |
| O That We Two Were Maying | September 15, 1927 | Columbia | 78 |
| Old Folks At Home* | August 7, 1919? | Columbia | 78 |

| | | | |
|---|---|---|---|
| Ombra Mai Fu | July 16, 1909 | Gramophone Co. Ltd. (Label: Gramophone Monarch Record) | 78 |
| Ombra Mai Fu | 1915-1916 | Columbia | 78 |
| Peace | June 10, 1925 | Columbia | 78 |
| Peace And Rest | October 28, 1910 | Historic Masters | 78 |
| Rend' Il Sereno | 1915-1916 | Columbia | 78 |
| Rend' Il Sereno | May 29, 1925 | Columbia | 78 |
| Rend' Il Sereno | July 24, 1912 | Gramophone Co. Ltd. | 78 |
| Rock Of Ages | November 10, 1931 | Columbia | 78 |
| Rose In The Bud | September 12, 1929 | Columbia | 78 |
| Rule, Britannia | May 24, 1927 | Columbia | 78 |
| She Wore A Wreath Of Roses | May 29, 1925 | Columbia | 78 |
| Shenandoah | July 2, 1925 | Columbia | 78 |
| Ship Of My Dreams | July 9, 1925 | Columbia | 78 |
| Ships That Pass In The Night | June 10, 1925 | Columbia | 78 |
| Shir Temany | October 26, 1932 | Greenhorn Records* | CD |
| Si Mes Vers Avaient Des Ailes | July 20, 1909 | Gramophone Co. Ltd. | 78 |
| Smilin' Through | June, 1923? | Columbia | 78 |
| Snowdrops - Two Little Duets | July 20, 1909 | Gramophone Co. Ltd. | 78 |
| Soft-Footed Snow | July 9, 1925 | Columbia | 78 |

| | | | |
|---|---|---|---|
| Softly And Gently Dear Ransomed Soul | 1915-1916 | Columbia | 78 |
| Sposa, Euridice.. Che Farò | 1915-1916 | Columbia | 78 |
| Tell Me the Old, Old Story | November 11, 1931 | Columbia | 78 |
| The Better Land | March 23, 1921 | Columbia | 78 |
| The Better Land | May 15, 1924 | Columbia | 78 |
| The Better Land | July 11, 1929 | Columbia | 78 |
| The Birth Of The Flowers | 1915-1916 | Columbia | 78 |
| The Country Faith | 1917-1921 | Columbia | 78 |
| The Enchantress | Feb/March, 1917? | Columbia | 78 |
| The Fairy Pipers | 1917-1921 | Columbia | 78 |
| The First Nowell | August, 1922? | Columbia | 78 |
| The Fold | September 15, 1927 | Columbia | 78 |
| The Holy City | 1916-1921 | Columbia | 78 |
| The Holy City | April 1, 1924 | Columbia | 78 |
| The Holy City | July 11, 1929 | Columbia | 78 |
| The Keys Of Heaven | 1915-1916 | Columbia | 78 |
| The Keys Of Heaven | 1915-1916 | Columbia | 78 |
| The Keys Of Heaven | July 2, 1925 | Columbia | 78 |
| The Keys Of Heaven | February 7, 1910 | Gramophone Co. Ltd. | 78 |
| The Knight Of Bethlehem | April 12, 1927 | Columbia | 78 |
| The Leaves And The Wind | June 10, 1925 | Columbia | 78 |

| | | | |
|---|---|---|---|
| The Leaves And The Wind | July 20, 1909 | Gramophone Co. Ltd. | 78 |
| The Little Silver Ring | July 20, 1909 | Gramophone Co. Ltd. | 78 |
| The Lost Chord | 1915-1916 | Columbia | 78 |
| The Lost Chord | August 1, 1924 | Columbia | 78 |
| The Lost Chord | January 29, 1927 | Columbia | 78 |
| The Lost Chord | September 13, 1927 | Columbia | 78 |
| The Lost Chord | August 8, 1930 | Columbia | 78 |
| The Lost Chord | July 16, 1909 | Gramophone Co. Ltd. | 78 |
| The Lover's Curse & I Know My Love | 1915-1916 | Columbia | 78 |
| The Minstrel Boy | April 8, 1927 | Columbia | 78 |
| The Palms | 1916-1921 | Columbia | 78 |
| The Promise Of Life | 1915-1916 | Columbia | 78 |
| The Promise Of Life | September 12, 1929 | Columbia | 78 |
| The Promise Of Life | July 20, 1909 | Gramophone Co. Ltd. | 78 |
| The Rooks | August 11, 1930 | Columbia | 78 |
| The Rosary | 1917-1921 | Columbia | 78 |
| The Rosary | September 11, 1930 | Columbia | 78 |
| The Siesta | October 27, 1932 | Greenhorn Records | CD |
| The Silver Ring | 1917-1921 | Columbia | 78 |
| The Sweetest Flower That Blows | 1917-1921 | Columbia | 78 |
| The Sweetest Flower That Blows | September 12, 1930 | Columbia | 78 |

| | | | |
|---|---|---|---|
| The Willow Song | July 9, 1925 | Columbia | 78 |
| Then Shall The Eyes.. He Shall Feed His Flock | February 7, 1910 | Gramophone Co. Ltd. (Label: Gramophone Monarch Record) | 78 |
| There Is No Death | September 23, 1929 | Columbia | 78 |
| There Is No Death | August 8, 1930 | Columbia | 78 |
| There's A Land | April 26, 1923 | Columbia | 78 |
| Three Fishers | October 29, 1910 | Gramophone Co. Ltd. | 78 |
| Three Fishers Went Sailing | 1915-1916 | Columbia | 78 |
| Till I Wake | 1917-1921 | Columbia | 78 |
| Time's Garden | 1915-1916 | Columbia | 78 |
| Time's Garden | May 28, 1925 | Columbia | 78 |
| Time's Garden | October 29, 1910 | Gramophone Co. Ltd. | 78 |
| Trees | April 12, 1927 | Columbia | 78 |
| Two Letters | October 26, 1932 | Greenhorn Records | CD |
| Until | September 23, 1929 | Columbia | 78 |
| Untitled | February 7, 1910 | Gramophone Co. Ltd. | n/a |
| Vale | May, 1925 | Columbia | 78 |
| We Now Have Passed The Gate | 1915-1916 | Columbia | 78 |
| Were You There | November 15, 1927 | Columbia | 78 |
| When All Was Young | 1915-1916 | Columbia | 78 |

| | | | |
|---|---|---|---|
| Where Corals Lie | September 16, 1920? | Columbia | 78 |
| Where Corals Lie | July 24, 1912 | Gramophone Co. Ltd. | 78 |
| Where Is My Wandering Boy Tonight? | November 10, 1931 | Columbia | 78 |
| Will He Come? | October 29, 1910 | Gramophone Co. Ltd. | 78 |
| Women Of Inver | July 25, 1912 | Gramophone Co. Ltd. | 78 |
| Ye Banks And Braes O' Bonny Doon | 1917-1921 | Columbia | 78 |
| Yonder | February 6, 1921? | Columbia | 78 |
| Yonder | August 11, 1930 | Columbia | 78 |
| (untitled) | November 1, 1909 | Historic Masters | 78 |

## Unreleased Recordings

| Title | Recording Date |
|---|---|
| A Banjo Song | 1917-1921 |
| A Fairy Went A-Marketing | 1917-1921 |
| A Joyous Song Of Easter | September 30, 1926 |
| A Land Of Roses | April 12, 1927 |
| A Perfect Day (with spoken message) | 1917-1921 |
| A Summer Night | October 29, 1910 |
| A Summer Night | May 9, 1925 |
| A Summer Night | May 28, 1925 |

| | |
|---|---|
| A Youth Once Loved.. & The Tears That Night | July 16, 1912 |
| Abide With Me | July 16, 1909 |
| Abide With Me | September 16, 1909 |
| Abide With Me | September 16, 1909 |
| Abide With Me | January 29, 1927 |
| Abide With Me | June 4, 1927 |
| Abide With Me | November 14, 1927 |
| An All-Night Lullaby | February 6, 1921? |
| An Epitaph.. When I Was One And Twenty | September 29, 1926 |
| Auld Lang Syne | September 15, 1927 |
| Barbara Allen | February 7, 1910 |
| Barbara Allen | June 27, 1910 |
| Bless The Lord | March 28, 1916? |
| Cleansing Fires | June 24, 1910 |
| Clouds And Darkness Are Round About Him | October 6, 1926 |
| Clouds And Darkness Are Round About Him | November 11, 1926 |
| Come Unto Me | July 17, 1912 |
| Cradle Song & Sunday | September 16, 1909 |
| Creation's Hymn | April 7, 1927 |
| Creation's Hymn | June 4, 1927 |
| Crown The King | June 24, 1910 |
| Daddy | July 16, 1912 |
| Daddy | September 14, 1927 |
| Das Mädchen.. & Mein Mädel... | September 16, 1909 |
| Dear Love Of Mine | October 28, 1910 |
| Dear Love Of Mine | September 15, 1927 |

# DISCOGRAPHY

| | |
|---|---|
| Deep River | June 4, 1927 |
| Der Wanderer | June 24, 1910 |
| Der Wanderer | December 12, 1910 |
| Die Forelle | December 12, 1910 |
| Divinités Du Styx | July 21, 1909 |
| Divinités Du Styx | September 16, 1909 |
| Divinités Du Styx | September 16, 1909 |
| Down Here | April 7, 1927 |
| Dreary Steppe | 1917-1921 |
| England, Land Of The Free | May 14, 1924 |
| Erlkönig | December 12, 1910 |
| God Is My Shepherd | October 6, 1926 |
| God Is My Shepherd | November 11, 1926 |
| God Save The King | April 24, 1911 |
| God Save The King | 1915-1916 |
| God Save The King | 1916-1921 |
| God Shall Wipe Away All Tears | March 2, 1915 |
| God Shall Wipe Away All Tears | January 26, 1927 |
| God Shall Wipe Away All Tears | January 29, 1927 |
| God Shall Wipe Away All Tears | November 14, 1927 |
| Hatikvah | October 13, 1932 |
| Have You News Of My Boy Jack? | September 20, 1919? |
| He Shall Feed His Flock | September 16, 1909 |
| Homing | September 1920? |
| How Pansies Grow | January 30, 1919 |
| Husheen | August 11, 1930 |
| Il Segreto | July 16, 1909 |
| In Questa Tomba Oscura | December 19, 1910 |
| In Questa Tomba Oscura | April 7, 1927 |

| | |
|---|---|
| Japanese Death Song | September 29, 1926 |
| Jerusalem | May 24, 1927 |
| Jerusalem | June 4, 1927 |
| Kashmiri Song | August 28, 1924? |
| Kathleen Mavourneen | July 20, 1909 |
| Kathleen Mavourneen | September 30, 1919? |
| Kathleen Mavourneen | May 27, 1925 |
| Kathleen Mavourneen | April 7, 1927 |
| Knights | July 16, 1912 |
| Land Of Hope and Glory | July 21, 1909 |
| Land Of Hope and Glory | June 24, 1910 |
| Land Of Hope and Glory | April 24, 1911 |
| Land Of Hope and Glory | April 24, 1911 |
| Land Of Hope and Glory | November 10, 1914 |
| Land Of Hope and Glory | November 10, 1914 |
| Land Of Hope and Glory | November 10, 1914 |
| Land Of Hope and Glory | 1915-1916 |
| Land Of Hope and Glory | June 4, 1927 |
| Light In Darkness | June 5, 1925 |
| Light Of The World | November 10, 1914 |
| Light Of The World | November 10, 1914 |
| Little 'Fleur-De-Lys' | June 5, 1925 |
| Lord, Thou Art My Refuge And My Shield | October 6, 1926 |
| Lord, Thou Art My Refuge And My Shield | November 11, 1926 |
| Love Has Come To Stay | September 30, 1919? |
| Love's Old Sweet Song | April 12, 1927 |
| Lusinghe Più Care | December 12, 1910 |

| | |
|---|---|
| Lusinghe Più Care | July 24, 1912 |
| Lusinghe Più Care | July 24, 1912 |
| Mon Coeur S'Ouvre à Ta Voix | December 19, 1910 |
| Mon Coeur S'Ouvre à Ta Voix | June 19, 1923 |
| Mon Coeur S'Ouvre à Ta Voix | September 12, 1930 |
| Moontime | 1917-1921 |
| My Ain Folk | July 16, 1912 |
| My Ain Folk | June 5, 1925 |
| My Ain Folk | April 12, 1927 |
| My Child Is My Treasure | February 1921? |
| My Dear Soul | July 25, 1912 |
| My Dear Soul | July 25, 1912 |
| My Dear Soul | July 6, 1921 |
| My Laddie O'er The Sea | February 6, 1921? |
| My Son | November 11, 1914 |
| My Treasure | July 20, 1909 |
| My Treasure | April 12, 1927 |
| Nearer To Thee | July 1, 1910 |
| Night, Gentle Shepherd | July 7, 1921 |
| O Divine Redeemer | November 10, 1914 |
| O Divine Redeemer | March 2, 1915 |
| O Divine Redeemer | June 21, 1923 |
| O Divine Redeemer | May 15, 1924 |
| O Don Fatale | July 21, 1909 |
| O Don Fatale | July 16, 1909 |
| O Gladsome Light | June 4, 1927 |
| O God, Our Help | May 24, 1927 |
| O Rest In The Lord | July 16, 1909 |
| O Rest In The Lord | September 16, 1909 |

| | |
|---|---|
| O Rest In The Lord | September 16, 1909 |
| Ombra Mai Fu | August 1, 1924 |
| Ombra Mai Fu | June 4, 1925 |
| On Guard | June 4, 1927 |
| Our Prayer | 1917-1921 |
| Peace And Rest | July 1, 1910 |
| Peace And Rest | July 1, 1910 |
| Printemps Qui Commence | June 19, 1923 |
| Rule, Britannia | May 14, 1924 |
| Sabbath Morning At Sea | July 24, 1912 |
| Sapphische Ode | December 19, 1910 |
| Sea Slumber Song & Sabbath Morning... | June 24, 1910 |
| Shenandoah | September 30, 1926 |
| Shenandoah | April 7, 1927 |
| Shepherd's Cradle Song | July 16, 1909 |
| Shepherd's Cradle Song | April 8, 1927 |
| Shir Temany | October 13, 1932 |
| Si Mes Vers | 1917-1921 |
| Silence Of The Night | 1917-1921 |
| So Little Time | July 9, 1925 |
| Sorrow No More | 1917-1921 |
| Sunday | November 15, 1927 |
| Sweet And Low | July 20, 1909 |
| Sweet Memories | June 27, 1910 |
| The Beautiful Land Of Nod | April 26, 1923 |
| The Better Land | July 17, 1912 |
| The Company Of Heaven | June 29, 1933 |
| The Early Morning | November 15, 1927 |

| | |
|---|---|
| The Enchantress | 1915-1916 |
| The Fairy Pipers | November 11, 1914 |
| The Fairy Pipers | November 11, 1914 |
| The Fold | September 30, 1926 |
| The Garden Of Sleep | August 29, 1922 |
| The Holy City | September 13, 1927 |
| The Home Flag | November 10, 1914 |
| The Homecoming Of The Unknown Soldier | July 6, 1921 |
| The Keys Of Heaven | July 21, 1909 |
| The Keys Of Heaven | September 16, 1909 |
| The Keys Of Heaven | April 8, 1927 |
| The Knight Of Bethlehem | September 29, 1926 |
| The Land Of Might-Have-Been | August 31, 1922 |
| The Land Of Might-Have-Been | May 15, 1924 |
| The Lost Chord | Feb/March, 1917? |
| The Lost Chord | January 26, 1927 |
| The Promise Of Life | Feb/March, 1917? |
| The Promise Of Life | June 3, 1925 |
| The Promise Of Life | July 8, 1929 |
| The Rosary | June 23, 1930 |
| The Rose Shall Bloom Again | August 30, 1922 |
| The Snowdrop | November 15, 1927 |
| The Voice Of The Father | June 24, 1910 |
| The Voice Of The Father | October 28, 1910 |
| The Voice Of The Father | October 28, 1910 |
| The World's Thanksgiving | September 30, 1919? |
| Then Shall The Eyes.. He Shall Feed His Flock | February 7, 1910 |

| | |
|---|---|
| There Is A Green Hill | July 17, 1912 |
| There Is A Green Hill | July 17, 1912 |
| There Is A Green Hill | April 26, 1923 |
| Three Fishers | October 29, 1910 |
| Three Fishers Went Sailing | June 24, 1910 |
| Three Fishers Went Sailing | June 24, 1910 |
| Three Fishers Went Sailing | August 7, 1930 |
| Three Score And Ten | July 17, 1912 |
| Time's Garden | October 29, 1910 |
| Time's Garden | July 29, 1924 |
| Trees | September 29, 1926 |
| Untitled | July 9, 1909 |
| Untitled | November 1, 1909 |
| Untitled | July 9, 1909 |
| Untitled | July 9, 1909 |
| Untitled | January 17, 1910 |
| Untitled | January 17, 1910 |
| Untitled | January 17, 1910 |
| Untitled | January 17, 1910 |
| Untitled | December 12, 1910 |
| Untitled | January 5, 1911 |
| Untitled | January 5, 1911 |
| Untitled | January 5, 1911 |
| Untitled | January 5, 1911 |
| Untitled | 1915-1916 |
| Untitled | Feb/March, 1917? |
| Untitled | June 4, 1927 |
| Vale | June 19, 1923 |
| Were You There | April 8, 1927 |

| | |
|---|---|
| When The Mind Is Without Fear | October 6, 1926 |
| When The Mind Is Without Fear | November 11, 1926 |
| When The World Is Without Fear | July 9, 1925 |
| Where Corals Lie | July 24, 1912 |
| Woe Unto Them | February 7, 1910 |
| Women Of Inver | July 25, 1912 |
| Ye Banks And Braes | July 8, 1929 |
| Ye Banks And Braes | September 12, 1929 |
| Yonder | June 3, 1925 |

# ACKNOWLEDGEMENTS

Especial thanks to: Catherine Pope, Tanya Izzard, Trevor Midgley, Barbara Thorn, Sheila Keevill, Kevin Hubbard, Alan Woodhouse, David Drummond of "Pleasures of Past Times", City of London: London Metropolitan Archives, Peter Allanson of Guy's and St Thomas' NHS Foundations Trust, Mrs. P. Hatfield the College Archivist of Eton College Library, Mrs. Margaret Alford of the Worshipful Company of Musicians, the Society of Authors, the EMI Group Archive Trust, and most expressly the British Library.

## ABOUT MAURICE LEONARD

Maurice Leonard was for many years a television producer, working on shows such as *What's My Line*, *This is Your Life*, and *Strike it Lucky*, and studied singing with the Maryinsky soprano Oda Slobodskaya. His previous books include biographies of Kathleen Ferrier, Mae West, Montgomery Clift, Dame Alicia Markova, Oda Slobodskaya, and *People from the Other Side: The Enigmatic Fox Sisters*. Maurice is currently working on a biography of Madame Blavatsky for Victorian Secrets.

# INDEX

Adelaide Mary, Duchess of Teck, 46
Aguari, Lucrezia, 34
Albani, Emma, 38, 80, 109
Alboni, Marietta (Countess Pepoli), 6
Alvarez, Albert, 66
Aspinall, Michael, 206
Baker, Janet, 7
Barnby, Sir Joseph, 36, 42, 48
   asks Clara to audition, 36
   *Rebekah*, 36
Barre, Carl, 121
Barton, Marmaduke, 33
Beecham, Sir Thomas, 6, 162-163
Beerbohm Tree, Sir Herbert, 72
Bemberg, Herman, 72-3, 75
   *La Ballade de Désespéré*, 73
Benson, A.C., 108
Berliner, Emile, 131
Berneche, Alicia, 184
Besant, Annie, 18-19, 164, 180-181, 198
Bible Christian Society, 15
Bingham, Clifton, 54
Blavatsky, Helena (Madame Blavatsky), 18, 180
Blower, Henry, 33, 49, 80
Blume, Alfred, 88
Bouhy, Jacques, 63
Boult, Sir Adrian, 89, 160
Brahms, Johannes, 23
   *German Requiem*, 23
Bristol, city of, 13, 25, 27, 31, 72, 96, 175
Bristol Festival Choir, 22-23
Brooke, Rupert, 149
Brooks, Romaine, 32-33
Butler, Samuel, 19
Butt, Albert, 13
Butt, Bertie (Henry Albert) 13
   death from diphtheria, 15

Butt, Clara (née Hook, Clara's mother), 11, 24, 25, 28, 51-52, 77, 80, 93, 94
   marries Henry Butt, 11
   amateur singer, 13, 17

**BUTT, DAME CLARA**
critical reception, 40-41, 43, 47, 80, 85-86, 124, 147-148, 163, 177, 188, 193, 197-198
health, 15, 35, 48-49, 59, 75, 77, 79, 105-106, 108, 150, 176, 194-196
quality of voice, 6, 9
recording career, 51-52, 130-132, 138, 155, 164, 192, 194
religious beliefs, 15, 18, 20, 49, 57, 154, 170, 176, 181
Royal command performances, 44, 46-47, 51-55, 63, 154
taste for flamboyant dress, 25, 73, 142
vocal range, 19, 22
vocal technique, 35, 86, 160, 184
vocal training, 17, 19, 22-23, 25, 33, 60, 63-64, 67
**Personal life**
birth, 11-12
education, 14
learns piano, 14
contracts diphtheria, 15
early poverty, 15
scalding accident, 15
attends South Bristol High School, 20
first sings in public, 20
auditions for Royal College of Music, 26-29
wins scholarship to Royal College of Music, 30
enrols at Royal College of Music, 31
first professional performance, 31

Butt, Dame Clara - *cont.*
moves to Kensington, 31
awarded Morley Scholarship, 35
contracts tonsilitis, 35
friendship with German royal family, 54, 69
injured falling from a horse, 59
visits Berlin, 67-69
provides financial support to family, 73
has adenoids removed, 75
awarded the Victoria Badge, 76
friendship with Alice Keppel, 76
involved in car accident, 79, 142, 176
moves to Hyde Park Mansions, 79
funds her sisters' musical studies, 80
courted by Bertie Kennerley-Rumford, 87-89
engagement to Bertie Kennerley-Rumford, 82, 90
awarded the Diamond Jubilee Medal, 89
marries Bertie Kennerley-Rumford at Bristol Cathedral, 96-97
provides financial support to family, 97
moves to Compton Lodge, Hampstead, 100
birth of daughter Joy, 104
lives in Hove, 104
birth of sons Roy and Victor, 104
boating accident, 105
love of practical jokes, 134-135
relationship with Bertie, 135, 152, 201
friendship with Empress Frederick of Germany, 150-151
war work, 152-157
home burgled, 155
created Dame Commander of the British Empire, 164
enjoys gambling, 165, 179-180
death of son Roy, 169-170
silver wedding anniversary, 175
visits India, 179-181
anti-communism, 185
moves to North Stoke, Oxfordshire, 190
collapses during concert in Japan, 191
pets, 191
diagnosed with spinal cancer, 194
collapses during concert in Australia, 198
last illness, 199-200
suicide of son Victor, 200
buried in North Stoke, 202
death of, 202
will, 203
birth of grandchild, Oliver Cross, 206
**Professional career**:
able to shatter glass with voice, 34
auditions for Sir Joseph Barnby, 36-37
biography by Winifred Ponder, 188-189
debut in New York, 85-86
earnings, 145, 149
European tour, 77
first solo recital, 63
inclusion of popular songs in repertoire, 198
insists on performing for Saint-Saëns, 65
inspiration for Trilby, 56
invited to perform at Folies Bergères, 61
opera, 18, 37, 162-164
perfect pitch, 50
performance fees, 107, 110, 124
performs at Empire Day Festivals, 136, 182
performs in *Pageant of Fair Women, 1917*, 156
performs in Paris, 73-73
performs *Orfeo ed Euridice* at Covent Garden, 162-163
performs with Bertie Kennerley-Rumford, 87
radio broadcast, 175
response to criticism, 147
Royal Albert Hall debut, 38-39
sings at Buckingham palace, 51-52
sings at coronation of George V, 131, 137
sings at Queen Victoria's funeral, 102
sings at Romaine Brooks's soirées, 33
stage technique, 172
West End debut, 39

Butt, Dame Clara - *cont.*
wins Royal Society of Musicians medal, 62
**Tours:**
Australasia, 110-111, 121-129, 139, 146-149, 176
Australia, final tour, 194-196
Canada, 171-174
Japan, 191-194
North America 82-85, 139, 144-146
South Africa, 137-138
**Key repertoire:**
*Abide with Me*, 8, 15, 25, 103, 155
*Creation Hymn*, 193
*Dream of Gerontius, The*, 107, 154
*Elijah*, 42, 59
*Fairy Went a-Marketing, A*, 8, 88
*Four Cautionary Tales and a Moral*, 8
*Holy City, The*, 8
*In the Silent Night*, 193
*Israel in Egypt*, 42, 48
*Kathleen Mavourneen*, 51
*Land of Hope and Glory*, 108, 125, 137, 146
*Lost Chord, The*, 8, 53
*Mon Coeur s'ouvre à ta Voix*, 52, 55, 147
*Night Hymn at Sea*, 131, 145
*O Rest in the Lord*, 24, 59
*Orfeo et Euridice*, 39, 40, 44-47, 162-163
*Sea Pictures*, 90-92, 144
*Golden Legend, The*, 38
*Si mes vers avaient des ailes*, 72, 132

Butt, Ethel, 14
  singing career under name of Ethel Hook, 14, 80, 161
Butt, Frances, 13
Butt, Frederick, 13
  singing career, 81
Butt, Hazel, 24
  singing career, 80-81, 161
Butt, Henry Albert (Clara's father), 11, 28
  amateur singer, 13
  business difficulties, 15, 64-65
  marries Clara Hook, 11
  moves family to Bristol, 13
  religious beliefs, 15
  works as trawlerman, 11
  works as shipbuilder, 13
Butt, Herbert, 13, 180
Butt, Pauline, 80
  singing career, 80, 161
Butt, Warwick, 144
Butt, Wilfred Lawson, 13, 81, 143
  acting career, 143-144
Callas, Maria, 204
Cardus, Neville, 198
Carnegie Hall, New York, 85
Caruso, Enrico, 53
Cary, Annie Louise, 6
Charlton, Loudon, 141
Christian Science, 49, 170, 176, 179
*Chu Chin Chow*, 165
Clara Butt-Rumford Fund, 152
Clemens, Clara, 141
Cole, Belle, 21, 54, 97
Colles, H.C., 177
Collier, Constance, 201
Collins, Madeleine, 163
contralto voice, 6-7, 19, 33-34, 92
Cook, Miss (headmistress of South Bristol High School), 20-21
Corelli, Marie, 56
Cowen, Sir Frederic H., 176, 183
  *Light in Darkness*, 24
  *Promise of Life*, 54
  *Voice of the Father, The*, 73
Craxton, Harold, 137, 142, 156, 167
Cross, Oliver (Clara's grandson), 206
Crouch, Cora Pearl, 51
Crouch, Frederick, *Kathleen Mavourneen*, 50-51
Davies, Ben, 38
Davies, Clara Novello, 57-58, 72-74, 80-82, 93-94, 96, 99, 102, 125, 200, 203
  *A Voice from the Spirit Land*, 57, 72
  Clara's accompanist, 73
Dawson, Peter, 198
diphtheria, 15

Donizetti, Gaetano, 9, 35, 73
   *Lucrezia Borgia*, 9, 35, 73
   *Segretto, Il*, 73
du Maurier, George, 56
   *Trilby*, 56-57
Duvernoy, Henri Louis, 60
Dvořàk, Antonìn, *Biblical Songs*, 184
Eddy, Mary Baker, 49, 170
Edward VII, 44-47, 52, 72, 76, 103, 111
Elgar, Sir Edward, 7, 90-91, 153
   *Dream of Gerontius*, 107, 154
   *For the Fallen*, 153
   *Land of Hope and Glory*, 7, 108, 137
   *Sea Pictures*, 90-92
Elwin, Dorothy, marries Bertie Kennerley-Rumford, 205
Farrar, Geraldine, 145
Ferrier, Kathleen, 7-8, 50
Festival of Empire 1911, 136
Fields, Gracie, 201
Fifield, Christopher, 121, 186
Fincken, Adelaide, 14, 16, 19
Fitz-Lyon, April, 66
Foli, Signor (Alan Foley), 73-74, 82, 84
Folies Bergères, 61
Foster, Roland, 140-142, 148, 182, 198, 199, 201, 202
Francis, Duke of Teck, 55
Frederick, Empress of Germany (Princess Victoria), 54, 69
   friendship with Clara, 54, 69
Fyleman, Rose, *A Fairy Went a-Marketing*, 8
Galli-Curci, Amelita, 173
Gandhi, Mahatma, 180
Garcia, Manuel, 34
George V, 55, 104, 146, 158
   coronation, 131
   death of, 202
George-Dolby agency, 42
German, Edward, *Have You News of My Boy Jack?*, 158
Gerster, Etelka, 64, 68-69, 150

Gluck, Christoph, 8
   *Che Faro*, 40
   *Divinités du Styx*, 124
   *Orfeo ed Euridice*, 8, 39, 46-47, 162-163
Godfrey, Arthur E., 121
Goodhart, Arthur, *A Fairy Went a-Marketing*, 8
Gounod, Charles, 18, 36
Gramophone Company, 130
Grove, Sir George, 28
Gudagni, Gaetano, 40
Hahn, Reynaldo, 78
   *Heure Exquise, L'*, 79
   *Si mes vers avaient des ailes*, 72, 78, 132
Hall, Radclyffe, 32
Hammerstein, Oscar, I, 123
Hanbury, Lily, 158
Handel Festival, 42
Handel, George, 40
   *Angels Ever Bright*, 17
   *Israel in Egypt*, 37, 42, 48
   *Messiah*, 23, 48
   *Largo*, 132
   *Rend' il sereno*, 145
Harding, James, 98
Harrap, George W., 188
Harris, Sir Augustus, 41
Hatton, J.L., 29, 136
   *Enchantress, The*, 29, 136
   *Sleigh Ride, The*, 29
Hedley, John, 43
Henderson, Roy, 7-8
Henderson, W.J., 85
Henschel, Sir George, 23, 38, 88
Hetherington, John, 190
Hook, Clara see Butt, Clara
Hook, James, 12
   *Twas Within a Mile of Edinboro' Town*, 12
Hook, Theodore, 12, 134
   arrested for fraud, 12
   fondness for practical jokes, 12
   humorist, 12
   publishing career, 12
   *The Soldier's Return*, 12

# INDEX

Ibbs and Tillett (agency), 42, 107, 110, 140, 186
Ibbs, Robert Leigh (Bob), 42, 110-111, 124-125, 127-128, 139
Irving, Henry, 46
Jenkins, Alice, 24
Karim, Abdul, 52
Kathleen Ferrier Memorial Competition, 7
Kennerley-Rumford, Joy, 143, 151, 176
  birth of, 104
  presented at Court, 166
  engagement and marriage to Major Claude Cross, 182
  wedding, 183
  birth of son Oliver, 206
  death of, 206
Kennerley-Rumford, Robert (Bertie), 82-84, 87
  awarded Diamond Jubilee Medal, 89
  courtship of Clara, 87-89
  engagement to Clara, 82, 90
  marries Clara, 96-97
  singing career, 88-89, 121, 194
  serves in First World War, 151, 158
  assaults music critic, 177
  second marriage to Dorothy Elwin, 204
  death of, 205
Kennerley-Rumford, Roy, 143, 149
  birth, 104
  attends Eton, 168
  death of, 169-170
Kennerley-Rumford, Victor, 143, 149, 176, 194
  birth, 104
  becomes farmer in Africa, 177
  suicide of, 199-200
Keppel, Alice (Mrs George Keppel), 76
Kipling, Rudyard, *My Boy Jack*, 157
Kirkby-Lunn, Louise, 67
Klein, Herman, 19, 46
Kreisler, Fritz, 109, 188
Lablache, Luigi, 34
Lehmann, Liza, 133
  *Birth of Flowers, The*, 161
  *Four Cautionary Tales and a Moral*, 134
  *In a Persian Garden*, 133
  *In Memoriam*, 134
  *There are Fairies at the Bottom of Our Garden*, 133
Licette, Miriam, 163
Liddle, Samuel, *Abide with Me*, 102-104
Lind, Jenny, 5, 6, 48
Lizst, Franz, 18
Locker-Lampson, Commander Oliver, 185
London Symphony Orchestra, 136
Lyle, Henry F., 15
Mahler, Gustav, 7-8
  *Das Lied von der Erde*, 8
Mary, Queen *see* Victoria Mary, Princess of Teck
McCormack, Count John, 184
Mela, Eugenia, 34
Melba, Dame Nellie, 22-23, 55, 77, 97, 104, 123-127, 141, 159-160, 172, 176, 188
  complains about anecdote in biography of Clara, 189
  death of, 192
Mendelssohn, Felix, 5
  *Elijah*, 5, 23, 29, 37, 42, 59
  *O Rest in the Lord*, 23, 29, 43, 59
  *Six Songs*, 5
  *Woe unto Them*, 29
Merrick, Frank, 121-122
Meyerbeer, Giacomo, *Les Huguenots*, 67
Moiseiwitch, Benno, 165
Molloy, J. L., 7
  *Golden Bells*, 72
  *Kerry Dance, The*, 17
  *Little Tin Soldier*, 17
  *Love's Old Sweet Song*, 17, 54
Moore, Thomas, 132
  *Believe Me if all these Endearing Young Charms*, 132
  *Two Little Duets*, 132

Mozart, W.A., *The Magic Flute*, 34
Newton, Ernest, *The Keys of Heaven*, 87
Newton, Ivor, 133, 170, 173, 174, 182, 194, 195, 204
   as Clara's accompanist, 167-168
   *At the Piano*, 167
Nordica, Lillian, 23
Novello, Ivor, 57, 81, 93-94, 99-100
   pageboy at Clara's wedding, 97-98
   *Keep the Home Fires Burning*, 99
   *Land of Might Have Been, The* 99
   *Spring of the Year*, 99
Orchard, William Arundel, 147-148, 176
Oxenford, Edward, *The Harbor Bar*, 5
Parratt, Sir Walter, 28-29, 43
Patey, Janet, 19, 38
Patti, Adelina, 67
Plançon, Pol, 77
Podles, Ewa, 7
Ponder, Winifred, 15, 16, 41, 77, 154, 173, 190, 206
   writes Clara's biography, 187-188
   *Clara Butt: Her Life Story*, 16, 189
   biography of Clara recalled, 189
Prince's Theatre, Bristol, 31
Procter, Adelaide, 53
Proust, Marcel, 78
Puccini, Giacomo, *Vissi d'Arte*, 34
Purvis, Maggie, 44, 48, 58, 64
Reszke, Edouard de, 109
Radcliffe, Charles, 75
Ravogli, Giulia, 46
Ravogli, Sofia, 46
Rebroff, Ivan, 34
Richards, Jeffrey, 102, 136, 153
Riseley, George, 27
Robin, Mado, 34
Ronalds, Fanny, 53, 64
Rootham, Cyril, 22
Rootham, Dan, 22-29
Rossini, Giachono, 6, 7
Royal Albert Hall, 8, 28-29, 94, 99
Royal College of Music, 26-28, 31, 33, 39, 80

Royal Society of Musicians, 62
Rumford, Robert Kennerley, *see* Kennerley-Rumford, Robert
Saint-Saëns, Charles-Camille, 18, 65-66, 147
   *Mon Coeur s'ouvre à ta Voix*, 52, 65, 147
   *Samson et Delila*, 18, 51, 63-67
Sainton-Dolby, Charlotte, 5-6, 9
   *Harbor Bar, The*, 5, 6
   *Legend of Dorothea, The*, 6
   *Story of the Fruitful Soul, The*, 6
Santley, Sir Charles, 59, 108-109
Sargent, Sir Malcolm, 175
Sbriglia, Giovanni, 88
Schubert, Franz, *Der Tod und das Mädchen*, 72
Schumann-Heink, Ernestine, 6
Scott, Michael, 78
Shaw, George Bernard, 47, 187-188
   reviews Clara's performance, 48
Smith, Rodney "Gipsy", 20
Smyth, Ethel, 162, 164
South Bristol High School, 20
   Cook, Miss, headmistress, 20-21
Southwick, 11-12
Spiritualism, 57, 139, 154
Squire, W.H., 109, 156, 171, 188, 202
   *For Me Alone*, 171
Stanford, Sir Charles, 40, 44-45, 48, 91
Stead, William T., 139
Sterling, Antoinette, 18
Stoker, Bram, 47
Sullivan, Sir Arthur, 7, 51-53, 55, 77-78
   composes anthem for Clara's wedding, 96
   *God Shall Wipe Away All Tears from their Eyes*, 155
   *Golden Legend, The*, 37, 51
   *Light of the World*, 155
   *Lost Chord, The* 53, 94, 103
Sullivan, Sir Arthur - *cont.*
   *O God, Thou Art Worthy to be Praised*, 97
   *Onward Christian Soldiers*, 94, 97
Sumac, Yma, 34

# INDEX

Sutherland, Dame Joan, 203
Tagore, Rabindranath, 181
Terry, Ellen, 47, 164
Tetrazzini, Luisa, 127
theosophy, 18, 181
Thomas, Arthur Goring, *Night Hymn at Sea*, 131, 145
Tillet, Emmie, 42
Tillett, John, 42, 110
Titanic, sinking of, 139
Tosti, Francesco, 54, 88, 188
   *Goodbye!*, 54
Trebelli, Gloria, 6
Troubridge, Una, 33
Tubb, Carrie, 156
Turner, Eva, 22
Turner, Mary, 44
Verbrugghen, Henri, 176
Verdi, Giuseppe, *Rigoletto*, 68
Vert, Narciso, 42, 81, 90, 110
Viardot, Pauline, 66
Victoria Mary, Princess of Teck, 46

Victoria, Queen, 45-46, 49, 51-56, 64, 69, 71-72, 89, 97
   Command performances from Clara, 46-47, 51-55, 63
   funds Clara's musical studies, 59
   Diamond Jubilee, 76
   death, 102
Visetti, Albert, 32-33
vocal range, 34
Wakefield, Augusta Mary, 6
Weatherly, Frederic E., 165
   *Holy City, The*, 165
   *Danny Boy*, 165-166
   *Roses of Picardy*, 165
Wedmore Vale Church, Bristol, 20
White, Maude Valérie, *Three Little Songs*, 89
Wilhelm II, Kaiser of Germany, 151
Wolfson, Alfred, 34
Women's Freedom League, 164
Wood, Sir Henry, 136, 177
Yorke, Albert, Earl of Hardwicke (Lord Hardwicke), 64

# Victorian Secrets

*The Perfect Man: The Muscular Life and Times of Eugen Sandow, Victorian Strongman* **by David Waller**

Eugen Sandow (1867-1925) was the Victorian Arnold Schwarzenegger – a world-famous celebrity, and possessor of what was then considered to be the most perfect male body. He rose from obscurity in Prussia to become a music-hall sensation in late-Victorian London, going on to great success as a performer in North America and throughout the British Empire.

Written with humour and insight into the popular culture of late-Victorian England, Waller's book argues that Sandow deserves to be resurrected as a significant cultural figure whose life, like that of Oscar Wilde, tells us a great deal about sexuality and celebrity at the fin de siècle.

"Hugely entertaining ... Waller skillfully places Sandow within the context of the age." Juliet Nicolson, *The Evening Standard*

"Waller...furnishes a narrative rich in stories reflecting Victorian life." Valerie Grove, *The Times*

"Waller's lively, colourful and fascinating book should help restore interest in an unjustly forgotten icon." Miranda Seymour - *The Daily Telegraph*

www.victoriansecrets.co.uk

Lightning Source UK Ltd.
Milton Keynes UK
UKHW021427180419
341242UK00005B/116/P